The Clock of the
COVENANT

Nyle Kardatzke

xulon PRESS

The Clock of the Covenant
by Nyle Kardatzke

Editorial Services: Karen Roberts, RQuest, LLC

Printed in the United States of America.

ISBN 9781498482240

For permission to use material, contact:
Nyle Kardatzke
Email: nylebk@gmail.com

Front Cover Photo: Rod Holz, Innovations Studio, Genoa, Ohio

Back Cover Photo: Rob Nichols, Sycamore School, Indianapolis

www.xulonpress.com

Readers have said...

Like a collection of photographs telling a story in a family album, The Clock of the Covenant captures an era and a culture in a series of vivid snapshots, framed by a local church in small-town Ohio. Nyle Kardatzke's recollections of life in the 1940s and 1950s read with irresistible ease, reminding us of days gone by, but also thoughtfully challenging us to take stock of markers that must never pass away. The Clock of the Covenant is nostalgic, yes, but much more: it provides a compass for roads still to be traveled. Open its pages and you will be drawn into life, whatever your age or circumstance.

Jim Lyons
General Secretary of the Church of God
Anderson, Indiana

The book is enjoyable reading. It is interestingly entertaining. It is inspirational. It is informative. It is well written. *The Clock of the Covenant* should have wide appeal because so many people will identify with it, as I have done, not only because I lived through some of it with the author, but also because it rings the bells of my memory about other churches.

W. Curtis Lee
Pastor at Elmore, 1948-51

The author offers a unique "view from the pew" detailing the life, love, and losses of those who crossed paths with the Elmore Church of God during its formative years. The stories, based loosely on historic fact and oral tradition, portray a poignant and personal view of the people of Elmore that played a part in this century old institution. *The Clock of the Covenant* gives an entertaining and heartfelt look into the past of the Elmore community from both a spiritual and secular perspective

Katie Blum & Jennifer Fording
Local History Department
Harris-Elmore Public Library

The Clock of the Covenant would be a winner if it was fiction. Realizing the stories are real makes them even more intriguing. These true stories are so different from anything we experience today. Here you can discover what church life was like sixty or seventy years ago. These stories will show the role of church and faith in people's life crises in those earlier, turbulent times.

Donna Thomas
Christian Vision Ministries
Phoenix, Arizona

The Clock of the Covenant is full of moving and inspirational stories of life values, the reality of life and death, and the faith of the children of God and their commitment to family and God. Written in the delightful imagination of children, this is a poignant journey into times gone by written from a grateful heart. It is very delightful.

Sherry Minton
Anderson, Indiana

OTHER BOOKS BY NYLE KARDATZKE

Widow-man: A Widower's Story and Journaling Book, 2014

The Brown House Stories: A Child's Garden of Eden, 2015

DEDICATION

This collection of experiences and stories is dedicated to my parents, Arlin (1911-2004) and Ruth Bruner (1914-2006) Kardatzke. They met in 1931 at the short-lived Warner Memorial University in Eastland, Texas, and they were married in 1934 in Old Main at Anderson College by my uncle, Dr. Carl Kardatzke. They enjoyed sixty-nine years of married life before my father's death. The Kardatzke and Bruner families both have roots in the Church of God (Anderson, Indiana) that go back to the early 1900s, and both are now large extended families.

Arlin and Ruth raised six children, a feat that was already becoming rare in the mid-1900s. Both attended one-room schools through eighth grade and later attended college. My father's main career was as an instrument repairman at the Sun Oil refinery in Toledo, Ohio. My mother taught in Ohio public schools in Rocky Ridge, Gibsonburg, and Northwood, Ohio when her own children were far enough along in school.

In their love for God and for each other, my parents were reflections of the Holy Trinity. My father seemed to me like God the Father: constant in his love, truth, work, and creative power. My mother seemed to me like Jesus: the seeking, reaching, communicating, and demonstrative personality of God. Like the eternal love within the Godhead, their love and joy radiated like an expression of the Holy Spirit. My siblings and I were nurtured in childhood and throughout our adult lives by the continuous, conscious, unconditional love of our parents for each other and for us. I'm thankful for the way of life they showed us and gave us as a spiritual inheritance.

CONTENTS

PREFACE

This book is about life in a small church in Northern Ohio as I perceived it in the 1940s and 1950s when I was a young boy. There are comical stories ("Grandpa Webert's Pants) and serious descriptions of church beliefs and practices ("Getting Saved" and "Footwashing"). I have included stories about some of the "saints" in our little church and a few people whose paths through life seldom brought them to church. There are stories of tragedies that changed people's lives, dangers evaded, and happy holidays and summer picnics.

The book is an appreciation of the vital Christian life I saw and experienced as a kid, and it's a remembrance of Christian practices and passion that have changed so much over these decades. It's also an act of repentance for my rebellious nature as a boy, traces of which I probably carry as an older man.

Readers will glimpse some of the funny, personal quirks of people in our church, where attendance seldom exceeded one hundred souls. I hope those personalities suggest in microcosm the great diversity that exists in much larger and seemingly homogeneous congregations today. The reader may also experience some of the devotion and fervor in the church I saw as boy. There's no going back to the church of the early postwar world, but its character is worth remembering, at least for a moment.

Pastors and lay leaders may benefit from reading about the Evangelical Christianity of the postwar period. It may lead to a "revival" of interest in the nature of the church in those days, even though the word "revival" has been expunged from the vocabularies of most church people. In the ongoing rapid change in styles and content of worship since at least the 1980s, there may be some value in these glimpses of the church we are changing *from*.

I suspect the book will primarily be of interest to people born before 1950 who remember the church world I share here or something like it. Possibly some younger people will read it for the funny stories and for a nostalgic look at the church's past. The church in this book closely resembles hundreds of churches from similar denominations in the 1940s and 1950s. Older people who have read or heard some of these stories have told me they attended churches like this, often down to the last details of the Christmas treat and the conduct of Sunday school. Many could write about similar churches, and perhaps they have, but no one else can write so authoritatively about my church and the people in it.

Surely there are hundreds of large and small churches today in which most of the personalities and practices I describe are seen. I suspect some readers will nod with knowing smiles as they recognize their own churches here.

Had I written this book when I first thought of the scene in the title story about the church clock, many people still would have been living who could have contradicted, corrected, and refuted some of what I have written. Now that the twenty-first century is well under way, I am one of the few surviving witnesses of the scenes, people, and practices in this book. Most of the people I mention are now dead. Although they aren't here to edit the stories I tell about them, what I have written is as close as most of them will come to a biography other than the vapid texts of their obituaries. Having waited this long to publish *The Clock of the Covenant*, I am now a living authority on my topic.

If you read this book, perhaps you can think of it as spiritual time travel. But here you will travel back into the past rather than forward to the hope of all Christians.

ACKNOWLEDGEMENTS

I' m thankful I have lived long enough and have retained enough mental health to write this account of life in the church of my childhood. The book would not have been possible without the blessing of health I have received.

Inspiration for the stories came from more individuals than those that are spotlighted here. They somehow loved and encouraged me and other restive, irreverent children and young people in the years I have reported here. No doubt many of us would have come to worse ends had it not been for those people, their life stories, and their prayers for us.

My editor, Karen Roberts, clarified my writing time and again as we revised the book. Her youthful experiences in similar church settings made her an especially astute partner in making the book a faithful portrayal of the church life we both knew. She has been endlessly patient and skillful in her work on this book, as well as my two previous books.

I am deeply indebted to Jennifer Fording, the Local History Librarian at the public library in Elmore, Ohio, and her assistant, Katie Blum. When I couldn't find a fact I needed in the library's excellent online holdings, they researched the topics and sent me scans of newspaper clippings and other documents, some from more than one hundred years ago. I could not have asked for more skillful and willing research assistance.

Spenser Benefield, the unofficial but endlessly informative historian of the Elmore Church of God, provided many pieces of information that make this book more historically accurate than would have otherwise been possible.

Doloris Dellinger of Toledo provided helpful details about Harry Klinger, the one-hundred-year-old man who appears in several stories. Harry Klinger was her grandfather; Alice Klinger was Doloris's grandmother as well as my Sunday school teacher. I met Doloris "by chance" at the funeral of a cousin in 2015 when I had long since dismissed hope of firsthand information about Harry and Alice Klinger.

Curtis Lee, the pastor at Elmore from 1948 to 1951, read a late draft of the entire manuscript and made helpful comments, correcting some of the history. He was the pastor when the new church was dedicated in 1949.

Dr. James Cook read portions of an early draft and made helpful comments. Gerald Goldsby of Elmore read three chapters and affirmed their accuracy.

I apologize to others I have overlooked whose stories, advice, and encouragement have gone into the book. My wish is that they will find joy in seeing that their memories have been recorded without attribution and I hope accurately. I have included a few errors and unclear passages for all other astute readers to find.

Where there are theological or historical errors, I invite readers to report them at my blog site, nylek.com.

PROLOGUE: AN APOCALYPTIC PAST

By 1948, when the little Church of God of Elmore, Ohio, moved to its new brick building, the people had experienced an apocalyptic past. Older members of the church had fought in the First World War, and many of the young men were veterans of the Second World War. The oldest members had been born shortly after the Civil War and knew of that maelstrom. The Great Depression had shown that the robust capitalist economy of the 1800s and early twentieth century could fail. "Hard times" now could be worse and last longer than in the nineteenth century. People were out of work, businesses closed, and farms were sold.

In the midst of the Depression, demonic political leaders had arisen in Europe and Asia. Satan seemed embodied not only in those leaders but in the crazed multitudes that followed and idolized them. War had erupted around the world, and everyone was involved either directly in war zones or indirectly at home. Young men died. Privation even reached the safe fields of home. Truly the world seemed to be near its end, and that vision of chaos turned the people in our church to God in ways that might not have happened in more tranquil times.

Our church itself had started in the wake of a shocking tragedy. A train had collided with an open touring car in 1913, killing a prominent woman and her talented adult son on a quiet Sunday afternoon. Life was uncertain.

Events like these prepared members of our church and thousands of similar churches for a spiritual view of the world that might seem unfamiliar in our more prosperous and seemingly stable times. These people had seen the end of the world and were living in a world beyond it, but they knew their new world could end even more disastrously. Beyond the comic events in church, the sumptuous Sunday school picnics and delicious Christmas treats, there was a world in disorder. Only within the church did our people find lasting peace and harmony. This book shares a little of what the peace was like.

I. IN THE BEGINNING: HOW PEOPLE HEARD FROM GOD

WHEN THE TRUMPET SOUNDED

George Gleckler grasped the iron crank while twenty-one-year-old Clarence, the eldest of his four sons, set the choke and throttle and advanced the spark on their new 1913 Model T Ford. On the second turn, the engine roared to life, and to George it was a beautiful sound. Life is good, thought George Gleckler as he hopped into the passenger seat and Clarence took the wheel. The entire world was at peace, his brick and tile factory was thriving, he was in good health, and here he was with his wonderful family, off to pick watermelons on a beautiful Sunday afternoon. It was September 7, 1913. His attractive wife, Kate, was in the back seat behind Clarence, and alongside her their very young "surprise" son, three-year-old Teddy; their eleven-year-old daughter, Malinda; and Clarence's fiancée, Miss Jessie Henry. George and Kate's other two sons, Rollin and Arthur, were spending the afternoon with friends.

George looked around at the flat farm fields of corn, beans, and sugar beets along Graytown Road. He was happy that he was managing his little factory instead of guiding a team of horses in hay fields or driving one of the noisy new tractors that had recently begun to invade the farms in this part of Ohio. And he thought also of his good fortune to live in Ohio rather than in the family's native Germany. His father, Christ Gleckler, had brought his industrial skills from the Old Country, but little else. Had the family remained in Germany, George probably would not have become what some of his neighbors called "prosperous." His brick yard had burned down in 1899 and 1900, but the family had amassed enough wealth to restart a brick and tile factory. It was full of fire itself, but the fire was well contained in the brick-lined kilns, and there was little to burn except the coal that had helped make him truly prosperous. The clay his workers scraped out for his factory had left three large ponds that were the marvel of the neighborhood. He enjoyed a little chuckle at the thought of his relative wealth and the idea of his being "prosperous."

"What are you laughing at?" Kate called from the back seat. She had seen his smile and the little laugh, though she couldn't hear over the roar of the car.

"Nothing, Kate, nothing," George yelled, "except the thought of having two beautiful women in the back seat of a new car on such a nice day! Shall we see if we can pick up Em or some other good-looking girls on the way?"

"You better not, George!" Kate shouted. "Not even Em!"

Em was George's sister, Emma Kardatzke, and the Model T had just passed the well-groomed barns and house where Emma and Fred Kardatzke lived. Emma had given birth to their sixth child, a boy they named Elmer Edward, six weeks earlier. George and Kate didn't have such a sprawling, large family as Fred and Emma, and they were happy for what they had. It was enough.

As they fairly flew over the smoothly packed gravel roads, George and Clarence mostly gave up on talking. The rush of the wind and rattling gravel added to the roaring engine, and they didn't want to spoil the day by making themselves hoarse shouting to be heard. The day was beautiful, and farm smells flitted through the open car as they passed newly mown fields, plowed ground, and occasional barnyards that made them happy they were moving so fast.

"How fast we goin'?" George yelled to Clarence as they passed one of those barnyards.

"Can't really tell," Clarence said, "maybe 20 or 25 miles an hour."

The car hadn't come with a speedometer, a rare device at that time, so they had to guess their speed. No matter. They were going fast enough. No horse could go this fast for so long, and the road wasn't good enough for the car's advertised top speed of 45 miles per hour. So they roared along, scaring chickens and geese near the road and waking people from their after-dinner naps. They themselves had finished dinner shortly after noon to allow enough time to reach Green Springs, talk with the watermelon farmer, and load several melons into the car. They had invited Fred and Emma to come for a watermelon feed that evening, and they wanted time for the melons to cool in cold water in the stock tank.

They crossed the Portage River, passed through the village of Lindsey, and were soon on the outskirts of Fremont, a small city that gave them a feeling of having arrived somewhere important. It was, after all, the hometown of a former president, Rutherford B. Hayes, and was named for the famous explorer, John C. Fremont. Gliding over the paved streets in Fremont made them feel they were joining the twentieth century with a flourish.

Just beyond the downtown streets, George shouted to Clarence, "Get ready to turn. Take Smith Road. Turn right."

On Smith Road, they were on gravel again, and the clattering gravel punctuated the roar of the engine and the wind in their ears. Tall stalks of ripened corn lined both sides of the road, and it was planted so near the road that they could have reached out and touched the leaves. Fresh corn tassels perfumed the air. The road ahead was clear, and only at the last moment they could see the slight rise where the road went over railway tracks. Clarence slowed for the bump. Suddenly there was a terrifying shriek. When George thought of it later, he realized the sound was Kate's scream when she saw the oncoming locomotive. There had been no warning sound from the train.

"Train! Clarence! Train!" George yelled out.

Clarence glanced up and saw the train bearing down on them from his left. Instinctively he tried to stop, but the car skidded and stopped on the tracks in the path of the oncoming train. He tried to back the car off the tracks, but not soon enough. George could only watch in horror as the cowcatcher on the front of the engine plowed into their car, spun it around, and slammed it against the steel driving rod that connected the train's large driving wheels.

George slammed against Clarence as the car was blasted off the tracks. Kate's scream stopped suddenly, and little Teddy was thrown from her lap into the air over the back of the car. To George, the entire world seemed to be moving. The train rumbled past the intersection, its brakes and steel wheels screaming and smoking as the engineer tried to stop.

For a moment it was quiet. Trees along the track swayed gently in the breeze, and in the distance crows were quarreling. Then George heard voices. Teddy, crying somewhere off in the cornfield. Miss Jessie

Henry, moaning, not able to cry out loudly. Nothing more. When his senses returned enough for him to look around, George found himself a few rows inside the cornfield but unhurt. He stood and pushed his way through the corn to the edge of the field. There he stared at his smashed car, trying to take it all in, trying to know what he should do. Clarence and Kate were lying beside the mangled car, which sat parallel to the tracks. No sound came from their motionless bodies. Where were the others?

And then he saw his daughter, Malinda, dazed, standing in the shallow ditch next to the tracks. Jessie Henry lay nearby in tall grass, seemingly asleep. Little Teddy was climbing up the roadbed, looking for his family. A young boy rode up on a bicycle. Malinda was about his age, so he went to her.

"What happened? Didn't they see the train? Is that your Pa? Where is your Ma? Who's that little kid?" he asked.

Malinda was too shocked to answer, so the boy went over to Clarence and Kate, calling out, asking if they were okay. No one answered.

The five-car passenger train was backing up slowly toward them, so George pulled Clarence and Kate clear of the tracks. Teddy came to his side, and George picked him up and held him, for his own comfort as much as Teddy's. He watched numbly as the conductor and the brakeman ran along the track to them.

"Oh, God! Oh, God! Help them!" the brakeman yelled. When he was near enough to see Kate's and Clarence's lifeless bodies, he screamed and cried, "Oh! No! No! No! They're killed! They're killed!"

"Quiet, man!" the conductor yelled. "Help the living! Help the *living*! Get them all on the train. Get men from the train! Get help!"

Soon passengers from the train surrounded the terrible scene, and people came running from nearby houses. A sound of general moaning and crying and prayer rose from the crowd, and the conductor shouted again over the din. "Get them all on the train! Be careful with the dead! They may not be dead! We'll take them all to town!"

Passengers joined the train's crew to lift Kate and Clarence carefully onto the floor of the baggage car. Kate still held Teddy's cap tightly in her grip. Jessie Henry had awakened and climbed aboard with help from the men. George, Jessie, Malinda, and Teddy sat down beside Kate and Clarence with the brakeman. A man in a dark suit clambered in and identified himself as a doctor.

"We're alright!" George yelled. "Help *them!* Help *them!*" he said, pointing to the silent Kate and Clarence.

The doctor felt for pulses and then pulled a stethoscope from his coat pocket. In the silent, still air of the halted baggage car, he listened intently for breathing or a heartbeat. In a few moments, he folded the stethoscope and returned it to his pocket. He looked somberly at George. "I'm very sorry, sir, very sorry, indeed."

Jessie Henry screamed, fell to the boxcar's floor, and began to cry so piteously that all the others in the baggage car joined her, in their own ways. Malinda huddled on the floor and sobbed. But George Gleckler and Teddy couldn't cry. They could only stare at Kate and Clarence. For them it wasn't real. It hadn't happened. They just stared and listened to the others.

When the train started again, another man climbed aboard. He said he was from a local church and wanted to help in any way he could. Surveying the scene, he saw the bodies, the injured young woman, the young girl, and the silent man and little boy. The brakeman nodded toward George, and the man sat down next to him.

"Your wife?" he asked.

George nodded.

"Is she gone?"

George nodded again and added, "The boy too," pointing to Clarence.

"I am so terribly sorry," the man said. "May I pray?"

George nodded. It was too late for what he wanted, too late for his wife and son, too late for the lovely watermelon party they were planning, too late to stop for the train. But the man offered to pray, and that was right.

As the stranger prayed, the train slowly slid forward, bearing its sad cargo westward toward Fremont, so near that the train moved only at a walking pace. Someone from a house near the crash had called the train station, and wagons awaited the survivors and the two bodies. One group of men led George, Teddy, Malinda, and Jessie to the closest wagon. Another group of men carefully slid stretchers under the lifeless bodies. The first wagon would go to the Fremont hospital, while the second would take the bodies to a funeral home for immediate embalming. A policeman spoke to George and then called Emma and Fred Kardatzke from a hospital phone. They were the closest neighbors and among the few with a phone, and they were family.

By late Sunday afternoon, Kate's and Clarence's bodies had been washed and embalmed. The funeral home in Fremont provided two caskets and a basket for the bloodied clothing. George's surviving sons, Rollin and Arthur, came with a truck and a car to take the caskets, clothes, and the survivors to Kate and George's home.

Two neighbors buried the bloodied clothing behind the house at the far end of Kate's garden. A man from the funeral home in Elmore brought two casket stands, called catafalques. With help from his young assistant Fred Sabroske, George's brother-in-law, the caskets were placed on the stands in the parlor for viewing the next day. Though the bodies were badly bruised, it was customary to show them. Women draped the windows in black cloth. Candles, as a sign of grief and respect, were arranged to temporarily replace the modern gaslights. The Gleckler home had become a funeral parlor for the dead and the garden a cemetery for their clothing.

Jessie Henry had broken bones, damaged joints, and emotional trauma, all of which would affect her for the rest of her life. George, Malinda, and Teddy had survived without visible injuries, but they were deeply wounded where only God could see.

Jessie Henry's family took her home, and George put Teddy and Malinda to bed. That night he sat in the living room, staring at the caskets, so huge in the small space. From time to time, he looked into the caskets and then sat again, just staring. Clarence was strong and young and handsome. Kate was beautiful and still young at forty-four. Their deaths still weren't real. He couldn't think about the life he would face the next day, to say nothing of the days, weeks, and years ahead. He could only stare, get up to look in the caskets, and sit and stare again. Unable to think, he just waited for thought and understanding to come, if it ever would.

It was nearly morning when George awoke to screams from Teddy's room. He jumped up, fearing the worst, and found a neighbor woman in the room. She was consoling Teddy after a nightmare. The neighbor must have slipped in silently while George slept. Malinda was there, and she was crying too.

"Papa! Papa! Where is Mama? I had a bad dream!" Teddy sobbed.

"She's not here," George stammered. He realized he had spoken the truth, but she *was* there—or her body was. How would he explain it all to the small boy? He had run his business successfully, but he wasn't prepared for his little son's questions. He felt he had had all the answers for questions in his business, but he was not prepared for the questions of life and death.

"She's with Jesus now," the neighbor woman told the children. "She is happy with Jesus."

Malinda and Teddy had heard stories about Jesus, and they knew that Jesus could take care of Mama and everyone else. They smiled at the woman and at their father, and they settled back down to sleep. George returned to the parlor, looked into the caskets one more time, and slumped into his chair again.

The rising sun the next morning comforted George with a peace he couldn't feel during that long night. The smell of coffee brewing in the kitchen awakened him to the awful day he knew he would have to face.

AUTHOR'S NOTE: *The title of this story, "When the Trumpet Sounded," is also the title of a 1951 book on the history of the Church of God (Anderson, Indiana) by Charles Ewing Brown, usually known as C. E. Brown. The title seems appropriate for this account of an event that led to the formation of the Church of God congregation in Elmore, Ohio. Tragically, the trumpet that called the Elmore Church of God into being may have been a train whistle even though some witnesses said the train had sounded neither its whistle nor its bell.*

Soon after the funeral for Kate and Clarence, George Gleckler brought a lawsuit against the Wheeling and Lake Erie Railroad Company for the engineer's failure to sound a warning. George Gleckler's attorney concluded that Kate and Clarence's skulls were crushed when the car struck the train's right hand driving rod. The outcome of the lawsuit is unknown to me.

George Gleckler was a brother to my grandmother, Emma Gleckler Kardatzke. He was a great-uncle to me and lived next door to my family from 1943 until his death in 1945. Teddy Gleckler and my father were cousins and were about the same age. They were childhood playmates.

The ponds created by the Gleckler tile yard are still visible on Graytown Road between State Road 105 and State Road 163, about two miles south of Graytown, Ohio. An ice house and one residence made from Gleckler clay are still standing.

CASKETS IN THE PARLOR

Sunlight was already piercing the gaps in the black window coverings when George Gleckler awoke on Monday morning, facing the caskets that were somehow even sadder in the dimly lit room than in full darkness. His clothes felt clammy, and he needed a shave. It was painful to move, but he heard men at work in the tile yard behind the house, shaking ashes and clinkers from the kilns. He needed to go to work. No, he couldn't work today. He *shouldn't* work today. But if he didn't work, what would he do?

His head was still buzzing from shock and lack of sleep. Eleven-year-old Malinda and three-year-old Teddy came in and looked at the huge, new objects in their living room. George thought it best to get them out to the kitchen.

"Let's get you some breakfast, kids," he said in a voice that he hoped sounded normal.

In the kitchen, bacon was on the stove. The aroma of fresh bread wafted from the oven. Fresh coffee was welcoming, but the smell of food nearly made George ill. On a typical day, Kate would have been doing this, cooking a hot breakfast, but not today. Not ever again.

"You up a'ready, George?" his sister Emma said as she came back into the kitchen from an errand in the yard. "I got ya some breakfast started. I bet them kids can eat something."

George stared blankly at his sister's health and energy. He felt life returning to his foggy mind as he watched her fairly stomping around the kitchen on her morning rounds. When their eyes met, they both struggled for composure in front of the children.

"Yeah, let them little kids eat, Em," he mumbled. "Do 'em good."

He sat down and stared as Emma placed bowls of oatmeal and a plate of bacon and bread in front of the children. They ate eagerly, since last night's supper had been scant and disturbed. George knew he must eat, so he chewed on bread and butter and sipped the second large cup of coffee Em placed in front of him.

"Man from the funeral home is coming pretty soon to talk about the funeral," Emma announced. "Wants to know if you want it at the church and wants to know about the cemetery. It's awful to be talking about such things, but we hafta do it."

"Am I going to school today?" Malinda asked. Before George could say he didn't know, Emma said she could go a little later and play with the kids in morning recess. That seemed to assure Malinda that some things hadn't changed. She understood better than Teddy what had happened, but for now she was cried out and wanted to do something else.

"Laurie's comin' pretty soon to git Teddy," Emma said. "He can play at home with Arlin. They'll be good company for each other."

Arlin was two years old, several months younger than Teddy. Laurie Deacon was Emma's sister-in-law. She lived in Elmore, about three miles from the Gleckler home. She could come out for visits, which she did frequently, either by buggy or on the interurban train.

When the children were out of the house, George tried to speak. "Why did this happen, Em? Why? Why are Kate and Clarence out there, out in the front room?"

"Oh, Georgie! I don't know, I don't know!" Em cried out, and she sat down and sobbed great heaving sobs that frightened George.

Caught up in her emotions, George cried too, calling out, "Kate! Kate! Come back! Clarence! Stop for the train!" He felt he would never stop crying. When he did stop, he could hear the big machine at the tile yard, pressing clay into the tile forms. He felt dead himself, and the factory work was going on without him.

George and Emma were drying their faces when they heard a knock at the kitchen door. It was H. E. Burman from the funeral home in Elmore, dressed as he should be in a black suit with a vest and shiny black shoes. People called him either "Mr. Burman" or sometimes just "Burman." His given name was Henry, but his work was so serious that, out of respect, most people didn't use his first name. George knew him well enough to call him Henry, but he almost never did.

"George, I came to help with the service," the visitor said cautiously.

"I know. Come in. Sit down. Tell me what we have to do," George said, feeling he could face this task now that it seemed like a management problem. Emma left the two of them in the kitchen to complete their work while she dusted and cleaned the front parlor.

Burman went through a list of questions. He asked where the visiting and the funeral would be. He said the funeral service could be in the church in town, where George and Kate sometimes went, or it could be in the little showing room at his funeral parlor. After a long pause, he allowed that, well, the visiting and the funeral could be right there at the house if George wanted it that way.

George couldn't bear the thought of sending Kate and Clarence off to town, whether to the church or to the funeral home. "We'd best do it right here, Burman," he said with conviction. "I know that's what Kate would want. This is her house more than anybody else's. We'll do it all right here."

"That's fine," Burman said, "a wise choice and in keeping with your family's history."

His formal tone made George feel he was on solid ground. Burman then made suggestions about visiting hours this day and the next, the minister to preside, the music, the flowers, the notices to the local papers, plans for food for visitors, and the location of the grave. George agreed to nearly all the suggestions, entering only a comment or two before the plans were complete. Things would move swiftly.

"Better tell Emma the plan too," George advised as Burman rose to go, "and probably some of the others. I won't remember much of this by dinnertime."

Still in the clothes he had slept in, George went out to the tile yard. The men were loading dull red field tile onto a farmer's wagon. They stopped and stood silently as he approached. No one knew what to say—not George, not the men, and not the foreman. They could only manage to hold their hats. Finally George spoke.

"I guess you heard."

Some men looked at the ground, and a couple nodded silently with tear-filled eyes. One blew his nose. George could see that he would only make matters worse for himself and the men if he stayed.

"Thanks for keepin' the work goin'," he said. "Best thing to do."

The men seemed relieved when he said no more. "We're sure sorry, Mr. Gleckler," one of them said as George turned toward the house.

The house was now silent with Emma and the kids gone. He went to the parlor for another look into the caskets. All he could feel was shock and unreality. He managed to climb the stairs to the bathroom, carrying enough hot water to warm a bath. He shaved, bathed, and dressed in a suit. People would be coming soon.

In the early afternoon, visitors began to arrive, mostly in wagons but some in cars and some on bicycles and three on horseback. Neighbors walked down the road or cut across fields from other roads. George watched the first arrivals from upstairs and heard Burman greet them, as he and Burman had arranged. Young Fred Sabroske was there as well to help Burman handle the crowd. George wondered how many would come out of curiosity, just to see the bodies and any visible damage to them from the accident.

Some of the nearest neighbors, the Harmons, arrived earliest. George knew he should go down to greet them. Then relatives began to arrive, some from as far away as Toledo. The women were crying. George buttoned his suit coat and went down, already sweating in the abnormally warm weather. Emma was downstairs greeting people too, while Laurie Deacon corralled the children.

The afternoon was a blur of greetings, most of them seeming hollow to George. Some of the conversations brought the visitors to tears, and he himself cried twice. Finally it was dark and candles were lit around the room. Visitors left, and Laurie Deacon, who had stayed all day, was there to put the children to bed. Eventually it was quiet again, so he sat where he had last evening, staring at the open caskets. Burman had offered to close and lock the caskets before he left for the night, but George said he wanted them open so he could look at his son and wife if he should awaken in the night. After staring at them in silence for an hour, he knew it was time for bed. Tuesday would be a very long day.

HOME FUNERAL AND BURIAL

The funeral for Kate and Clarence Gleckler was scheduled for two o'clock Tuesday afternoon at George's home on Graytown Road. Visitors began to arrive mid-morning, some with picnic baskets of food to eat in the former schoolyard next to George's house. Others came to pay their respects and go back to work in the fall harvest, but even those farmers came in dark suits to show their sympathy before returning to their work. Emma's sisters-in-law came to help around the house, and one of them, Minnie, made George eat a ham sandwich. Elizabeth Sabroske hurried around the parlor, dusting and tidying for the service. By one o'clock, the schoolyard was filling with buggies and cars, and vehicles were parked along the road.

George looked over the crowd from the front porch from time to time, and he thought it looked like a scene at an auction sale. When he returned to the darkened, candle-lit room, now prepared for the coming service, he kept thinking that Kate and Clarence might wake up. He knew it was wrong thinking, but he couldn't help himself. He wondered where they were. Had they gone straight to heaven? He couldn't bear to think that they might not be in heaven. Other disturbing thoughts crowded in. What would happen to him if he died today? What would it have felt like if he had died on Sunday?

"Where should Teddy and Arlin be during the funeral?" Laurie came in to ask. She had spent the night at George's house with Teddy and Malinda. Emma had come earlier with her six children, including Arlin. Teddy and Arlin were both toddlers and would have to be watched. George was startled by the simple question and didn't have an answer.

"How about I keep them on a blanket out in the yard?" Laurie offered. "They can't sit still in the hot room for the funeral. I'll have to keep baby Elmer outside anyway."

George welcomed that solution and waited in a daze for others to solve other problems of the day. He didn't even try to think about his young daughter, Malinda, and all of Emma's children; the women would somehow manage. Thinking ahead to the burial, he was relieved to remember that places were available in the Gleckler cemetery plot, and that Burman had arranged for the graves to be dug. Burman and Fred Sabroske would handle all of that.

George Gleckler was a prominent businessman. Some of his business associates came as well as friends and family members. Many people came simply because they had heard of George Gleckler. Kate had been known as an attractive woman and a skilled hostess, and many community ladies had attended her parties. Some of them had come to pay their respects. Clarence had been a popular and talented young man, and he and Jessie Henry had been a popular couple. Clarence's death in the presence of his fiancée was a tragedy too great for anyone to bear alone, so dozens of their friends came to support Jessie.

Finally the funeral began. George, Malinda, and his older children, Rollin and Arthur, were directly in front of the caskets. Close family members were pressed in behind them, and a few neighbors filled the remaining space. A large crowd stood outside or sat in the yard, silently listening for any sounds of the funeral. For the sake of the crowd outside as well as for those inside, the funeral should have been short.

In spite of the heat and the cramped room, the service was long. E. V. Huffer from the Christian Church gave a sermon for Clarence, and Reverend Yeager from Elliston gave another in memory of Mrs. Gleckler. Miss Marvel Guthrie accompanied a trio of ladies on the foot-pump organ. These details were reported in the *Elmore Tribune*.

The two sermons and the heat dictated that only two hymns be sung before the closing prayer. Then Burman asked everyone in the room except the family to go outside. His black suit and solemn manner gave him high rank at this moment, but so many members of the extended family remained that he had to clarify. "All but the *immediate* family may leave," he said, more insistently this time.

At last only an intimate few were left inside, but the room was still crowded. George, Malinda, Rollin, and Arthur were nearest the caskets along with Jessie Henry and her parents and a few members of Kate's immediate family. George's six sisters and two brothers stood for a few minutes, gazing on their lifeless family members for the last time. They watched as the lids were closed, and then everyone went outside to waiting cars.

Already the line of vehicles along Graytown Road had reached nearly a quarter of a mile to the north as people prepared for the procession to the graveyard. Before he and the children climbed into a car, George watched as the caskets were brought out and placed in the two black, horse-drawn funeral wagons, one of them borrowed from Burman's place in Oak Harbor. The wagons pulled onto the road to lead the way, followed by the car carrying George.

The procession slipped slowly along Graytown Road, crossed the interurban tracks, turned right, and followed River Road to Elmore. At the bend where the old brick schoolhouse had stood, George looked back at the line of motorized and horse-drawn vehicles behind the two funeral wagons. He couldn't see the end of the line. The newspaper reported later that there had been one hundred and fifteen conveyances in the funeral procession.

As the procession came into Elmore, a church bell tolled slowly, and people came from shops and homes to watch the mournful line of friends and family pass by. Women and girls cried, and men held their hats. A flag hung limply at half-staff. Seeing it all, George broke down in great shuddering sobs, crying in a way he never had before. He had kept his composure until now, but the grief of so many others overwhelmed him. The whole town saw him, and those who had been merely curious were drawn into his grief.

All was ready at the cemetery. The two prepared gravesites were side by side. The crowd formed a great circle around the freshly dug pits, and the caskets were brought to them. The beating sun seemed unnatural. The day should have been cold with rain, George thought. The bright sun seemed indifferent to the scene of grief below.

The graveside service was brief, just long enough to punctuate the sadness of the day. The caskets remained suspended on straps above the graves until the crowd dispersed, leaving George alone. Burman then nodded to George to tell him it was time for him to leave too. George turned away from the grave. He was unprepared for the world without Kate and Clarence, a world that had begun on another sunny afternoon only two days earlier.

SISTERS, WILL YOU COME AND HELP US?

Sisters, will you come and help us?
Moses' sister aided him;
Will you help the trembling mourners
Who are struggling hard with sin?
Tell them all about the Savior –
Tell them that He will be found;
Sisters, pray, and holy manna
Will be showered all around.
(From "Brethren We Have Met to Worship," or
"Holy Manna," a nineteenth century Christian
hymn, sung to the tune "Holy Manna".)

George Gleckler lived as if he were totally alone in the days following the funeral, even though he had remaining children in the house. And he was more than alone; he was lonely. And he was frightened. He knew Kate and Clarence both had been Christians—real Christians. They didn't just go to church, as he did irregularly; they had prayed, read the Bible, and sometimes went to prayer meetings in other people's homes. George hadn't joined them in these things, but now he wished he had.

He was comforted to know that Kate and Clarence had been like that, what he thought of as real Christians. He felt assured that they were in heaven, and that thought eased his loneliness. But he was frightened about his own future, his life beyond this one. He knew his success in the Gleckler Tile Yard would do nothing for him after he died, and he knew he wasn't prepared spiritually as Kate and Clarence had been. The realization gave him a sick, guilty feeling whenever he thought how differently he had gone through that Sunday of their deaths. Unlike him, they had been up early for breakfast and household chores, and Clarence had taken Kate and the younger children to Sunday school classes at church. George had remained at home, checking to see that the kilns were properly banked and then pulling a few weeds around the flowerbeds on his way back to the house. He had enjoyed the beautiful morning and the time for himself, and he hadn't thought of God or of church.

Now he felt empty, wishing he had been with Kate and Clarence in church that morning, wishing he had listened to Kate more closely about such things, wishing he could ask her about them now. Even his son Teddy's obvious enjoyment of church life now felt like a rebuke. Why had he remained so distant from it all?

The lonely days after the funeral stretched into a week, then two, and George felt like a walking dead man. Nothing meant as much to him as it had before the accident. He just went through the motions of his work and his care for the children. But everything began to change one day in late September when a letter came from his sister, Elizabeth Gross, whom he always called by the affectionate nickname Lizzie. There had always been a special bond between them. Lizzie wrote from her home in Michigan.

"Dear Georgie," the letter began. Though she was six years younger, she usually addressed him in that affectionate way, as she would a small boy. It often annoyed him, but this time he was touched by her sisterly intimacy. The letter went on to say, "Anna and I are coming to see you at the end of the week. We have been praying for you, and we want to come to help with the children. We know Emma has been a big help, and we want to help as well. Also, Georgie, we want to talk with you about something very important, something that may help you more than anything else."

The Anna she referred to was George's sister Anna Weihl, who was three years older than George. Lizzie was six years younger. He hadn't seen either of them since the funeral, but he'd received a stream of letters and a card from each of them. George regretted that these two sisters had married and moved out of state, but he was on good terms with their husbands. Anna and her husband, George, lived outside Coleman,

Michigan. Lizzie and her husband, Herman Gross, lived in Midland, Michigan, only twenty miles away.

By the time George received the letter, their visit was only two days away. They would ride the train to Toledo and take the interurban train to the end of Graytown Road. From there they would hope for a ride on a farm wagon or a car for the final half-mile to his place. George looked around the disorder in his house. In spite of several women who came to help, the kitchen wouldn't have passed Kate's inspection. The parlor was still disarranged, and the space where the caskets had been was still empty. At least the black cloth was off the windows, and the candles were gone.

On the day Lizzie and Anna arrived, he happened to be in the yard and heard the interurban train screech to a stop at the end of the road, about half a mile from his driveway. It didn't normally stop there, so he knew the reason. He took a truck from the tile yard to meet them. The women were carrying small valises and chattering as they walked up the road. They waved frantically when they saw the truck coming. When they saw it was George driving, they yelled and laughed, though he couldn't hear them over the roar of the engine. When he climbed out to greet them, they offered tight, tense smiles and tear-filled eyes.

"Oh, Georgie, it's so good to see you!" shouted Lizzie. "How did you know we were here?"

"Heard the train stop, and it don't usually stop. The truck was there, and I just jumped in and came," he said. He took their small bags and put them in the back, and the two sisters managed to jam into the tiny cab with him. They all tried to talk on the way back to the house, but it was useless to compete with the noisy engine.

Soon the sisters were buzzing around the house, tidying, cleaning, and making plans for dinner at noon. They had brought a ham from Michigan, and there was enough bread in the house for sandwiches. Their sister Emma came over with little Arlin and baby Elmer for a short visit while they ate. Emma's older children and Malinda were at the Leatherport School. Rollin and Arthur were working in the tile factory behind the house.

Sitting there with his sisters, George felt some of the old life returning as they talked, catching up on life before Kate and Clarence were killed and about life after the tragedy. It helped to tell them details he hadn't told anyone else, and he could feel, just barely, that his life might come back together and go on. But that feeling was only a glimmer. After dinner he broke down and cried again, harder than he had cried since the trip to the cemetery. The sisters cried too and hugged him.

George remembered that Lizzie's letter had said they wanted to talk to him about something important. Now that they were together, he wanted to know. "What was it that you wanted to tell me—what you said in your letter you wanted to talk about, Lizzie?"

The women all fell silent for a moment, waiting to see who should speak first. The Michigan sisters looked at each other quickly and then glanced away. Their silence alarmed George. What else could be wrong? What *else* had happened, he wondered.

"Let's go in the front room to talk," Lizzie suggested. There they found places around the room to sit, moving chairs to fill in the spaces where the caskets had been. The other sisters looked to Lizzie to start the conversation.

"George, we have been praying for you," she began.

"Thanks," George mumbled out of politeness.

"George, I mean we have been *really* praying for you," she continued. "How have you been, living without Kate and Clarence?"

George looked down at the floor. He wanted to say he had been doing fine and just didn't want to talk about it, but it wasn't true. He heard himself say, "Not very good."

"We know," said Anna, finding her voice for the first time, "It has been so hard for all of us too, but not like it is for you. We can't really imagine."

Suddenly George couldn't contain his grief. He shook and sobbed. All of his sisters jumped up and gathered around him, and they all wept too.

"It's too much!" George said. "I can't stand it! Why did they die? Why didn't I die? Why do I have to keep living?"

"Oh, Georgie!" Lizzie said tearfully, "We love you! We all do! So does everybody!"

When their crying subsided, they all sat down. By now the afternoon sun was illuminating golden leaves outside, and the beauty outside made the pain in the room even more poignant. Once again George remembered the letter from Lizzie.

"You said there was something important you wanted to tell me, Lizzie. What else has happened? What else has gone bad?"

To his surprise, Lizzie turned to him, smiling through her tear-streaked face. "Nothing *bad* has happened, Georgie. It's something *wonderful!*"

George looked around the room. Anna and Emma were smiling too. How could they be smiling at a time like this?

"What do you mean?" George asked cautiously. His sisters weren't ones to exaggerate or to be dramatic for no reason.

"George, we have found new life in God. We all have been saved!" Lizzie said. All of the sisters, including Emma, were smiling and nodding. "We heard a message right from the Bible in a new church. It was about being saved. Our lives have started all over. As it says in the Bible, we have been born again!"

George knew some people talked about religion like this, but not people he knew well, not people in his church. At his church, people believed in God and believed they should live good lives to be approved by God. The people had all been baptized as children and had gone through confirmation classes to learn the standards of the church. He had done all of that, and he was relieved when it was over and all he had to do was go to church with his family and avoid bad habits as much as possible. He had become leery of people who were too religious, especially after he had become prosperous and a leading member of the community. He didn't want to seem odd or out of step with other businessmen. Now this news from his sisters stirred his feelings. He wanted to pull back inside himself, but he also felt something pulling him to hear more from his sisters. He just remained silent.

"We think this may seem strange and new to you," said Lizzie. "Does it?"

George nodded.

"Can we tell you more?"

George nodded again, and Anna continued. "Last spring Lizzie and I heard there would be a revival in a tent at the fairgrounds in Midland, so we went to see what it was about. A small bunch of men and women were there singing new Christian songs that were so lively and happy, not like what we had been singing in our church. It was wonderful. Then a man got up to preach. His name might have been Brother Byrum. He was so confident and sure, and he talked right from the Bible. He said we all needed to turn right to God and not depend on special rules in any of our churches. He said we needed to be like the first Christians and let the Holy Spirit lead our lives. And he said that even if we were church members, we needed to be saved and be born again."

George's mind was fairly reeling at this revelation, but he said nothing. His sisters were sensible, mature women, so he listened, and now not just politely. He began to feel that they might be telling him something that would break his grief and fear and loneliness.

"At the end of that service," Lizzie said, "a lot of people went to the front and prayed at an altar. Everybody in the tent watched and prayed too. It seemed that God was right there. Other people went to the front and prayed with those who had gone forward while everyone else sat back down. After a while, everyone got up again, and the preacher said that ten people had been saved right there that night. We sang another song, the preacher prayed, and we all went home."

Lizzie paused, choosing her words carefully for what she was about to say. "The next day, we talked about the revival. We said we all wanted to go back that night, so we did. The service that night was like the first night, and the preacher said that all we needed to do to be saved was to believe in Jesus, be sorry for our sins, and give our lives to Jesus. Somehow we knew what he meant, and we felt God calling us. At the end of the service, both of us went to the altar, and we were saved! Suddenly we felt that God had made us new and had taken away our sins, just as the man had said."

George wondered what their husbands had thought about all of this, and it seemed that Lizzie had read his mind.

"On the third night," Lizzie said, "Herman and George went with Anna and me because we had told them about the revival. They liked the meeting too. Well, we all went back a couple more nights, and the men were saved too!"

George liked both of these brothers-in-law, and he considered them honest, sensible men, but he had to think hard to envision them in this new way. Hearing that they shared this experience with his sisters nearly made his head spin. He felt alone is his limited, skeptical view of life and the church. Finally he asked, "What kind of a church is this, anyway? Where do they come from?"

"They call themselves the Church of God," Anna explained. "They have church meetings all over this part of the country, but their main location is in Indiana. They have a magazine called *The Gospel Trumpet*, and it's good. A lot of people have been saved after reading it."

"I thought all of Christianity was the church of God. Isn't that right?" he replied.

"Well, that's the only name in the Bible for the church, the real church, so that's why they call themselves the Church of God. The name is meant to include everyone in the world who really believes in Jesus," Anna said.

"Don't worry about that," Lizzie said. "What we mostly wanted you to know is that we have been saved and we are going to heaven. We think Kate and Clarence are there already. You know how true they were to the church. God knows people's hearts, George, and he is the judge."

George felt better. They are safe with Jesus right now, he thought. He couldn't contain his relief, and he began to cry again, this time softly. When his sisters saw his response, they wiped tears from their eyes too. Kate and Clarence were safe with Jesus! They were all thankful.

George suddenly felt happy, but then he was alarmed as well. What if he never could see them again? What if he wasn't saved and wouldn't go to heaven? He knew his dutiful, reluctant relationship to the church was not the same kind of thing his sisters described. He didn't think he was saved. His life now didn't seem right at all. "How can I get saved?" he asked. "Is there another revival around here?"

"You can get saved right here, right now," Lizzie said. "You just have to believe that Jesus is God's son and that he can forgive your sins and help you with your life. You just have to talk right to him and tell him you trust him and you are sorry for your sins and you want to live for him, and you will be saved. Do you want to pray like that now?"

George couldn't resist this offer of peace and assurance and release from his sense of selfishness and hardheartedness. He wanted to get rid of all of it and have the new life his sisters had. He nodded. He did want to be saved.

"Just pray like Lizzie said," Anna told him. "Say those things to God. He's right here."

So George began to pray, and for the first time in his life he felt that he really did believe in Jesus. He began to feel healed, just like some of the people in Bible stories who were healed of illness and madness. He prayed for only a few minutes, but when he was done, he shook and cried again, and all of his sisters gathered around him and cried too. But this time they were all happy. At that moment, the setting sun was casting a ray across a corner of the room. When they all saw it, one of the sisters said, "Praise God!" and other said, "It's heavenly sunlight!" And then they all hugged and laughed and cried again and were thankful for the new life each of them had begun, including George.

That day was the beginning of the Church of God in Elmore, Ohio. George Gleckler, recovering from the shock and grief of losing his beloved wife and his firstborn son, turned to Jesus when his life could have gone very badly. He was saved, and he became one of the leaders in the new congregation. He could have become bitter, angry, and selfish. Instead, he became known for his faith, his generosity, and the beauty he maintained around his brick house in the country.

The church began with home church meetings as the people migrated from home to home around the Elmore area to worship, and sometimes they met in the town hall. In 1925, George Gleckler and Henry Otte, another spiritual pioneer in the Elmore church, gave money to help buy a one-room schoolhouse to use as a church building. Others followed their lead, and before the end of the year, the church had its first home on Harris Street, a quiet side street in Elmore.

AUTHOR'S NOTE: *George Gleckler met and married his second wife, Mary Steiner, in 1915. He and Mary lived together on the Gleckler property for thirty years, and Mary cared for George in his later years. George died on a cold, sunny day in March 1945 at age seventy-eight. Mary had walked to the next house that day to see Ruth Kardatzke, George's niece by marriage, for a break from her bedside duties while George's son Rollin stayed with George. When Mary saw Rollin pull into the driveway at Ruth's home, she gasped and gathered up her purse and coat. Rollin's arrival could mean only one thing. Mary and Ruth hurried to the back door. Rollin stood at the base of the back steps, tears welling up in his eyes.*

"Dad's gone," he reported simply.

"I'll have a lot to do," Mary said matter-of-factly, pulling on her coat.

George's funeral was held in his home a few days later, like the service for Kate and Clarence in the same house many years before.

ROBBERS IN THE NIGHT

It had felt like snow all day. The sky was heavy and gray, and the air was damp and cold. In 1921, there were no reliable weather forecasts, even though weather observation stations had been communicating weather reports since telegraph by the mid-1800s and later by telephone and then radio. These reports helped but did not provide accurate forecasts. Most people just had to learn to judge by the feel of the air and the look of the sky and hope they were right.

Fred Kardatzke was bringing in the last two buckets of milk near sundown when the snow began. It started fast, like sharp pebbles, first bouncing on the gravel and then settling on it and covering it. He turned his face a little to the east, away from the wind, and walked faster to the milk house. He shut the door while he poured the milk into the ten-gallon collection cans floating in cold water. By the time he was done with his final chore of the day, the storm had gained energy, and he was glad to reach the house before it hit with full force.

"Gonna be a real blizzard," he said to Emma as he came in, his coat loaded with snow pebbles.

"Yep. I seen it comin', and I hoped you'd git in fast," she replied without looking up from her cooking.

He left his boots and coat in the mud porch and took a cup from the cupboard. Hot coffee was always good at a time like this. "Where the kids?" he asked.

"Some in there and some upstairs," she said, nodding toward the living room. "They got their studies to do."

He looked in and could see three of the youngest, sprawled on the floor with their books near the heat register. Recently he had installed

40

a large coal-burning furnace in the cellar that warmed the downstairs and sent a little heat drifting up the stairs to the kids' bedrooms. The kids didn't look up when he came in but kept reading, so he thought it best not to start any talk with them just then. Time enough for that at supper. Anyhow, he didn't want to talk about their schoolwork. A little of that went a long way for him. He slipped into his chair for another look at last Sunday's paper. It was the main thing he read, and the Sunday paper usually lasted him all week.

Elmer, the youngest boy, noticed his father and broke the silence. "Pa, do you think we'll have school tomorrow if it snows really hard?"

Fred was a little annoyed at the question. The one-room school was right across the road from their house. Why wouldn't they have school? Of course, there was the little matter of the schoolteacher getting there. "I dunno," he said. "Depends on whether Miss Wainwright can make it out from town." He thought for a minute and added, "Course, if she can't come, I could come and teach you kids a thing or two!"

All the kids laughed at that idea. "Would you really teach school?" one of the little girls yelled. All of them laughed again, and Fred laughed a little too and shook his head.

The kids knew Pa only visited the school a couple of times each year, unless one of them got in trouble. He had only gone to eighth grade when he was a boy, and he didn't understand why any of his kids needed to go further than he had. Carl and Harris were already in high school, and there might be more of that kind of thing soon. The way Carl talked about school all the time convinced him he hadn't heard the last on that topic.

"Supper's ready," Emma announced. "I need some help in here."

Three of the kids hopped up, ready to move around and make sure suppertime was a happy time. Pa didn't like his supper to be served cool or late. Soon the family had gathered around the kitchen table, all eleven of them. Ma asked Harris, the oldest boy, to pray. When he finished his prayer, the food began to disappear. There wasn't a lot of talk around the table; Pa didn't like to hear a lot of talk when he was eating. But when the wind blew hard against the house and, snow pelted the windows, Ma said, "Sounds pretty bad out there. Good thing we got the new coal furnace."

After supper, three of the girls helped Ma in the kitchen. Two of the older boys bundled up in their coats and went to the barn with Pa to make sure the animals were inside and the doors were all shut. This evening would be a bad time for a cow or pig to go wandering.

Back in the house, it was bright and warm. The checkerboard was out, and so was the carom board. Expert fingers would flick the wooden shooter carom rings, hitting the red and green rings into the corner pockets to earn the right to shoot in the black ring for added points. Many snowy nights were enlivened by checkers, caroms, Old Maid, other card games, and popcorn.

An evening of fun began. The click of the carom rings and the tapping of checkers measured off the time before bedtime. Pa checked the furnace one more time, shook out the ashes, and added more coal. When he came back upstairs, he announced, "Pert near bedtime," and looked around the kitchen and living room to see if all the kids had heard.

They had all heard; they had learned that it was best to hear when Pa made one of his announcements. The games were put away, and the race was on for the stairs. Pa ignored the thunder of feet and turned off lamps in the living room. As he did, he thought about how fortunate they were to be the first people on their road to have electricity. Their house was near the state route that ran along the river, and the electric poles came only as far as their house.

Quiet settled in for the night. Chatter and giggling ended upstairs. The only sound was the moaning of the winter storm. Fred and Emma prepared for bed in their own ways. It would be good to settle down under the blankets and let the storm blow itself out. As he pulled thick blankets over his shoulders, Fred began to think about the animals in the barn and the other buildings. He could see himself checking them in the morning, and soon he drifted into sleep and dreams.

Sometime in the middle of the night, a shot of fear went through him and he was awake. Then he remembered his dream. What remained of it was mainly a feeling, but in the dream he had seen dark figures coming to the house. Even awake, he felt overwhelming fear. He felt sure the dream figures were robbers, and it was a warning. He sat up in bed, awake with the fear of death. After listening for a minute, he lay back down.

"What is it, Fred?" Emma asked.

"They're coming," he said, almost in a whisper.

"Who's coming?" she asked.

"Robbers. I dreamed that robbers are coming."

They both listened, and all they heard was the wind outside. She was about to tell him it was just a dream when a wave of fear swept over both of them. They lay motionless and listened. No! There were men's voices just outside the house! It must be the robbers! They didn't dare to move, and the voices were coming closer. Soon feet were stomping on the side porch and there was a loud knock on the door.

Fred thought about his shotgun, but it was at the other end of the house and he didn't know if he had any shells. It was a crazy thought, he knew, but his fear was taking him over. He should just find out who it was. Maybe his dream was wrong. Maybe these were neighbors needing help.

"Stay here," he said to Emma as he put on his heavy grey sweater and went to the door. She could hear him open the door and begin talking with someone. When she heard him say, "Well, better come on in," she got up quickly and put on a warm housecoat. In the kitchen light she could see two men, quite young and unknown to her. They weren't dressed for the cold. They were so poorly dressed that it seemed as though a careless mother had dressed them. She looked at Fred for an explanation.

"They got car trouble," Fred told her. "Car slid in the ditch up the road. I kin get 'em out in the morning. Have enough blankets for 'em to sleep on the floor?"

Emma looked the men over, and they now seemed like just big boys, not much older than her older sons.

"Sure, we got blankets," she said and went to pull them out of the back closet. They always had extra blankets because it was common to have relatives drop in for the night. They had no extra beds, so the kids would usually sleep on the floor and let the company have their beds. This time the visitors would sleep on the floor.

Fred talked only a little with the men while Emma made them beds on the floor. He never liked to talk much, and he especially didn't like to talk in the middle of the night with strangers he still thought might be robbers. He looked them over carefully while they talked, and they seemed like simple town boys. They didn't seem to be armed or dangerous, and it was clear they were grateful to be in out of the storm. They told Fred they had gotten lost on their way to Toledo. But how did they manage to be out on this country road, and why so late at night?

When Emma finished making beds out of blankets on the floor for the men, she said, "We don't have pillows. Can you sleep without pillows?"

The men looked at each other and at her. "Sure," they said with a shrug.

"We all better git to bed," Fred said, making his words sound like a warning. "My wife cooks a good breakfast, but she cooks it early."

The house was soon quiet again, and the only sound was the storm. Fred didn't fall asleep quickly this time. Thoughts continued to bother him. What if they really were robbers? What if the dream was true? He thought he was still awake thinking about robbers all night when he heard a pan in the kitchen and smelled coffee. Emma was frying some ham from the hog they had butchered two weeks earlier. It was still dark and would be for a time, but it was time to get up, nearly five o'clock in the morning. Fred pulled on his shirt and overalls and walked in his socks to the kitchen. Emma set a cup of coffee on the table, and he sat down to put on his shoes. They looked at each other and then toward the living room, but they didn't speak. They didn't want to wake up the sleepers.

The next sounds they heard were squeaks from the floor upstairs. Some of the kids had smelled the ham and were up. Sometimes they were noisy in the morning, but today the first ones awake were very quiet. Fred saw Lucille and Forrest enter the living room and stop. They looked at the sleeping bodies on the floor and then tiptoed around the mysterious guests to the kitchen.

"Who is that?" Lucille whispered. "Are they the cousins from Michigan?" Emma had sisters in Michigan, and their kids were among the favorite visitors.

"No, those are no cousins of yours," Ma said. "We don't even know who they are."

The words startled the children. They looked at their mother and then again at the sleepers. "Why are they here?" Forrest asked.

"Car slid in the ditch in the storm last night," Ma explained and kept fixing breakfast. "Musta been ten o'clock when they come knockin' on the door. Pa let 'em in to sleep here. He's gonna git their car out after breakfast."

The kids quickly tiptoed to the south windows to see the car in the ditch. Sure enough, there it was, halfway to the river. Then they scampered upstairs to tell the other kids the exciting news. "Strangers are sleeping downstairs! Their car is in the ditch! They came in the middle of the night and slept here! Come down and see them!"

Emma heard the commotion upstairs, so she hurried breakfast along. Soon all the kids came down the stairs, making a noise like rolling thunder. They stopped in their tracks and fell silent when they saw the bodies on the floor. They crept through the living room and past the sleepers, looking them over cautiously. Emma put a finger over her mouth to tell them to stay quiet, and they slipped into their places at the table. The ham and eggs and bread were disappearing when a man appeared silently at the living room door. Everyone was startled that he had made his way there so quietly.

"Well, did ya sleep okay?" Ma asked the stranger, who replied with a nod of his head.

Pa didn't say anything; he just looked at the young man suspiciously. The dream of robbers was still on his mind, but how could he tell if somebody was a robber by looking at him? He particularly didn't like the looks of this one. He was skinny with blond hair and pale eyebrows that made him look like a criminal. Just like me, he thought, when he realized the young man looked something like he had at that age. That thought didn't decrease his dislike for the man.

"How 'bout wakin' up your friend and havin' breakfast?" Ma offered. "Then you'll both have time to eat before for our morning worship."

No one was surprised at Emma's announcement. She always led the family in worship after breakfast with prayer, a Bible verse, a song, and sometimes even her version of a little sermon. This time Fred felt a little embarrassed. What would these men think when they had to "go to church" for their breakfast? Then he thought, what do I care? It serves them right to have church with their breakfast after waking us up in the middle of the night. If they are robbers, Emma's little "church service" will be just what they need.

Fred was never really in the spirit of morning worship, but he sat through it for the sake of his wife. Her brother George Gleckler had become a Christian after a family tragedy, the train accident that had killed his wife and son. Emma and all of Fred and Emma's older children were Christians as well. The church that formed as a result of the Gleckler family tragedy was meeting in several homes in the area, and Emma was one of its most active leaders. She thought and talked about

45

God and the church every chance she had. Fred knew she wouldn't miss this chance.

The other man appeared at the living room door, and Fred decided he didn't like his looks either. His brown hair was rumpled and he had a dishonest, shifty way of looking around the kitchen. The kids slid their chairs aside, and two of the older boys brought extra chairs from the mud porch. The strangers were placed side by side at the end of the table facing Fred. Plates of food were handed to them, and it seemed they hadn't eaten for a while. The children noticed their poor manners but kept their eyes on their own plates. Fred noticed everything.

After the table was cleared, Emma started morning worship with a short prayer of thanks for breakfast and shelter from the storm. She gave thanks that the mysterious visitors had found safety in the family's house and had not frozen in the storm, going out into eternity in whatever their spiritual condition might be. Then Emma asked Lucille to read a short passage from the Old Testament about the Ten Commandments, after which she told a short version of the story of the prodigal son. To end, everyone sang "The Way of the Cross Leads Home," and then Emma asked Harris to give the closing prayer.

Morning worship took only a few minutes, but Fred felt it was very long. All the time, he kept watching the two visitors, who were barely older than his boys. Both looked down at the table most of the time, only peeking around the room a few times. Fred thought they probably never had to sit through morning worship at the breakfast table before.

"I guess we better see if we kin git that car outa the ditch," Fred announced. Then he thought he would quiz the boys a little.

"You boys brothers?" he asked.

"Just friends," the blond one said.

"Where ya from?"

"Toledo."

"Whatya doin' way out here?"

"Seein' friends in Oak Harbor," the dark haired boy answered.

"Oak Harbor? I know lots of people in Oak Harbor. Maybe I know your friends there," Fred replied. He thought the boys became pale when he said that.

"Well, they don't live in Oak Harbor anymore," the blond one said nervously.

"What're their names?" Fred pressed.

After a pause, the blonde-haired one said, "Johnson. Tom Johnson." It was the most common name he could think of.

Fred thought a minute. He was sure the name wasn't real, but he thought it best not to press the issue. Anyway, if the friends didn't live there anymore, why did they come out to Oak Harbor? He doubted these boys knew anybody in Oak Harbor, so he just said, "I hope I get to meet him sometime. I'll ask about him next time I'm in Oak Harbor."

Everyone got up from the table, and the children went to find their warmest clothes. Fred got his boots and coat from the mud porch. He wasn't going to leave these men in the house with his family, so he said, "You can come with me to hitch up the horses. They can probably pull your car out of that little ditch. Ennaway, I don't think the tractor will start in this cold."

Before Fred and the men left the house, Emma came in from the living room with two gospel tracts. Giving one to each of the young men, she said, "Take these with you and read them. They will tell you the way of salvation."

The men looked at her sheepishly and tucked the tracts into their pockets. One of them mumbled, "Thank you, ma'am." Fred burned with embarrassment and pushed his way out the door.

Emma watched the two young men follow Fred to the barn. In a few minutes, the wide barn doors opened and the big team of horses emerged. Their breath made small clouds in the cold air, and they were beautiful to see. The men and horses trudged through the snow out to the road. The snow wasn't very deep, and most of it had blown off the road near the car. Emma moved around to the south-facing windows to watch the car come out of the ditch. By this time, the children were dressed and joined her.

"Looks like ya just drove off the road," Fred observed at the car. "Couldn't see the edge in the snow?"

The boys both shook their heads. "We thought we were in the middle of the road. We couldn't back out when we drove in there."

Fred moved the horses past the car and attached a long chain to the rear bumper. It wouldn't take much to pull the car out of the shallow ditch.

"See if you can start it," he told the boys. The dark haired one got in, and the car started with no trouble.

"Okay, when I say go, you back up the car but make sure you stop when you're out of the ditch. I don't want you runnin' over my horses," Fred ordered. They could see it would be best to follow this man's instructions exactly and not run over his horses.

Fred urged the horses forward until the chain was tight. "Okay! Go!" he yelled, and the driver started backing the car out of the ditch. The horses leaned into their collars and pulled, and the car was soon up on the road. It hadn't seemed hard at all to these huge draft horses. Fred unhooked the chain and turned the horses back toward the barn.

"If you're goin' to Toledo, you can go on up this road to the first big road. That's 163. Turn left, and you can find your way to Woodville Road," Fred said.

They nodded, looked up the road, and then down at their feet. Their shiftiness heightened Fred's suspicions.

"Thanks, mister," one of them said, and they climbed quickly into the car and started up the road. The car looked too good for those scruffy young men, Fred thought as they drove away.

Fred put the horses away and went back to the house to get a better coat.

"Whatcha doin', Pa?" Emma asked.

"I'm goin' to town. I gotta see the police. Them men were too suspicious." Emma shuddered when he added, "My dream was right. They were robbers."

Fred was glad that his car, inside the corncrib, started easily. The snow had stopped, so he drove carefully into town with no trouble. Elmore had a small police station, but it wasn't open all the time. He went there first, and to his surprise, he found the local policeman, Ernie Sondergeld. He described his night's adventure, the men, and the car they were driving.

That's them, alright," Ernie Sondergeld said. "They stole that car in Oak Harbor. I got a call last night. Which way did they go?"

"They went north on my road. I told 'em how to go to Toledo," Fred explained.

"We'll get 'em," Ernie said. "Toledo police are already lookin' for 'em." He reached for his big black phone and placed the call in very serious tones. When he put down the phone, he turned to Fred.

"You have any other trouble with them boys?" he asked.

"Like what?" Fred asked.

"Well, it sounds like them same two got pretty rough with a man at a gas station in Oak Harbor. Hit him and stole some gas too," Ernie said.

Fred felt the chill of fear he had felt the night before. "No, pretty peaceful at my house," he said.

"Well, we'll get 'em," Ernie said. "We'll get 'em."

As Fred drove back to the farm, he wondered what would happen to those young men. He didn't know much about the police or the courts or the prisons. He didn't know how long they would be in prison if they had to go there. At last he was getting over his fear, and he was surprised to be feeling sorry for the boys. He hoped they wouldn't be in prison too long. He felt sorry for their parents too. Then he remembered the tracts Emma had given them and the morning worship she made them listen to. Maybe it was the right thing to do, he thought. Maybe they still have a chance to go right. They can even read the tracts in prison.

Work on the farm continued that day. Leta Wainright, the schoolteacher, made it out to the Leatherport School from town, so there were classes all day for the school-age children. At supper, the kids asked, "Who were those men at breakfast?"

Emma looked at Fred. "Well, it turns out they were robbers," he said. "They stole that car. They were car thieves."

The kids gasped at this news. "Robbers! How did you find out, Pa?" one of them asked.

"I went to town and told the police," Fred said. "They were already looking for them and the car they stole."

The kids asked many more questions about the men, the car, the police, and the danger of robbers coming to the house. Nothing like this had ever happened to them before. Pa said the men would probably go to prison, and the kids at first appeared to feel safer, but then they felt sad, imagining what it would be like to go to prison. Emma sensed their thoughts.

"The worst thing about it is that those men aren't saved," she said. "If they were, they wouldn't a done a thing like this. At least we had a chance to witness to 'em. I gave 'em tracts about salvation before they left."

The children looked at their mother and could see her determination. She had witnessed to the two robbers who had come in the night, robbers who might have robbed them if they'd had a chance. Ma is a good woman, they thought, a good Christian woman. And Pa did right too. They hoped they had done right too, and they hoped they would never steal a car, and they never did.

AUTHOR'S NOTE: *My father, Arlin Kardatzke, told me about this incident in detail in the late 1900s, including his father's dream about the robbers. Judging by Arlin's perception of the story, he may have been about ten years old at the time. If so, this incident happened in 1921.*

The game of carrom, or carroms as we called it, is a form of billiards or table shuffleboard. It's played on a board about three feet square with net pockets in the corners. The players flick shooter (or "striker") rings against the red and green rings that more sophisticated players might call carrom men. The player who first clears the board of his colored rings may shoot for the black ring called the queen. The game originated in India and became popular after World War I. Until I did a little superficial research for this book, I thought everyone grew up playing carroms.

GRANDPA'S SUNDAY MORNING

Bacon was already frying when Fred Kardatzke woke up. Breakfast usually came after the first chores in the morning, but then he remembered it was Sunday. Emma was cooking breakfast early so she could get to church on time. In the past, she had to get all nine kids ready and cook breakfast for them before church, but no more. Now only Fred and Emma still lived on the farm.

"I guess I'll have to have breakfast with her before I feed the stock," he said to himself as he buttoned his blue work shirt. "I wonder if that new calf is okay," he continued, pulling on his blue bib overalls. He tied his work shoes and noticed a little manure on the side of one. He didn't want to have to talk about that again, so he cleaned it off. He had meant to take his shoes off in the mud porch, but he forgot. It always upset Emma when he tracked manure into the house.

As he stepped into the living room, the breakfast smells lifted his spirits. Emma glanced up when he entered the kitchen, but they didn't talk. Their Sunday morning talks were usually short and careful. Finally he said, "Anybody comin' home for dinner?"

Without turning around, Emma said, "I dunno. Mebbe Harris and Delorous and Elaine. I din ask 'em yet." She sometimes invited a family from church to have dinner with them, but Fred preferred a quiet afternoon. Sunday was his day of rest, and he didn't need any help with that.

They ate breakfast silently. Once or twice Fred looked up and caught Emma's glance and immediately looked back at his bacon, eggs, and fried potatoes. Even to meet her glance was to know her wish that he would go to church with her. He didn't want to go, and he didn't want to say no, so he just ate his breakfast. By now Emma knew his ways well enough that she wasn't newly disappointed each Sunday, but his absence was a matter of continual heartache for her. She knew their time must be short, and as difficult as her life had been with Fred, she still wanted him to accept the Lord and meet her in heaven. He knew it, so she didn't have to mention it again.

"Good eggs, Ma," he said in an effort at conciliation.

"Yep," she said as she took their plates to the sink. "From that same old brown hen. I dunno why her eggs taste the best, but they do. I been savin' the three of 'em just for you."

"Thanks, Ma," he mumbled and felt the old guilt rising in his chest. He always felt that when she was especially good to him. "Goin' out for chores now," he added.

It was a beautiful spring day, but the prospect of his work that day seemed heavier on his mind than other times. Maybe it was all of the plowing and harrowing he had done that week or having to catch the cows that somehow got out yesterday. What would be wrong when he got to the barn today?

After trudging through the bright sunlight, Fred thought the barn seemed especially dark. The familiar smell of dust, straw, and aging barn timbers greeted him. As his eyes adjusted, he looked for anything that might be wrong. A silent movement in the haymow was just the cat. He liked this one particular cat, though he hated dogs. He wouldn't tolerate a dog on his property, ever. Farther inside, the two white-faced steers looked at him calmly and waited for their hay. The new calf was fine, still wobbly but healthy in its stall. Out back, the cows shambled amiably to the milking shed when he opened the door, and the pigs as usual squealed a greeting, hoping for some corn. All was well in the barn.

After bringing two large buckets of milk to the little milk storage house halfway to the house, he went into the house for his bath. Emma had left for church with their son Harris, who lived nearby and had a car. Fred rarely went to church, but he did honor the Sabbath by bathing and getting dressed as though he had gone to church. Having the house to himself was a luxury, especially after the years of raising nine children and lately the frequent thunderclaps of grandchildren and family visits. He could take his bath in private and dash in his underwear across the living room to the bedroom for his dress clothes. It was part of the Sunday ritual he lived by. Fred had only two suits, and the one he wore on Sundays was almost always the dark blue, pinstriped one. He felt secure in that suit, almost like a preacher or a judge, though he was far from either. A little splash of Old Spice after shaving, and he was ready for the trip to town.

Fred checked his hair and his tie. He glanced down at his shoes and brushed away dust that had gathered on them during the week. The garage was only a dozen steps across the gravel driveway from the side door. The shiny, black 1941 Buick was always a joy to drive, especially for his Sunday trip into town for the paper. It was one of the last models built before World War II and was eight years old, but it hadn't lost any of its power or shine. With the war over, Fred felt that things were starting again in a better way than ever before.

In town there was only one place he could buy a paper on Sunday, at the only business whose owner chose to be open in the face of local sensibilities about doing business on Sunday. Fred and the owner shared the desire to avoid church, but probably for different reasons. Fred didn't really know why Arnold kept his restaurant open and didn't go to church with his wife, but here he was, ready to sell the *Toledo Blade* and maybe some breakfast. Since he had already eaten and wanted his privacy, he went inside only to pick up a copy of the *Blade*.

"How ya doin', Fred?" Arnold asked as he rang up the sale.

Fred knew he was just making conversation, but even this much talk felt irksome to him this particular day. "Pretty good," he said flatly.

"Been okay, have ya?" the man persisted.

Now Fred was annoyed. Turning his powerful gaze directly on his friend, he said in a level tone, "Yep, I bin okay. What'd ya mean?"

Arnold saw that he had crossed a line. "I din mean nothin' by it, Fred. I just wanted to be sure."

Fred let the remark pass, paid for his paper, and got back in the Buick. Angry thoughts filled his mind. What was Arnold getting so nosy about? How am I? Why did he want to be sure? I'm about the same as always, but older. And this is a hard time of year for any farmer. So what? Anyhow, why doesn't Arnold go to church?

Fred knew his own reasons. He had been mad at the church for about twenty-five years. It all went back to that preacher, one of the temporary preachers before the church people bought the church building in town. Fred had seen him with a woman one night in Toledo, and it wasn't the preacher's wife. At first he thought the woman might be from the church, but he didn't recognize her. The next day he went to some of the leaders in the church, but they said he was just trying to cause trouble. He *had* caused trouble a few times, but it was for good reason, he told himself. Those things were before that sneaky preacher came, and they had no right to turn the tables on him. Worse yet, when the church leaders found out later that he was right about the preacher and there was trouble in the church, no one came to him and said he'd been right. After the trouble ended, he felt justified in staying away from church. He was angry every time he remembered that part of his past. It gave him a reason to stay home and have his own kind of Sunday, just like this day.

Back home it was good to see his old chair waiting, and he laid the paper on the table next to it so he could stop in the bathroom. When he washed his hands, he glanced in the mirror and it gave him a start. He looked pale—almost green—and not pink and "ruddy" as he was usually described. No wonder Arnold was getting nosy. I better get a nap, he thought.

He felt a lot more tired than he usually did at this time of day, and he settled in his chair to read. The news was mainly bad, as usual. Truman was trying to keep the Russians from taking over the whole world, and men were out of work after coming back from the war. Unions in the cities were stopping work while other people wanted to work. Farm prices were down, and he wondered how much he would ever get for his six feeder pigs. He laid the paper down and waited for Emma to return from church. He dozed off, but he woke up suddenly with a stabbing pain in his chest. He tried to get up, but his arms and legs were too heavy. He loosened his tie to breathe better, and sweat broke out all over his body. He looked nervously out the window to see if Emma was back. Not yet. He would just sit still till she came.

Finally the crunch of gravel in the driveway alerted him that Emma was home. Harris and his wife, Delorous, had brought her home. They were talking as they got out of the car, and he could tell that they were all coming in, including Elaine, their daughter.

"Pa, where are ya?" Emma called. "We got company!" She followed her own voice through the kitchen and then thought she was being too loud. Fred hated to be awakened from a Sunday nap. He was in his chair as usual, but something was different.

"Fred, you okay?" Emma asked, going over to him. By now their son Harris and his family were close behind.

"I dunno, Ma," he said softly. "I had a pain, and I feel real tired."

The very softness of his voice startled them. Emma looked at Harris and Delorous, but none of them knew what to do.

"Yer not havin' a heart attack are ya, Pa?" Harris asked.

"I dunno," Fred murmured. "What if I am?"

No one dared answer. They knew what could happen, and they knew he was not prepared, and *they* weren't prepared for him to die like this either.

"We hafta call the doctor," Harris said, and before Fred could object, he went into the kitchen to get on the telephone. The house was the only one on their road with a phone, and Fred and Emma were glad to have it, especially now that they were living alone on the farm.

Harris came back in a few minutes. "Doc Willet is on the way," he reported.

"Pa, can we pray for ya?" Emma asked.

Fred felt the "other sickness" in his chest just then. He knew that people had been praying for him for years, especially his family members, and it made him feel even more guilty. But this time was different, and he knew it. "Okay," he said, and the family gathered around him and all of them prayed except Fred. They prayed that his life would be spared and that he would rise up again to do his work and that God's power would be seen in his healing. Then Emma broke down and cried and they all cried. Even Fred cried quietly, though it hurt his chest. They were still crying when Doctor Willet's car pulled into the driveway. He knew the family and had cared for them well for years.

"Where's the patient?" he asked quietly as they led him into the living room. Taking one look at Fred, he opened his black bag and pulled out his stethoscope.

"I need to listen to your chest, Fred," he said, and Emma helped unbutton his shirt. The cold stethoscope gave Fred a chill, but Dr. Willet's expression chilled him even more. He was listening too carefully in too many places.

"When did this start?" he asked.

Fred had to think. How long had he been in his chair? Had he been sleeping? Maybe he could tell from when he got back from town. Yes, that would tell it. "I guess I bin here since 'bout ten," he said.

Doc Willet looked at his watch. "Over two hours. That's good, since you're still here to talk with us."

No one felt better after that comment. The doctor kept checking and finally stood up and said, "He better go to bed. I'll give you a prescription and I'll call one of the Ghering brothers at home so they can open up the pharmacy and get it for you today."

"What's wrong with him, Doctor?" Emma asked. "Can you tell?"

"I think it's his heart, but it might be something else," he replied. "His heart is not sounding the way it should. Other things can seem like a heart attack, but this seems like one. Like a heart attack, I mean. He shouldn't do anything to make this worse right now. Let's get him into bed."

Harris called his brothers and sisters in the area, and one of them was going to those without phones to tell them the news. Before too long, many family members were in the house learning the details and being asked to pray. From his bedroom, Fred could hear someone praying out loud for him. For once, on this Sunday morning, he welcomed the prayer.

AUTHOR'S NOTE: *Fred and Emma Kardatzke had a telephone installed early, perhaps about 1910. There were so few other subscribers that they had the phone removed after a couple of years. They had it reinstalled again in about 1938.*

In 1948, when these events took place, congestive heart failure was one of the leading causes of death, but it was little understood, and there was no effective treatment. Following the death of President Franklin D. Roosevelt in 1945, major studies of cardiovascular disease were launched, notably the Framingham Heart Study, the first long-term study of its kind.

GRANDPA'S AFTERNOON VISITOR

T he day after Fred Kardatzke's first heart spell, Dr. Willet gave him some medicine and told him to "take it easy." He didn't say he would get well. When Fred asked him point blank, Dr. Willet just said, "We'll have to see how things go."

After that first bad day, Fred was in bed much of the time, but not all of the time. He was always tired, and he sometimes went to bed in the afternoon and didn't get up until breakfast the next day. In the mornings, he could sometimes help Emma with light chores outside, like feeding the animals and gathering eggs. He could sometimes milk the cows if she got them into the milking shed. He could put out hay for the cattle, but only if one of his sons came over and threw it down from the hayloft high in the barn. He couldn't drive the tractor, so he couldn't get out away from the house to see the fields. He knew he would never be able to do all the things he used to. It was a lot of extra work for Emma, helping with the animals and other farm chores besides taking care of him. He was sorry for that, and sorry for the time that his grown children had to spend helping on the farm. They were being so kind to him, but he had not always been kind to them.

As he shuffled around the few hours he was out of bed each day, it felt as though someone was sitting on his chest. The pressure made it difficult to breathe, and sometimes he felt a sharp pain. Something else was bothering him too. He could feel another weight in his chest, one that made him sad and even more tired. This other weight was heaviest when people told him they were praying for him or came to visit and prayed for him. And why shouldn't they pray for him? They prayed about everything else, so it was natural that they wanted to pray for him, and sometimes he really wanted them to. He knew his time was short, and he hadn't prayed for many years. Whenever they came to see him when he was in bed and prayed for him, he always just looked away, lay there quietly, and said, "Thanks."

One afternoon in the week after his heart attack, after he had helped with chores outside in the morning and had eaten dinner at noon with Emma, some good chicken and noodles and potatoes, he had gone back to bed as usual. When he woke up after a short nap, he could hear someone talking with Emma in the kitchen. They weren't whispering, but they were talking quietly. He listened for a while but couldn't hear what they were saying. Finally he recognized a voice.

"Ma," he called out, "is that Art? He wanta come in and see me?"

Chairs scraped the kitchen floor as they pushed back from the table. He was right, it was his nephew Art Gleckler, the one who had lost an ear many years earlier. Art had been working in the fields when his horses bolted. He fell under a cultivator and was being dragged by the horses. Fred, working in the next field, ran over and stopped the horses, saving Art's life. There was a special bond between the men ever since. Art was a quiet, thoughtful man, and Fred was fond of him. They had worked the fields around the area for many years before Art became a carpenter.

"Hi, Fred," Art said cautiously as he approached the bed. "How are ya?"

Fred looked at his nephew and thought about giving a smart answer, but he knew he shouldn't joke with him, especially now. Art looked sad and seemed to have something to say. Fred didn't want to hear what he had to say, but he greeted him well.

"Right now I'm doin' pretty good," he said, "for an old man with a bad heart."

He wished he hadn't put it that way. He did have heart disease, as people called it, but he knew Art would see a double meaning in what he'd said. Sure enough, Art looked at him closely to see what he'd meant. Fred glanced at Art and then looked away into the other room, so Art didn't press the matter.

"Yep. I know, Fred," he said softly and shifted his weight to the other foot because he was nervous.

"Got time to set down, Art?" Emma asked, pointing to the chair at the foot of Fred's bed.

Art silently sat down and looked at Fred again. There was a long silence before he asked Fred about the farm work and the cattle. It was easier for Fred to talk about things like that than about his illness and his life. After the milk cows and the pigs and the horses had been talked over, both men fell silent. Art looked sad, and Fred knew he still had something to say.

"We prayed for you at prayer meeting last night," Art mumbled, looking down at the side of the bed. Then he said what he had come for. "We prayed for your heart."

Fred's heart thumped and beat harder. He knew what Art meant, but he didn't want to talk about it. "Thanks, Art. I 'preciate that," he said.

The two men sat quietly for a minute, not knowing what the other might say next. Emma stood in the doorway, covering her mouth with her handkerchief.

"I better go now," Art said at last, putting on his cap. "I got some work to do."

"Yep," Fred muttered. "Good to see you, Art."

Fred could hear emotion in Emma's voice as she talked with Art again in the kitchen. Fred, too, felt so sad he nearly cried. "Art!" he called out to them, and he heard Emma and Art quickly crossing the living room to his bedroom to see if something had happened. But Fred couldn't say any more. He just said, "Thanks again for comin', Art."

Art knew what he really meant, but he couldn't say much either. "I wisht you was better, Fred," he said awkwardly.

When Art was gone, Emma came back to the bedroom. "Art's really worried about you, Fred. He asks me ever time I see him. He feels real bad."

Again Fred swallowed hard. Art was so gentle, not like him. Art probably worried more about him than anybody, including Fred himself. Fred felt lonely, even with Emma with him, but he didn't understand why. He thought of Art's kindness and wondered if he had ever been that kind to others. He wondered too how Art could be so patient. Why couldn't he be like Art? He remembered Art's near-fatal farm accident, and how he had rescued him, and how Art's recovery had made him gentle, not angry. Maybe Art had come to save *him* this time, he thought. He began to remember past years and was soon asleep.

THE "LITTLE PROFESSOR" COMES TO VISIT

A week after Fred's heart attack, there was a phone call from Carl, Fred and Emma's second eldest child. Carl said he wanted to come for a visit. He was living in Anderson, Indiana, where he was a professor at Anderson College. Fred dreaded seeing Carl. This son was cut from other cloth than he was, and he was different from the other children too. Carl had been shaping his brothers' and sisters' thinking ever since he was in high school. In some ways, Fred thought, Carl had shaped their lives even more than he had himself. Just the thought of a visit from Carl made him anxious, especially because he knew why Carl was coming.

Of their many battles, Carl had won the biggest—the one about education. He had left home to go to college in Anderson, and he had become a professor of education. Education, of all things, Fred thought. He had never favored excessive education, and now his son taught it like a science! But those battles were now in the past, and Fred felt grudging admiration for what all of his children had accomplished, much of it through Carl's example, prodding, encouragement, and even financial support.

Fred saw Carl's intelligence and his different ways of looking at the world even before Carl started school. Carl was able to read even before he entered first grade at the one-room Leatherport School. Fred could read, but he thought there was something odd about a kid who read so young without even being taught. It was surprising but vaguely annoying. A kid like that couldn't be counted on for farm work.

Carl entered first grade in 1909 along with his older brother, Harris. Emma had kept Harris out of school until the school building was moved away from the smoke of George Gleckler's brick and tile factory, so Harris was six years old and Carl was five when they started school. Carl learned so much first and second grade material that the following year he was placed with the third grade students. Even there he excelled. In fact, he was always the top student in the Leatherport School during his seven years there.

Outside of school, Carl was full of questions and little jokes. He puzzled over pictures in the paper, but he also puzzled over words, sometimes words that were too big and too serious for a boy his age, Fred thought. Carl caused Fred no trouble growing up. He pitched into the farm work whenever he was needed, and even though he was the smallest of the sons, he worked on the farm better than Fred had expected. He often made a game or a story out of his farm tasks, and Fred found some of his stories funny.

Fred had gone to the Leatherport School up through fifth grade, and he finished his last three years of formal education at the German Lutheran School in Elmore. All of his life he'd worked for his father on the farm, so he took up full-time farming after his eighth grade graduation. His choice of career was a good and respectable way to live, and he expected his children to do the same. His plan seemed in place until Carl was in his last year at Leatherport School. Storm clouds began to gather soon after Christmas that year. Carl would graduate in the summer, and his brother Harris would graduate the following year. The problem was that Carl wanted to go to high school in Elmore, and he had planted the idea in Harris's mind too. High school? Where did they get ideas like that, Fred wondered?

By this time, the idea of high school was difficult to avoid. A high school of sorts had existed in Elmore since about 1855, and a two-story brick high school had gone up in 1871. High school was an ambition many parents held for their children. Even some farmers were talking big about their sons going to high school, and some were thinking of sending their girls. Emma told him people in the church were talking about high school for Harris and Carl, people who didn't have farms and didn't need their sons to help. They could afford to talk, Fred thought. Why didn't they stick with their Bibles and Sunday school lessons? High school was not a proper topic for church people on Sunday, he thought, and not even on Wednesday nights.

The high school talk continued, and even Emma joined in. She talked about school at the dinner table and talked about the good work all the children were doing. Fred could tell she was proud of them, and he tried not to think that she actually was bragging on herself as well as on her children. After all, she'd read Bible stories to the children since they were young and had encouraged them in their schoolwork while he was busy in the fields. She'd learned alongside the children and almost sounded like a schoolmarm herself. Fred was badly outnumbered in his own home. To make matters worse, Ohio law said that schooling was required for kids from age six to eighteen even though farm boys and girls could be exempted from school after age sixteen. Harris and Carl were farm boys! If he could somehow convince them to stay out of high school, he could have them on the farm.

Carl and Harris didn't leave school after eighth grade. Emma wouldn't let them, and they didn't want to leave. Carl especially loved school and always had, ever since first grade. Instead of working with their father on the farm, as Fred had wanted, the boys went to the new high school in Elmore, one year apart. To get there, they rode the interurban train into town and walked the rest of the way to the school. In 1921 Carl and his brother Harris were the first Kardatzke family members to graduate from high school. Not only did they finish high school, but Carl also went on to college in Anderson, Indiana; and a year later, Harris went to business school in Detroit. After college, Carl kept trying to talk the other children into going to college, especially after he became a college professor. Fred felt grudging pride in his son, as he did for all his children, but it sometimes seemed he was all alone in his farming and in his hope for good lives on the farm for all his children.

Truth be told, Fred was worried about Carl's visit for a much bigger reason than the old school issue. This son was also a preacher now, like his younger brother Elmer. It was difficult for Fred to think of Carl as a preacher because he didn't preach like other preachers, especially not like Elmer. Elmer was an evangelist, and he could be forceful in his preaching. In contrast, Fred thought Carl preached like a schoolteacher, or maybe a college teacher. But Carl believed strongly in what he preached and could be quite persuasive in his own, mild way. Carl knew his father's attitude about church and his bitterness, and Fred knew that Carl knew. As Fred thought about Carl's visit, he sank a little lower in his bed. He was not looking forward to facing this "little professor," as he sometimes thought of this educated son.

Carl arrived on a Friday night, and Fred was pleasantly surprised that the visit was mild, as mild as Carl's own temperament. His son sat beside him on the bed, talking fondly of life on the farm and asking Fred questions he could answer: how many hogs were there now? Did Ma still get enough eggs from the chickens? Did they have any trouble when the ditch ran over last spring? Are the cows giving a lot of milk? Fred almost felt well again just thinking of those practical things.

Then Carl began to talk about his Christian beliefs. He told Fred how God had made a way for him to go through school and be the first Kardatzke to graduate from high school. An even greater miracle was his graduation from college and then becoming a doctor of education. Carl also talked about his spiritual conversion at a revival meeting in Toledo, a conversion that had surprised Fred because Carl had been raised as a Christian and had been a good boy even before his conversion. Carl told his father how easy and happy his conversion had been and how it had given him direction in life. Finally, he told Fred of the peace he felt about his work for God as a professor and a preacher. Carl emphasized the peace he felt when he thought of his own future death and how thankful he was that he had remained true to God all the years since his conversion.

That was as far as Carl's evangelistic appeal went that day. To Fred's relief, his son had merely said the obvious things and left his father to think about them. After Carl left his room, Fred could hear Emma and Carl talking softly in the kitchen. They probably were talking about him, he thought, and it gave him that other sick feeling, that almost unbearable feeling of weight and sadness. He understood all that Carl had told him and why he had said it. And he knew he would hear more the next day and even more when his youngest son came to visit. That son was not only a preacher. He was an evangelist.

AUTHOR'S NOTE: *Carl Kardatzke became the family's intellectual leader. Through his influence, each of his eight siblings received some college education; six of them received four-year degrees. When Carl died in January 1959, he was vice president at Anderson College in Anderson, Indiana.*

GRANDPA COMES TO GOD

Fred heard the phone ring from deep within his cave of sleep and heard Emma exclaim, "You are? When?" After a pause, she said, "Oh, Mit, I'm glad ta hear that. How will you git to the house?" After another pause, he heard her say, "I'll tell Harris and Arlin. One of 'em can git you. What time does the plane land?"

The plane? Fred thought. What plane? Is she talking to Mit?

"Okay, I'll tell 'em. Ten thirty tomorrow. We'll all pray the plane makes it to Toledo," she said, her voice starting to waver. "Bye now. I can't talk no more now, Mit. I'll cry. Bye."

Fred heard her hang up and hurry in to him. "Fred! You awake?" she asked.

How could I sleep through that, Fred thought to himself. "Yep, I ain't sleeping. What's that all about?"

"It was Mit, callin' long distance on the phone all the way from Wichita. He's coming right away to see you, riding on an airplane!"

"What's he doin' that for?" Fred mumbled, though he knew the answer. Mit, as he was called, was their youngest son, but his real name was Elmer. He was a preacher, an evangelist actually, and his job was to get people saved. Fred knew the reason for the sudden trip. Mit thinks I'm gonna die, he thought. And he didn't know which he dreaded more: dying or having Mit come to save him.

"Ain't that gonna cost a lot of money, flying on an airplane?" Fred asked. "Where's Mit gonna git that much money?"

"Mit can figure it out. Remember, he's got businesses he does out there, fixing up trailers for the soldiers that come home and all that."

Fred had forgotten his youngest son's energy and optimism. Besides his success as a preacher, he also had business talent. He had never understood Mit's way of business. To him earning a decent living meant doing things right here on the family farm, not looking all around for other things to do. But Mit could find ways to make money, even when he was the preacher for a pretty big church in Wichita. Big church or not, Fred thought, it should pay his son enough to support his family.

"When's he comin'?" Fred asked.

"He gits to the Toledo airport in the mornin'. I 'spect he'll be here about dinnertime, 'bout noon or so," Emma replied.

"Okay," Fred muttered, and he settled down for another nap to get ready for the visit. He felt very tired and wanted sleep to cover him up and take away his thoughts.

It was dark outside and the house was quiet when Fred awoke. The dim lamplight showed Emma sleeping in a chair across the room. He gazed at her for a few minutes, this woman he had married nearly forty-five years earlier. She had changed after the hard work of raising nine children, cooking, washing clothes, and helping with the farm. Her beauty of early years was covered by the lines and flesh of a long life, but there she was, still with him.

Emma sensed he'd awakened even though he said nothing. "You okay, Fred?" she asked cautiously.

"Yep. Been sleeping pretty good," he said with more energy than usual. "What time is it?"

"'Bout ten, I think. You bin sleepin' a few hours and now it's bedtime again," she said. They both chuckled a little.

"It's pert near always bedtime for me now, Em," he said.

He seldom called her the affectionate nickname he had used when they were young. He usually didn't even call her Emma, only "Ma," since that was what their children called her. She smiled and watched him for a moment and then came to his side and touched his hand. She felt warm and soft to him, even after all these years on the farm.

Emma was startled by how cold and damp his hand felt. "You been sweatin', Pa?"

"Mebbe just a little. 'Tain't nothin'."

She knew better than to believe things like that, but there was nothing to be done. "I'll go turn off more lights and git to bed myself," she remarked.

Fred felt that old, heavy tiredness coming over him and the sadness. Em was right here, but he felt alone. He began to imagine the visit from Mit the next day. He was afraid of seeing his young son, but he knew he must. Then memories of the kids in other years crept in followed by images of farm machinery and cattle and crops. His mind drifted to a time when he could work all day in the sun.

The next morning, Harris came over earlier than expected. "Anybody up?" he called as he stomped through the kitchen and into the sitting room. Fred heard him but felt too tired to answer. Emma called from the bathroom. She had just gotten up and had only made coffee so far.

"Mind if I have coffee?" Harris asked.

"Go right ahead, help yourself. I made 'nuf for you," Emma called through the bathroom door. When she came out, dressed and ready for the day, she asked, "Whatcha doin' here so soon? Plane don't come till ten thirty."

"I just thought I better come check on Pa before I go. Mit will wanna know the latest when he gets there. 'Sides, I wanna see some planes land and take off. We don't see that out here."

"We sure don't, and I hope we never will," Emma said. "Them big planes would scare the chickens out of layin' eggs for sure."

Taking his coffee with him, Harris went to see his father. He was the oldest of the nine children, and he was a farmer like Fred. But the two of them were far from the same in many other ways. Harris had gone off to school, too much in Fred's mind. And he had some big ideas that Fred would rather not hear about. Still, he trusted his son and liked the fact that he farmed nearby.

Fred opened his eyes when he felt Harris come in and sit on the edge of a chair next to him. "Goin' to the airport, I hear," Fred offered as a greeting to his son.

"Yep. Mit's comin' all the way from Wichita. I guess I better get him the rest of the way home," Harris said.

"Pretty sudden, Mit comin' all the way here. 'Taint even Easter or Christmas," Fred mused.

"Pretty sudden you having heart trouble too, Pa. Everybody's worried about you."

Fred knew what he meant. He knew the double meaning about his heart trouble even if Harris didn't say so. Both meanings made Fred feel tired and helpless. "Well, I guess it's a good thing he's comin,'" Fred mumbled.

Harris didn't reply, but his pulse quickened. Maybe his father was softening. Maybe he would listen to Mit and respond. He didn't want to ask and risk stirring up his father's stubborn side.

"Better get going," Harris said, getting up. "Haven't been to the airport enough to know how long it takes. I think I can find it though."

"Just watch where them planes are landing," Fred said with a chuckle. "They'll be the big noisy things way up over your head."

Harris laughed at that and headed out.

It was after dinnertime, nearly two in the afternoon, when Harris and Mit reached the house. Fred heard them pull into the gravel driveway. Emma let a pan clatter to the stovetop when she heard them, and she ran to the door. Fred couldn't hear what was said, only the voices, especially Mit's. After all, he *was* a preacher.

"You wanna see Pa right away, Mit?" Emma asked as the three of them came into the living room.

"You bet!" Mit said with his usual bounce. "Where you got him, Ma?"

"You know where. He's in bed. Come on in here," Emma said, leading the way.

Fred managed a smile when his son entered the bedroom. Mit paused at the foot of the bed first and then came around to shake his father's hand. Fred was reassured by the feel of his son's mammoth hand gripping his now weakened one. That grip was the reason for his nickname. His childhood friends called him "Mit" because his hands were as big as baseball mitts. The nickname stuck, and people who knew him well called him Mit, not Elmer.

Mit was startled by the cold, clammy feel of his father's hand. He let it rest again on the blankets. "How are you, Pa?" he asked earnestly.

"Been pretty good. Milked ten cows this morning and kilt two hogs. Ma's prob'ly got them put up already." He smiled at his own little joke. He couldn't resist adding, "Might go out and plow some later."

Mit laughed and slapped his knee. "Well! I guess I didn't have to come. Now that I'm here, I hope you don't put me to work!"

Fred smiled at that. For all of his energy, Mit had never been happy with farming. He was good with words though, even Fred could see that, and he knew Mit was considered a good singer too. He didn't expect his son to do any farming on this trip. This trip was for something else.

Soon Emma had supper ready, and another son, Arlin, came in from down the road. Arlin would help with some of the evening chores, maybe more than his growing family at home liked. Fred knew Arlin felt obliged to help, and he appreciated all that he did for him and Emma. He could hear Harris, Mitt, and Arlin all talking with Emma in the kitchen, but he was content to have a small plate of food brought to him in bed. It would be too difficult for him to get up and eat in the kitchen, especially with the other people there.

When supper was over, Harris and Arlin went out to milk the cows and feed the other animals. Both of them had enough experience on farms to handle whatever was needed out there. While Emma was cleaning up the kitchen, she talked with Mit about Fred and the farm and things at the church. Mit was mainly listening, for once, Fred thought. He heard Mit ask something about him, but it wasn't clear what was said. He heard Emma's answer though. "No, he hasn't, but we all bin prayin' for him. You here to talk to him 'bout that?"

Fred didn't hear an answer, but he soon heard footsteps and Mit entered his room, looking serious. He even looked powerful, like he had something inside him that was more than his muscles and his brains, something he couldn't hold back. Mit sat down next to the bed again.

"You been thinking things over, Pa?" he asked. "You know what I mean?"

Fred didn't want to answer, but Mit came right to the point. "You been thinking about what comes after this?" he asked. "After this life?"

Again Fred didn't want to answer, but this time he did. "Yep, I bin thinkin'. Yep."

"Can I talk with you about it, Pa?" Mit asked. "I'd like to tell you some things to think about tonight. We can talk again in the morning. Would you want that, Pa?"

Fred felt the old fear and sadness coming over him, but here was his son who had come a thousand miles to try to help him. He knew he couldn't stop things now. "Yeah, okay," he said. "I raised a preacher, but I haven't give him a chance to preach to me much."

Mit smiled. "I won't be preaching to you, Pa," he started. "I just want to tell you a few things that you've known a long time."

Fred looked away but listened.

"Pa, I know you've been staying away from church a long time. And I know something about what happened to you and why you stayed away," Mit said.

Fred began to feel the old anger rising up again. He remembered how the church people had turned on him when he found out about that preacher and told them. He remembered how nobody believed him or took his side, and then later none of them said they were sorry when they found out he was right and the preacher was wrong. The old anger started burning in him again and his chest hurt.

"That was a hard time, Pa, and it's been a hard time for you ever since. I want you to know that I'm really sorry that happened to you," Mit said.

Suddenly the anger turned to tears. Fred began to shake and cry hard, so hard that he gasped for breath as he was crying and Emma came running into the room. "What's happened to Pa? What's happened? Will he be all right?" she demanded.

Mit was crying along with Fred. Emma guessed what was happening, and she began to cry too. "Oh, Fred!" she said between her tears.

Fred let his tears come out a little longer and then took a deep breath and looked over at his son. "I wisht somebody woulda said that to me a long time ago. I bin mad a long time."

"I know you have, Pa," Mit said and then added, "I guess you've done some things you shouldn't have too."

Those words didn't make Fred angry or sad now. Somehow it was a relief to hear his son say them. His son was right.

"But here's another thing, Pa," Mit said. "You've worked hard and taken care of Ma all these years. You taught us to work, and Ma taught us that too, along with a lot of things about the church. You didn't go to church with her much, but you didn't stop her. You mostly tried to do what was right."

Fred took that in, knowing that he had only "*mostly* tried to do what was right." He wished he had been different and had helped Emma more with teaching the kids what was right. And he remembered some things that he wished he couldn't remember.

"Pa, you've been a mountain of strength to us kids," Mit said. "I wanted to tell you that."

Fred didn't feel like a mountain of strength. He felt small and old and weak. Here he was, sick in bed, and his youngest son was looking right into his life in places nobody else had looked or talked with him about before.

"Pa, you know why I came, don't you?"

Fred nodded but didn't speak.

"My job as a preacher is to help people get saved. I want to talk with you about getting saved, Pa."

Fred knew this was Mit's mission, and he felt too tired to argue or resist or respond in any way. Mit could see his father's exhaustion. He didn't want to take a chance by leaving things until morning, but he knew it was time to let his father rest.

"Get some sleep, Pa. Mind if Ma and I pray here with you before we all go to bed?"

Fred had heard lots of prayers lately, including many for him. "Okay, sure. Okay," he said.

"Heavenly Father," Mit prayed, "thank you for my father here on earth, Fred Kardatzke. Thank you for his hard work and his help to his family. Thank you for helping him through hard times when people didn't understand and when the family took a different path than he wanted. I pray now that you will hold him in your loving hands tonight. Please continue to preserve his life as you have all this time. Please let him rest well tonight and have strength and hope for the new day tomorrow. I pray these things in the name of your righteous son, Jesus Christ, our Savior, amen."

Fred hadn't said it for a long time, but he added, "amen." Mit glanced up but didn't comment. Instead, he left the room without saying another word, letting the prayer close their day. Now his father could get some sleep.

At about 2:30 in the morning, Fred awoke with a start. Everything Mit had said and more came back to him: his anger, his hard words for some people, and his drinking that he hadn't thought was so bad but that had separated him from his family many times. Looking around the room in the dim light, he wondered how many more times he would awaken here. How soon would he awaken somewhere else, in another world? After the way he had lived the last twenty years, how could he turn to God? He felt sadder and more alone than he could ever remember. He felt that all of the work of his life had shrunk down to this moment, lying here in bed and waiting to die. Again he felt too tired to keep thinking about these things, and sleep mercifully overwhelmed him.

When Fred woke up again, the sun was well up, and he could smell breakfast cooking. He was about to call for Emma when he saw that Mit was sitting across the room reading. Just like a preacher, Fred thought. He was already dressed in a shirt and tie, and Fred could smell some shaving perfume across the room.

Noticing Fred's slight movement in the bed, Mit spoke. "Good morning, Pa," he said in a serious way, not with his usual bouncy cheerfulness. "How did you sleep?"

"Slept pretty good," Fred replied. "Woke up for a while in the middle of the night but got back to sleep."

"What woke you up, Pa?" Mit wanted to know.

"Nothin'," Fred muttered. Then he corrected that little lie. "I was thinkin'."

Mit waited a minute before asking, "Pa, are you ready to die?"

The question shocked Fred and made his heart race. But he wasn't surprised. He knew why Mit had come, and he didn't want to admit the answer to the question.

Again Mit asked, "Are you ready to die, Pa? Have you been saved since all the trouble happened?"

This moment was what Fred had feared ever since he'd heard his son was coming for a visit. Mit let the question sink in and waited for Fred's reply. Mit could hardly hear it when Fred whispered, "No."

Mit paused and started again. "Pa, you remember how to get saved, don't you? It's real simple."

Fred nodded. "But I can't do that anymore. I seen too much, and I bin away from church too long. I did some bad things. 'Sides, how do we know about God? What if he ain't there?"

Mit remembered the barriers of doubt that Fred had built around himself. He hadn't talked with him about those things for a long time, and Pa hadn't said any of those things around him, especially since he'd become a preacher. A little talk about it would lead to more talk, Fred had always felt.

"Pa, God is there. The Bible says so. And you know he saved Art Gleckler and Harry Klinger and a lot more. And remember how God healed Arlin when he coulda died from that kidney infection way back when we were in high school?"

"I just don't know, Mit," Fred said, using his son's nickname for the first time on this visit.

"Do you believe in God enough to give him a try?" Mit asked. "Think about this. If God isn't there, but you believe in him and call on him and then die, what's wrong with that? But what if you don't believe in him and don't get saved and then you die and find out God was there all the time? What if he is right here in the room with us now? What do you have to lose?"

Fred thought about those words. He had thought about them before, but he had pushed the thoughts away when he was busy and had plans and was working hard and didn't want to be trapped into being a Christian like everybody else. Now it was different, but still he resisted. Everyone would find out. Some of the men would say, "Old Fred Kardatzke finally got religion!" It was embarrassing. It seemed like giving in.

"Pa, I have to say a real hard thing to you," Mit said. "Pa, you might die pretty soon, maybe even today. Or maybe in a few weeks or a few months, but pretty soon. You know that, don't you, Pa?"

Suddenly Fred's life all came crashing down on him. He was at the end of it, and he couldn't see anything beyond this bed and this room. Tears stung his cheeks, and he felt embarrassed.

Mit reached over and touched his arm. "You want me to help you get saved, Pa?" Mit asked. "I can remind you how to pray to get saved and forgiven and start trusting God with your life. Can I pray with you? Will you pray too?"

It all seemed so sudden and impossible, but Fred wanted to try one more time to turn his mind to God. He had turned to God more than once as a boy and even as a young man when he could see his sins and couldn't stand to carry them around with him. He wasn't so scared of dying back then—he just had to get rid of the heavy, sad, guilty feeling in his chest, and he wanted to be right with the world. And he did live right for a while every time after he got saved. Back then he couldn't stand being wrong with the world. But over the years, he had hardened and toughened himself and had pushed his guilty feelings away. Now he had two things on weighing him down. He was scared of dying, and he had a larger weight of sin on his chest than when he was young. He couldn't get rid of the sin feeling on his own, and he couldn't get well either. What did he have to lose?

"Okay," he replied to his son.

"Okay what, Pa?" Mit said, pressing him to be clear.

"I want to get saved." Fred's voice was now firm. After a pause, he added, "You think I still can?"

"I *know* you can, Pa. You just have to believe that Jesus will forgive you for everything and he will take you into his kingdom. Let's pray, and later you will be with him in paradise."

Fred remembered the story from the crucifixion, and he hoped he could be like that one thief who was crucified with Jesus, who didn't live long enough to start sinning again after Jesus promised he would be with him in paradise that day.

"Let's pray now, Pa," said Mit, taking his father's hand. "You pray each part after me."

Mit began to pray. He thanked God for his goodness and greatness and love. He thanked God for the gift of salvation that was for anyone who would truly believe in his son, Jesus Christ. Fred repeated each sentence in his low, rasping voice. Then Mit began to tailor the prayer to his father. "Lord, you know that I am a sinner."

Fred repeated, "Lord, you know that I am a sinner."

"Lord, *I* know that I am a sinner too." Mit prayed. Fred repeated Mit's confession too.

"Lord Jesus, I'm sorry for all of my sins. I'm sorry for things I have done and things I have said."

Once again, Fred repeated every word his son Mit said.

"I'm sorry for the way I been thinking for a long time. Please take me back, Lord."

Tearfully, sincerely, Fred spoke those same words aloud. "I'm sorry for the way I been thinking for a long time. Please take me back, Lord."

After a long pause, Mit prayed and Fred repeated, "I want you to forgive me, Lord God, and save me, amen."

As soon as Fred had finished his part of the prayer, he felt the weight lift from him. He had held his grudges and habits so tightly for so many years that he didn't think he could ever let them go. But after giving in, letting go, they all went away. He suddenly felt light and young. He even felt happy that he was near death. He would soon go to heaven, and he wouldn't have many chances to throw away his salvation again. He turned to Mit and smiled.

When Mit saw that smile, he burst into tears, sobbing so loudly that Emma heard him in the kitchen. She came running into the bedroom, sure that Fred that had died. "Oh, Fred!" she cried. "Pa! Pa! Did he die just now, Mit?"

Mit was still crying, but he wanted to laugh. "No, Ma. Pa didn't die. Just the *opposite!* He started to live again! He got saved! Praise God! Tell everybody!"

All three of them were still crying and laughing when Harris and Arlin came over to do the morning chores. When the two of them heard the news, they blew their noses and wiped their eyes. Soon the whole family heard the great news: Pa was saved! Word went out to the whole church, and there was a prayer meeting that night. Everybody there thanked God too.

Some of Fred's friends heard of his conversion and shook their heads. They had a hard time believing it, but they knew that people sometimes did change when they were about to die. They wondered if they themselves would be ready when it was time for them to die. And some asked how Fred had changed so much just by a short prayer. Others who knew more about such things were brave enough to say, "It looks like God can change anybody," while some men just looked away and were quiet.

AUTHOR'S NOTE: *When Elmer said to his father, "What do you have to lose?" he was expressing a version of a proposition known as Pascal's Wager. It is named for the French Catholic mathematician, Blaise Pascal (1623–1662). In short, Pascal said it doesn't pay to bet against God by rejecting him in this life, taking a chance that he doesn't exist. When weighed against the infinite value of heaven, it's better to accept God, even if you aren't sure he exists. Some details of this conversation by necessity are fictionalized, but Elmer's use of Pascal's Wager was described to me by Elmer's son, Dr. Jon Kardatzke, as reported to him by Elmer. The "wager" evidently appealed to Fred's practical mind and opened it to God's own voice speaking through Elmer.*

FEAR AND BLESSING

Grandpa Fred Kardatzke had been sick in bed for several months, but by the summer of 1948, it was time for my family to take our annual trip to Kansas and Oklahoma to see our relatives. My mother was from Oklahoma, and my Uncle Elmer (Mit) had moved to Wichita about 1940. We had lots of aunts and uncles and more cousins than most kids. In fact, we had Kardatzke family relatives and Bruner family relatives all the way from Wichita to Western Oklahoma. The trips to the West to see them were always filled with adventures. We had unusual treats like soda pop, gum, and candy from gas stations, things we didn't have at home. We could buy fireworks out there that were illegal in Ohio. My aunts, uncles, and cousins always welcomed us with lots of hugs and embarrassing exclamations of how much we'd grown. The feeling of warmth and love in Kansas and Oklahoma made those places seem like mythical places.

On the way to Oklahoma in 1948, we stopped as usual to see Uncle Mit and Aunt Vera and their kids in Wichita. To us, Wichita was a vast, modern city, and we felt that our relatives there were among the most sophisticated and important people we knew. Wichita's population was 165,000 at the time, while Elmore had about 1,200. Riding bikes on city sidewalks and buying soda pop on our own made Wichita a center of sensual pleasures for young kids. This trip was like the others before, except four of us cousins would be spending a week at Camp Fellowship in the countryside about 25 miles west of Wichita while my parents and younger siblings went to Oklahoma to visit my mother's parents there. Kids attending the camp were supposed to be at least nine years old. My brother Merl and my cousin Jon were grown-up eleven-year-olds and were of legal age for the camp. My cousin Stan had turned nine in April and was of legal age. I was only eight, but it was decided that I could be "smuggled" in as a camper with my cousins because Uncle Mit was one of the major organizers and would make it happen.

That summer, in the middle of our week at camp, a tornado struck and demolished the camp, including the building in which two hundred children and adult counselors had taken refuge. Miraculously no one was killed, but it was a turning point in the lives of most who were there, including me. Sometime during that terrifying night, I prayed to God for salvation, as I had learned in church that I could. I don't remember the particular moment or how I said my prayer, and I don't think I knew the details of my experience even a few days after the event. But I did come away with the conviction that, faced with possible death in the storm, I had been saved for Christ through a prayer of faith.

During the remainder of our trip to Oklahoma, and among church people and neighbors when we arrived back in Ohio, we re-told the story of the tornado and our miraculous rescue. I had told my parents about being saved during the tornado, and they helped me tell others. I was thankful that I would go to heaven, even if I died in the next tornado. In spite of my prayer for salvation the horrible night of the storm at Camp Fellowship, the tornado had left me with an overpowering fear of storms. I discovered this fear a few weeks after our family's return to Ohio. The wind of a thunderstorm one night sent me running downstairs to sleep on the couch near my parents' room. From then on, for about three years, the slightest breeze at night, even in the winter, would send me into a frenzy of fright.

It was a time of fear for other reasons, some of which I barely understood. The Russians had blockaded American access to Berlin in the summer of 1948, and every news broadcast carried a message of fear. The world seemed on the brink of another war far worse than World War II, which had ended only three years earlier. There were even rumors that the Russians might be building an atomic bomb. That fearful world was far from my home on Graytown Road in Ohio, but pictures of World War II bombings made it seem that Toledo could be the target of a Russian bombing attack.

Even so, the summer of 1948 was calm and hot in Ohio as usual. The tall maple trees around our house barely swayed in the breeze on those sultry afternoons. The peacefulness of the past hung over the farms and homes on Graytown Road. Although all the homes had electricity and indoor plumbing by this time and everyone traveled by car, few homes had telephones, no one had television, and many farming methods were the same as they had been in the 1800s. Horses were still used for some work, and small family farms typically raised grain, hay, dairy cattle, beef cattle, hogs, chickens, and other poultry, much of it for home use. Cats ranged the barns and outbuildings to control rats and mice, much as they had in medieval times. To me it was a wonderful world where every ditch and pond and haystack was a place for adventure and imagination.

Although I looked forward to enjoying the rest of the summer in that child's paradise, something was wrong in the family that weighed heavily on everyone, including me. Grandpa Kardatzke was dying. He had heart disease, and there were no cures for it. He lay in bed most of the time in the house where he had lived nearly all his life. His life was gradually ebbing away. His body was filling with fluids, and his breathing was becoming more and more difficult. We children were not allowed to play in our grandparents' yard, as we had in previous years, because Grandpa needed quiet.

Not long after we returned from the trip to Kansas and Oklahoma, my mother and I went to visit Grandpa and Grandma at their farmhouse just down the road from where we lived. My dad and two of my uncles milked Grandpa's cows for him morning and evening now, since he couldn't get out to do much work anymore. Before getting milk to take home, my mother and I we went up to the house. Grandma was in the kitchen, cleaning up after supper.

"Well, hello, there!" Grandma called out as we stepped up on the porch. "How was that big trip?"

"It was good," my mother said, "but it's great to be back home. Things are so green here."

"Yeah, we've had lots of rain. I guess you had some rain out there, too, didn't you?" Grandma said.

"We sure did, especially during the tornado," my mother replied. "The water was waist deep in front of Mit's house that night."

"So you were in the tornado?" Grandma asked me. She'd heard some of the details of our family visit and what had happened at camp from her son Mit, but she hadn't seen me since we'd returned home.

"Yep. And Merl and Jon and Stan too," I answered.

"I'm glad you come out of it okay," she said. "Maybe you should come in and tell Grampa about it."

"Is he having visitors today?" my mother asked.

"Oh, yeah," she said. "He's feeling pretty good right now. Let's go on in."

Grandma dried her hands and took off her apron. We walked through the living room to Grandpa's bedroom. It was dimly lit with the curtains drawn, so Grandma turned on a lamp next to the bed. Grandpa was dozing when we came in, so Grandma went over to him and touched his shoulder.

"Looky who's here, Pa," she said just loudly enough to wake him.

Grandpa opened his eyes and straightened his head, looking across his toes at me. His head was round and nearly bald, and his ruddy cheeks again made me think of Santa Claus. I always thought of him as playful and kind, but I learned later that he was sometimes fierce and harsh in earlier years. It was strange to see him propped up in bed, covered with sheets on a warm summer day.

"Well, it's the boy," he said in a stronger voice than I expected. "Hoddy."

"Hi, Grampa," I mumbled.

"It's good to see you, Dad," my mother said. "We just got back from Oklahoma."

"Yeah, Ma tolt me. Good you made it back." Grandpa wasn't much of a traveler, so he probably always thought it was good when people made it back home.

Mama and Grandma and Grandpa started talking about farming and the trip and the relatives we had seen. I sat on a chair across the room from Grandpa's bed while they talked. I was thinking of something else when I heard my mother talking to me.

"You have something to tell Grampa, haven't you?" she asked me. When I hesitated, she prompted me. "About the tornado. Being saved."

I felt the eyes of the three adults on me. It was my time to testify to Grandpa. "I got saved in the tornado," I said, sitting on my hands and swinging my feet under the chair. "I was scared too."

For a moment, Grandpa just gazed at me across his toes. I knew he had been saved on this very bed after years of being away from God and away from the church. I thought this was why I needed to tell him that I had gotten saved in the tornado.

Finally Grandpa spoke. "That's the way to do it," he said, "while you're young."

I don't remember him saying more, but I felt that he was telling me not to live as he had, angry and away from the church, coming to God only on my death bed. But I also knew he was telling me that his salvation was real, and so was mine. Though he was sixty-five years old and near the end of his life, I felt sure that his salvation would take him into heaven and that I would see him there. He had given me his blessing with his approval of my salvation. I was so young and had come to God in such fear, yet Grandpa had smiled at me and said, "That's the way to do it, while you're young."

That visit was the last time I saw Grandpa even though he stayed in that bed for several more months. I sometimes heard the big people talking about him, about him being "full of water." People requested prayer for him in church on Sundays and at prayer meetings on Wednesday nights, and sometimes people repeated the story about how he had found the Lord. Then some people would say "Amen!" and "Praise God!"

On the bright, cold morning of Saturday, March 26, 1949, I was in my front yard, tossing a football in the air, when the news came. A car drove up the road, slowed down, and pulled into the driveway. It was Uncle Paul, who had been a bomber pilot in World War II. Uncle Paul stopped beside the house and got out. I walked over to him, and I thought I could feel the reason he was there. Uncle Paul never talked much, and he didn't say much on this day.

"Your grandpa just died," he said. "Your folks home?"

"They're inside," I said, nodding toward the house. Uncle Paul went to the back door, and I stood watching until he went in. I knew it was an important time, but I didn't know what to do. So I tossed the football in the air a few more times. Then Uncle Paul came back out and drove back to Grandma and Grandpa's house, but now it was only Grandma's house. Grandpa had died.

Grandpa's funeral a few days later was the first in the new church, and it was the first funeral I ever attended. I would miss Grandpa, but I wasn't worried about him. Grandpa had gone to heaven, but before he left, he had given me his blessing. It was a gift that would last a lifetime.

AUTHOR'S NOTE: *The full story of the tornado is included in the story titled "Tornado at Camp Fellowship."*

THE FIRST FUNERAL

F red Kardatzke's death in 1949 and the funeral in the new church were my first experiences with saying good-bye to a relative and attending a funeral. The church building on Congress Street in Elmore was simple and plain, but the funeral service was majestic and awe-inspiring, a wonderful way for family and friends to bid their final farewell to my grandfather. His death and the funeral were important events in my early life.

The customs that surrounded a family member's death and funeral were typically more intimate in the 1940s and 1950s than they are today. If death was not by a tragic accident, most people died at home, not in hospitals, and the body was often displayed in the home for the family in addition to public viewing at the funeral. After the funeral service and burial, family members ate together in the home of the deceased and spent hours crying, laughing, and telling stories.

Fred died early on Saturday morning, March 26, 1949, in the farmhouse where he had lived most of his life. When Emma, his wife, came in from feeding the farm animals, she found that Fred was not breathing. She called her eldest son, Harris, who lived nearest and had a phone. Emma's daughter Marion and her husband Paul Gottke were staying with Harris at the time. All of them came when Emma called. Emma's eyes were brimming with tears as she greeted them.

"I think Pa is gone," she said as she led them to the bedroom.

Paul had seen death many times during the war. He went right to Fred's side and felt for his pulse.

"There's no pulse," he said simply, looking at Emma.

"That's what I figured," Emma said. "He didn't wake up all yesterday."

They stood quietly. Fred's face was peaceful after his active and forceful life.

"We better pray," Emma told the men. "We got a lot to do."

After a long silence, Harris prayed. "Our Father in heaven, thank you for Pa. Thank you for taking him out of his weakness here and into your presence. Thank you for saving his soul. Now please take care of Ma and all of us. Amen."

"I better call Uncle Fred," Harris said. Fred Sabroske, the town undertaker, was his uncle by marriage. In 1949 the Kardatzke family was practically a tribe living in and around Elmore, Ohio. Among the close relatives, three men had been named Fred, and now there were two.

Within the hour after the phone call, the long black hearse from town pulled slowly into the driveway, and Fred Sabroske came to the door. He was tall, and his full-length, black overcoat made him look even taller. He was nearly always dressed in a suit, and today was no exception. Paul led him silently to the bedroom where Emma was sitting, gazing at her husband's lifeless body. Fred felt for a pulse.

"He's gone," he announced. "Feels like it's been an hour or more."

No one answered. They knew.

"Good thing you men are here," he said, "I'm gonna need some help. One of ya can help me bring the cart in."

The men brought in the stretcher. Together they slid the body onto it and then onto a cart. Fred Sabroske tightened straps to hold the body on, and they carried the cart out to the hearse. Emma followed them, dabbing tears from her cheeks. Her husband's death was a shock, even after months of decline. She felt guilty for feeling relieved and then sad, sad that Fred had died alone while she was in the barn. But she knew how it happened was Fred's way—to die alone. When the body was in the hearse, Fred Sabroske closed the door and turned to the others.

"I'll take him to town myself. I won't need help. Lizzie's there," he said, referring to his wife and helper, who was also Fred Kardatzke's sister.

Emma and the others watched as the hearse pulled slowly onto the gravel road. The black hearse on the white gravel road must have stood out and looked majestic as it stirred up a small white cloud of dust.

"You eat yet, Ma?" Harris asked when it was out of sight.

"Some bread and coffee before chores," she replied. "I better fix up some breakfast for all of us. We got a busy time ahead."

That day the word spread to the rest of the family and to the farms nearby. Only two of Fred and Emma's nine children lived far away: Carl was in Anderson, Indiana. Elmer was in Wichita, Kansas. They were called, and they said they would come soon. The minister, Brother Curtis Lee, came to the house as soon as he heard the news, and he prayed with the group that had arrived to offer condolences. By early afternoon, women from the church were bringing food for Emma and the family, and that night Emma's daughters, Marion and Elsie, stayed at the house with her.

Emma didn't go to church the next day. She felt it would be too hard to be there and hear Brother Lee tell everyone that Pa had died. Several family members stayed at home with her, and the day was quieter than Saturday had been.

On Monday Fred's body was ready for viewing at the funeral home, and visiting hours were posted. Emma stood by the casket all evening and greeted a long line of friends from town and farmers who had known her husband. Close family members were there and also some Emma could barely remember. It was another exhausting day, but she knew it was necessary. She drew strength from some of those who had waited so long in line.

The funeral was set for Saturday, April 2, to allow time for Elmer to drive from Kansas. Carl's trip from Indiana would take only five hours, but he had classes to finish teaching at Anderson College before he could leave.

The day before the funeral, the casket was brought to the house and opened for viewing in the same bedroom where Fred had died. All of the nearby family came at some time during the day, some staying for many hours. I was one of the grandchildren who came, and for many of us Grandpa was the first deceased person we had seen. He was dressed in his dark blue Sunday suit, a white shirt, and a dark tie, the same suit he used to wear on Sundays during his years of avoiding church. His hands were folded across his stomach, and he looked as though he was just sleeping. When no one was in the room, I reached in and touched his hand. It was cold, and his skin felt loose. I didn't do that again.

During the visitation, my aunts and uncles gathered at the kitchen table and read the obituary in the *Toledo Blade*. Their names were mentioned, along with their occupations and where they lived. Uncle Carl, as a college professor, sounded the most prestigious. He joked that the paper made him sound like "a big shot," and everyone laughed. I didn't know why that was funny so I didn't laugh, but I thought it was somehow good that Uncle Carl joked about himself. Knowing our family was mentioned in the paper gave me a feeling of importance and history. To me it was the first time we had been famous.

On the morning of the funeral, the hearse came to the farm to get the casket. Several family members followed the hearse in cars. Grandpa's open casket was at the door as people entered. Our extended family must have taken up half the pews in the main sanctuary. The piano was playing softly as we came in, and it seemed to make the day even sadder, Soon the church was packed. Every pew was filled, and the chairs in the overflow room were all taken. The casket was moved to the front of the church for the service, open there as well.

I don't remember all that happened during the funeral, but I do remember that we sang all the verses of "Rock of Ages," "Abide with Me," and another old hymn. There were prayers. There were a couple of speeches. One speech was about Grandpa and his life and his family and his salvation. The other speech was a sermon about Jesus and God and heaven. When the service ended, Fred Sabroske and one of his helpers went forward, closed the casket, and began rolling it to the back of the church.

Suddenly there was a scream from across the church and then another scream. Two women, Aunt Verda Stackhouse and Aunt Elsie Stagner, were crying hysterically and screaming, "Pa! Pa! No, no, no!" Uncle Jim and Uncle Roz tried to comfort them, and other people began to cry. After it was quiet again and the casket was placed carefully at the back of the church, it was opened one more time to show the body as people left. As I looked at him one last time, I was impressed with Grandpa's importance and the importance of the day.

A long line of cars followed the hearse to the cemetery at the edge of town. A grave had been dug already, and the hearse stopped beside it. The casket was suspended on straps above the open grave, and Brother Lee waited for everyone to gather close before he spoke. Most people couldn't hear all that he said, but they knew from other funerals what he would be saying. After he prayed, he said the service was over and everyone could leave. I had expected more, since this was my first funeral, but people just went to their cars. The cemetery returned to its natural peace.

That afternoon our vast family had a funeral meal at Uncle Harris and Aunt Delorous's farmhouse. A group of us grandchildren sat in a side room with food and talked about Grandpa and the funeral. We all felt famous and important because of the funeral, and we were proud of Grandpa. We were happy to be together as a large family, so we didn't think about missing him yet. We didn't know then that we would remember Grandpa for the rest of our lives, all of us in different ways. Most of us were too young to know that we would always be especially glad that he had given his heart to Jesus, even though it was near the end of his life. We didn't have to be told that Grandpa wanted us to do the same, and we understood that we should do it while we were still kids, not when we were old as he had done.

AUTHOR'S NOTE: *In 1942, Carl Kardatzke gave his mother, Emma, a copy of James Moffatt's translation of the New Testament. Inside that Bible, a rusting paper clip still holds a note in Emma's handwriting at that says, "I John 5:13-15." Those verses were underlined in the Bible in pencil. Emma may have clipped the note there so she could find those verses quickly and read them to Fred when he needed reassurance of his salvation. Here are the words of the passage she underlined:* "I have written in this way to you who believe in the name of the Son of God, that you may be sure you have life eternal. Now the confidence we have in him is this, that he listens to us whenever we ask anything in accordance with his will; and if we know he listens to whatever we ask, we know we obtain the requests we have made to him."

II. THE OLD CHURCH AND THE NEW

DISCOVERING THE CLOCK OF THE COVENANT

My religious consciousness awakened abruptly and for no obvious reason one Sunday morning in 1944 or 1945. About that same time, other areas of my awareness also were awakening, such as the prevalence of wild animals, especially after dark, and the magical powers of certain painted metal toys. Ironically perhaps, I emerged from the formless larval stage of my religious life while facing backward, balancing precariously on the edge of one of the folding wooden theatre seats in an old, one-room church.

To a four-year-old, acrobatic tricks on the folding church seats helped while away the time in church, that hour or more when the adults were strangely preoccupied and toys were in short supply for small children. One Sunday morning, as I rocked on the edge of the seat, something drew my attention to the back wall of the church and then up, up to a mysterious box on the wall that I already knew to be a clock. In a small glass house under the clock face, a pendulum swung back and forth, and between outbursts of worshipful shouting, I could hear the clock ticking its ancient rhythm. I sensed authority and meaning in this ceaseless ticking.

The pendulum bore a golden design that looked to me like a face. In my imagination, it seemed at first to be the face of one of the Philistine gods destroyed by the Israelites in the conquest of the Promised Land. That face, I thought with no little satisfaction, was all that remained of the evil Philistine god and the Philistines themselves. Perhaps the swinging pendulum induced a partial hypnotic trance that day, for I heard words that settled deep into my awakening consciousness and took on extraordinary significance: "And when Moses came down from Mt. Sinai with the tablets of the Law," the preacher said, "he ordered that the tablets be placed in the ark of the covenant to be carried wherever God's people went."

In my boyhood imagination, I thought he said the promises of God were locked in "the clock of the covenant." Indeed, I could see a door on the clock. Perhaps it was first opened when the promises of God were placed inside. And there before me was the actual clock, still with God's people, the people in my church. My spiritual forebears must have carried it with them into the Promised Land and then beyond, until at last they reached Elmore, Ohio. That ancient clock had marked time for God's people ever since. So it was that I first became aware of the religious life around me, while staring backward in church at the wall and the clock that hung there.

When I became old enough to think and to read, I learned that the ancient, mysterious clock was called a schoolhouse clock. By then my view of its religious significance could not be erased by the mere fact that such clocks had not always existed, and certainly not at Mt. Sinai. I remained enthralled by the clock and its spiritual significance.

THE OLD CHURCH

The clock of the covenant hung beside the door at the rear of what came to be known as "the old church," the small building on Harris Street in Elmore, Ohio, that the congregation used for worship until "the new church" was built in 1948. The old church was spartan, with clear glass windows, two sections of wooden theater seats on each side, and a single aisle down the middle. A coal-burning stove stood at a wide spot in the aisle during the winter, but the stove was moved out every spring to make the building more spacious. The simple, raised platform at the front was hardly needed to make the leaders visible in the little building, which at capacity could hold about seventy people.

The old church had been the one-room St. John's Parochial School. George Gleckler and another leader, Henry Otte, bought it in 1925 for two hundred dollars. George Gleckler had played a key role in starting the church after the death of his wife and son in 1913. Henry Otte was the patriarch of a family that has served the Elmore church since its very beginning. This old schoolhouse became the first building for the Elmore Church of God, whose people had met in private homes since the church's founding

The clock of the covenant may have been moved into the old church in 1925 from someone's home, or perhaps someone bought it for the church. The clock stayed in its place by the door, the only entry and exit, as long as the congregation worshipped there. It witnessed many crises, heartbreaks, and times of joy before being moved to the new church in 1949, just as I imagined it had been moved with God's people to Elmore from the Promised Land.

The wooden theatre seats in the old church were the kind with arm-rests between each seat and were attached by cast iron fittings at their backs. Perhaps eight or ten of these rows of attached seats were bolted to the floor on each side of the center aisle. The seat bottoms folded up for easy access in and out of the rows, so one of the common catastrophes was a small child falling through the opening at the back edge of the seat while standing with the adults for congregational singing. When a child stepped too far back on the seat, it would flip up and cause the child to drop to the floor and become lodged between the seat bottom and its back. Each time the catastrophe happened, the shrieking young worshipper could be heard above the congregational singing and had to be rescued quickly by adults in the vicinity so the singing could continue, more or less without interruption.

The theatre seats in the old church were the only contact that we in the church had with the theatre or movies in those days. The church was so staunchly opposed to movie going that it probably was difficult to acknowledge that the wooden and cast iron seats actually had been used as theatre seats before the church bought them. Movie going, like dancing and fishing on Sunday, were well beyond the bounds of Christian conduct for the people who worshipped in the old church and even for those who worshipped in the new church during its first few years. The ambiguities created by television had not yet penetrated the wall of separation that protected the congregation from the fabulously worldly fantasies of movies.

By the time of my spiritual awakening, earlier church strictures against neckties, buttons, and basic cosmetics had been lifted. Men and women in the church looked and smelled nice, and I often found a delightful smell of chewing gum and Sen Sens (tiny, powerful, licorice breath sweetening tablets) wafting from ladies' purses. Some of the war veterans chewed gum every Sunday, perhaps to tamp down their desire for cigarettes or in some cases to avoid suspicion of that pernicious habit. My first Sunday school teacher, Sister Klinger, always carried Sen Sens in her purse. Not everyone liked them, but no one thought they were sinful.

With or without neckties, chewing gum, and Sen Sens, the people of the Church of God on Harris Street strived to be a deeply spiritual, God-fearing congregation. They were so devout in their life of faith that I sometimes imagined I could see a pillar of fire crackling in the front of the church during services. I was certain that many sinners had been struck down in the old church by the spiritual equivalent of the blinding light that the apostle Paul encountered on the Damascus road.

One Sunday in my very early years of religious awareness, I looked up from my playing to see a most riveting and shocking sight. The service had ended without my noticing, but instead of leaving church, everyone remained. I looked toward the front and saw, to my amazement, a solid phalanx of grownups' bottoms. Nearly half the adults had responded to the altar call and were kneeling at the altar.

My father was just returning from the altar, so I asked, "What are they doing, Daddy?"

"They're giving their hearts to Jesus," he whispered. After a pause, he asked, "Do you want to go forward too?"

I stared for a moment at the people in the front of the church, wondering how I could possibly give my heart to Jesus the way they were. Since I had no idea what was going on, I whispered back a quick no. I would not take that all-important step of faith for a few more years, until I was scared into it during the great youth camp tornado of 1948.

While the adults' attention during services was fixed firmly on God, there were ample opportunities for children's minds to wander. The clear glass windows provided diversion during sermons too long for young minds. Through the windows, the weather and the sun's progress across the sky could be checked as often as needed. Sometimes the bright blue sky would call my young mind to wonder at the beauty of God's creation. Once a beautiful monarch butterfly danced outside and became lodged forever in my memory. On warm days when the windows were open, sweet smells of grass, tulips, bridal wreath, and lilacs drifted in. All the while, the clock of the covenant ticked on.

AUTHOR'S NOTE: *The original building of the old church is still there, although it is much smaller than it seemed to me in 1948. Since 1949, it has been used as a private home. All of the events in this part of the book came to pass between the time I became conscious of religious life in about 1944 and when the new church was opened in 1948. Few from those early years of the old Elmore church are still alive and remember those times, and fewer still can correct my memories or laugh at events that happened this way, perhaps only in my imaginings.*

SUNDAY SCHOOL AT THE OLD CHURCH

S unday school at the old church was to me a re-creation of the Tower of Babel. The sanctuary was divided into separate areas by curtains that hung from a grid of wires overhead. When classes were in session, people could hear what was going on in all of the classes at once. Simple stories of Jesus for small children blended with deep voices of the men and higher voices of women in the adult classes. As I listened to my teacher's stories, I imagined that the adults in the other classes might be recounting their personal experiences from historical events such as the march out of Egypt and into the Promised Land and the persecution there later under Nero.

My particular class of tiny people gathered behind curtains near the platform at the front of the church. Sister Klinger, our teacher, seemed very old to us. She dressed plainly and usually wore a turban style head cover, so I don't think I ever saw her hair. She seemed even more ancient than she really was, but she was dear to us. Her soft voice and wrinkled smile assured us of her love. She often opened her purse and shared Sen Sens with her little charges even though none of us had been smoking and some of us even had brushed our teeth before arriving at church. The sight and smell of Sen Sens still reminds me of that Sunday school class, though I now know Sen Sens have no spiritual significance.

Sister Klinger was so devoted to teaching small children about Jesus that a few years earlier, she had taught a very small class. The only member was my older cousin, Ellen Goldsby. Ellen told later how Sister Klinger always came prepared, and she even arranged for Ellen to have her own copy of the Sunday school story paper. Three years after Ellen graduated from her one-on-one time with Sister Klinger, the class swelled to eight or ten children, and each of us received the intriguing weekly Sunday school paper.

One of the great educational functions of Sunday school in the old church was preparation of the "Christmas pieces," as they were called. Two-line poems were assigned to the youngest children, or a longer poem was divided up so that it could be said, two lines at a time, by a number of children in sequence. The Christmas pieces were the children's portion of the annual Christmas program each year. One year I saw what could happen if a young orator was not adequately prepared for this ecclesiastical spectacle.

Each member of my class had been assigned to learn two lines of a poem about Christmas. We had done a little practicing during Sunday school, and we supposedly had rehearsed our lines at home until we could say them in our sleep. When the great day arrived, we were lined up in the proper order and marched up front onto the low platform. The church looked entirely different to me from this vantage point—much larger and suddenly foreign and filled with strangers. My heart began to pound, but before I could think of running away or falling on the floor myself, Sister Klinger nudged me and said the first syllables of my lines, which were to open our class's recitation: "The . . . shep . . . herds . . . ," she said slowly, drawing out each sound.

I picked up her prompting and barked without expression, "The shepherds saw the angels and to the manger went." What joy! What freedom! I had said my piece correctly for all of the big people, and I was off the hook! Toys and candy would surely be showered on me in abundance on Christmas Day! As these joyous feelings rushed through my entire body, I waited to hear my cousin Miles say the next two lines, "to see the Christ child to earth from heaven sent." The lines didn't come.

I stared at the congregation, waiting along with everyone else as the clock of the covenant ticked away five seconds. Then I heard a shriek and the sound of knees, elbows, and fists hitting the floor. Miles was there, and he was crying! He had forgotten his lines and had thrown himself down on the platform next to me, wailing and crying. The other children who had yet to say their pieces watched in frozen amazement. The more brazen ones, probably town kids, started to snicker. The more tender orators seemed about to join in the weeping. Suddenly

92

Aunt Eula was at the edge of the platform, plucking up the sobbing Miles and lugging him out of church while Sister Klinger droned out the missing words, "to see the Christ child to earth from heaven sent."

With order restored, the other pieces were rattled off without another hitch and without another sign of heartfelt emotion. Back in our seats, we children all giggled about Miles's attack of fright. We had survived. The clock of the covenant counted out a few more seconds. I imagined that something like a death angel had just passed over us, and we were free to anticipate the joy of Christmas.

SUNDAY JOYS AND CALAMITIES

S undays were a day of worship and rest, but they were also a time for joys and calamities, large and small. One of the more serious calamities was children falling out of cars on the way to or from church. These were the days before automatic door locks that could be controlled by the driver. Car doors had manual locks of sorts, but they failed notoriously, especially when kids tested them at roadway speeds. These were also the days before seat belts, and it was not uncommon for families to head out with six or more children packed into a car.

One Sunday morning, Uncle Joe and Aunt Eula's family was unusually late for Sunday school. When they finally arrived, the first woman who saw them coming in shrieked, "Oh, Lord! What happened?" My cousin Lauren had fallen out of the car, a pre-war Model A Ford. He was bruised and bloody, and pebbles were lodged in his face. Everyone gathered around to look at his wounds and hear the story. Somehow the car door he was leaning against had flung open on the gravel road near their farm, and he'd tumbled in the gravel before rolling into the ditch. Inside the church, we prayed for Lauren's complete recovery and gave thanks that he was not killed. He was dazed but sat through Sunday school under the watchful attention of the whole church. None of the Bible stories that day could match the drama of Lauren's injuries and his escape from death.

Another painful but less serious calamity happened later to that same family. One Sunday they arrived late amid some sheepish secrecy. The story of what had caused their unusual tardiness was shared in whispers. One of the boys, in his haste to zip his pants for the trip to church, had zipped a delicate part of his body into the zipper. There had been pain, tears, and blood, but at least the wounded boy was able to make it to church. Even today, those who were present and knew of the secret injury blush and suppress a shudder.

One of the most pleasant activities for children at the old church was playing outside after Sunday night services in the summertime. The church yard teemed with lightning bugs, and we younger ones all chased them and grabbed them until our palms were smeared with their pulsing, glowing bodies. Only the unpleasant sound of the little insects being crushed and the aroma that lingered on our hands marred the beauty of those hunts.

Another joy at the old church was congregational singing. Most of the people had grown up in homes where singing around the piano was valued entertainment, so we had good singers, many who could sing in four-part harmony. The building was so small and so full of people that the sounds of the voices fairly throbbed against my chest. I especially liked to hear the echoing parts and the rumbling basses. I could barely read in those years, and my frail, little voice wouldn't have reached the row in front of me, but I loved to hear the power and harmony of the adults' voices. Surely, I felt, the singing was an expression of our unity and faith.

A calamity that happened one Sunday evening at church was the result of a particularly heinous "crime" I committed, which I have waited until now to confess publicly. After the service, a number of us kids were playing around as usual in front of the church, waiting for the adults to stop talking. That evening, after we had worked ourselves into a frenzy of playing, a few of us ran into the tiny vestibule between the outer and inner door and tried to keep others out. Over and over the little mob would burst in and drag out the one who was "it."

When I was "it" and in the vestibule, I noticed the light switches. Without thinking, I reached for both switches, thinking I would turn off the lights on my friends outside the door who were about to capture me. I flipped the switches, and my little control booth was plunged into darkness. Screams and shouts erupted inside the church. I had turned off *all* the lights! I fumbled in darkness for the light switches. Just as I flipped the lights back on, my mother came from inside the church. At that moment, she was about seven feet tall and seemed to have come to me straight from the book of Revelation.

"I didn't mean it! I didn't mean it!" I protested, fearing the worst.

"I'll deal with you when we get home," she whispered in that menacing voice parents use to reprimand children for serious crimes in public places.

I scampered out of the church, feeling guilty about my crime and in terror about my coming punishment. I felt especially bad about scaring Aunt Willela, who was vulnerable to frights of any kind. As it turned out, nothing happened to me when we got home that night. I don't know why my mother didn't punish me, and I sure didn't ask. I guess she was too tired for another uproar at bedtime. Once again another seeming death angel had passed over me.

It would be pretentious and less than forthright to imply that the old church had indoor plumbing. The one restroom available for public use was an outhouse at the back of the church property, and it barely met Old Testament codes of sanitation. In order to avoid the outhouse, most families had a strict rule about everyone going to the bathroom before coming to church. I wish I could tell funny or alarming stories about this particular outhouse, like an accidental fire in the Sears catalog pages used for wiping or a wallet that slipped from a man's trousers into the reeking hole. But those are stories from other outhouses. Most people of the church avoided the church outhouse successfully, so its history, mercifully, is short and dull.

A small ceremony took place quietly and unannounced at the close of each Sunday morning service. One of the men, often Harry Klinger or Fred Webert, would step up to the clock of the covenant, pull the winding key from inside the pendulum window, and insert it in the slot in the face of the clock. Tat-tat-tat, tat-tat, the inner gears clicked as the key was turned. Several turns, and the spring was tight. To me the act was a signal that time would be measured for another week while everyone was out "in the world, but not *of* the world." In another week, we would come again to the house of God to unite in songs of praise.

AUTHOR'S NOTE: *These vignettes of life in the old church are the only ones I can remember. If the clock of the covenant could speak, it could tell about many more events that happened there. It saw and heard as the people sang and prayed. It saw all of those souls given to Jesus and heard all of the promises made to God. The clock heard the warnings preached to sinners and saw burdens lifted at Calvary. And it measured out the times the people of the Church of God in Elmore spent in that old church, now so ancient.*

The rhythms of worship, joys, and calamities continued in the old church until early 1949, when the people of the church made their own exodus. They left the old church forever, taking the clock of covenant with them to the new church on Congress Street. There, even today, the clock of the covenant still holds the promises of God. And there, for more than sixty-five years, longer than the children of Israel were in the desert after they left Egypt, the clock of the covenant has measured the hours of the lives of the people of the Elmore Church of God.

BURNING THE MORTGAGE

O ne Sunday morning four years after we had moved into and dedicated the new church, the pastor made an unexpected announcement. "I have important news for you today! I'll ask Brother Rollin Gleckler to come up here now. He can tell you the news."

The congregation drew a collective deep breath. Chairman of the Board of Trustees Rollin Gleckler had been a leader in developing the church, as had his father before him. Calling him to the front for an announcement meant either very good news or very bad news. It sounded as though it would be good news.

"I had a call this week from Mr. Magee at the bank," Brother Rollin began without drama, but he had everyone's attention. "He said our mortgage is paid off and. . . ." He couldn't finish his sentence. He choked, blinked, looked down, and was silent for a moment as he regained his composure. Brother Rollin was more deeply touched than most people knew. He had personally loaned the church $7,000 to get construction started, and the loan had been paid off quietly as fundraising gained momentum. To know that the external debt was lifted and announce it brought him to tears.

"Praise God!" Fred Webert shouted and broke the tension. Others said the same. "Thank the Lord!" said another.

Brother Rollin blinked again, looked up, and finished his short but momentous speech. "We got it paid off quicker than we thought. Mr. Magee said we can pick up the cancelled mortgage note any time."

Another chorus of amen and praise God followed. Several men and women wiped their eyes. Even Grandpa Webert blew his nose, but we kids knew he was hard of hearing and he probably hadn't heard the announcement.

Rollin Gleckler wasn't used to speaking in front of the church, and he was so nervous he could barely smile. Brother Witt, the pastor, had no trouble smiling. "Isn't that great news?" he said. "Now let's hear an amen from everybody who thinks it's good news!" And the church was filled with a roar of approval like never before.

"Two weeks from today," Brother Witt continued, "we will have a mortgage burning service. We all want to be here, and there will be people from other churches in town and from Toledo churches. Someone will even be here from Anderson, Indiana."

Burning the mortgage would be one of our congregation's rare symbolic moments. It would sum up years of saving building-fund offerings throughout World War II. To the kids in the church, this service sounded like something as splendid as inaugurating a president or crowning a queen. We would be there—in the front rows, we hoped.

The church had started accumulating money during the Depression, and a few dollars were collected each year to keep alive the hope for a new, larger building. Those offerings were so small that they were barely more than symbolic. The amount of money raised before the war wouldn't have paid for the front door of the new church, but the money set aside proved the congregation's commitment, and cash on hand grew penny by penny, dollar by dollar, and year by year.

During the war, money suddenly became plentiful. All the men who were not away fighting had jobs, and even some of the women worked in factories or on farms. Some men held two jobs. No one bought a new car, and few bought any new clothing or household goods. Even basic goods like sugar and gasoline were rationed by government command. The whole strength of the nation went into the worldwide struggle against tyranny. People were making money but were not able to buy much of anything, so offerings surged. Church business meetings became exciting because of reports on both the regular offerings and the money in the bank, small as it was.

In 1944, even before the war ended, enough money had accumulated to warrant buying a parsonage on Fremont Street with an adjacent property for a new building for $1,990. The new church would be on Congress Street where the Trinity Lutheran Church had once stood. Consumer goods were still scarce for a couple more years, but there was enough money by 1948 to justify starting construction on the new building. A building fund was established in early March 1948, and by April 1948, money flowed from the account as construction began. Still, a mortgage was needed to complete the work that had started with Rollin Gleckler's large private loan. The Bank of Elmore became a public partner; Rollin Gleckler was a silent partner. Soon footings were poured and the new church began to rise from the muddy ground.

Church families drove over to see the building's progress practically every Sunday after services in the old building on Harris Street. The construction was not without its sacrifices and dangers. During prayer meeting one Wednesday night, Verta Gleckler raised her hand. She rarely spoke in church, or ever, for that matter.

"Better pray for Sockie Wainwright," she said. "He fell off a scaffold and got hurt pretty bad."

Several women gasped, and men turned to see each other's reactions. Sockie Wainwright was the leader of the bricklaying crew and was the best of the bricklayers. How would the building be finished without Sockie? Would Sockie recover? Prayers for Sockie and the other builders were especially fervent that night. The people knelt in the pews and prayed, and they prayed standing. Sockie was mentioned each time.

Sockie Wainright was officially known in the newspapers as "Sox" Wainwright. From the 1920s to the 1940s, he had played for two different professional fast-pitch softball teams in Toledo, and he was famous as one of the greatest softball pitchers in Ohio. He even made some of the softball bats used in those professional games. We kids knew him as Sockie when he drove our school bus. We thought he was called Sockie because he had hit so many home runs, but he was more famous as a pitcher. We were lucky to have Sockie as our bus driver and the leader of our bricklayers.

Sockie didn't attend our church, but everyone admired his skill and determination. My dad told us how Sockie would yell, "More mud!" when he ran low on mortar. He led the charge, and the volunteers were glad to follow him. Once a softball star, he became a hero to our congregation, so the church rejoiced greatly when news came that Sockie was not seriously injured. He was soon back at the construction site, and the beautiful red brick walls continued to rise.

On a chilly, wet Sunday in March 1948, the congregation gathered at the construction site to witness the laying of the cornerstone. The men carried the church's pump organ from the old church into the front yard at the new church. The organ rocked precariously on a small wooden platform that looked like a raft in a sea of mud. Lucille Webert stepped onto the platform and played, and the congregation sang directly to the gray skies overhead. It was a time of thanksgiving, blessings, and promises to use the new building well. Sockie Wainwright was there for the ceremony. Dressed in a dark blue suit, he laid the cornerstone that is there to this very day. People who remembered his fall from the scaffolding gave thanks again for Sockie's recovery.

"It must have meant a lot to Sockie to be asked to lay the cornerstone," my mother said that day. "He did so much to help build the church."

Of course, many of the church men and women had volunteered to work on the building as well, including my dad. The volunteers could each see the parts they had helped build as it took shape. All of the people of the church looked at the building as it was being built and could see their money helping to wrap the building in its protective brick armor. When everything was completed, it was calculated that the new building cost $23,500—a lot of money at the time.

In a burst of enthusiasm, the congregation met in the unfinished building for the first time on October 31, 1948. The order of service for that day has been lost, but the signatures of ninety persons who attended have survived.

The great exodus from the old church to the new one took place in early 1949. The pulpit, two formal chairs from the platform, and the piano were brought on farm trailers pulled behind cars. The coal-burning stove was no longer needed and was left for the family that soon made the old church their home. A few of the theater seats were moved to the balcony of the new church. Hymnals, Bibles, and Sunday school materials were loaded into people's cars for the two-minute trip to the new church on Congress Street. The whole exodus took only a day, far less than the forty years it took the Israelites in the Bible. The clock of the covenant made the trip in the back seat of Harry Klinger's car, or his "machine," as he called it. Since the clock had hung at the back of the church by the door in the old building, it was placed by the door in the new building.

From the beginning, life in the new building was more elaborate than in the one-room church. The Christmas program of 1948 was larger and more glorious than any before, and all the Christian holidays were taken to new levels. The first funeral occurred in March 1949, and the first wedding was in June 1949. As the congregation had promised, they were using the new building well, as a gift from God.

On August 28, 1949, the new building was formally dedicated. The church was packed with all the regular and occasional worshippers, and visitors from around town, across the state, and around the nation. Everyone even slightly related to church was there, and friendly people from other churches in town came too. Some came from Church of God congregations in Toledo, and some came from the church headquarters in Anderson, Indiana. There were prayers of thanksgiving and Scriptures of praise. The singing was so powerful and harmonious it made some people think of heaven. Inspiring speeches and Scripture readings led to a prayer of dedication, to which many people said, "Amen." Prayers had been answered, sacrificial gifts of money and time were justified, and the new building seemed to glow with the promise of great things yet to come.

And so it came to pass, four years later, that the day was set for the burning of the mortgage on August 30, 1953. By that time, the church had grown to a congregation of more than eighty. People were praying that the day would soon come when a hundred worshippers would be there on Sundays. No one dared in 1953 to think that attendance would swell to more than a hundred and fifty, as it did by 1957.

When the great mysterious day arrived for the actual burning of the mortgage, the church was packed. At the moment in the service when it was about to happen, Brother Witt called all of the Board of Trustees to the platform. Rollin Gleckler stood next to Brother Witt, and the other Trustees surrounded them. Reaching inside the pulpit, the pastor produced a shiny metal plate, and Rollin Gleckler ceremoniously placed a paper on it. It was the mortgage, our promise to pay the bank the money we had borrowed.

Brother Witt held the plate and gave a short speech. He talked of the mortgage and our duty to pay our debts. He talked of the church's faithfulness in giving, sometimes with real sacrifice, and of our success in paying the debt. At last we would burn the mortgage. It was already marked "Paid in Full," he said, but those words weren't enough. We wanted something more visible to show how far we had come. We would burn the actual paper to show how completely we had moved beyond that debt and into new life in our new building.

Rollin Gleckler then pulled out a huge wooden farm match, struck it, and touched it to the mortgage. As it burned, I could hear "amen" and "praise God" all over the church. I don't think people clapped their hands. We didn't do that in church back then.

As a boy of thirteen looking for something sensational, I was a little disappointed. The flame from the burning mortgage wasn't very big. I knew it was an important fire, so I thought something much bigger would happen, a much bigger fire. I didn't expect a fire as big as those in the Bible when animals were sacrificed, but I thought there would be more to see. In truth, much bigger things had already happened in the life of the church to bring it to the point of burning the mortgage, and bigger moments were still ahead.

AUTHOR'S NOTE: *Burning mortgages was a tradition not only in churches but also in other institutions and even when private homes were paid off. In the 1940s and 1950s, it was more common than now for homeowners to pay off their mortgages. Moves were less common, and refinancing was even less common. My parents paid off their first mortgage in about a year during World War II. It was rarely the actual mortgage document that was burned in these ceremonies: the borrowers wanted to retain proof that their debts were paid, so they burned a facsimile or some other piece of paper.*

III. HOW KIDS SAW THE CHURCH

GOATS BEHIND THE CHURCH

People love the Christmas story of Bethlehem and the baby Jesus lying in a manger. They like the story, even if they have never seen a manger. The song line "the cattle are lowing" makes them think of friendly cows, sheep, goats, chickens, donkeys, camels, and cats and dogs coming peacefully to look at the newborn Christ child. The reality, for those of us who grew up in farm communities, is far from this imagined, idyllic scene.

In the oft-told story about the stable in Bethlehem, everything is clean and smells good. No one seems worried about a newborn baby sleeping in a cattle-feeding trough because everything seems to have gone well for Mary, Joseph, and Jesus in Bethlehem. The story is always quite sanitary. I have never heard anyone mention the possibility that the mooing cows and braying donkeys "went to the bathroom" in the stable. I don't remember any story where the animals actually smelled like animals. Goats rarely make it into nativity scenes, maybe because they smell. I don't even need to mention that pigs are never included in the Bethlehem stories.

At the Church of God in Elmore, it was easy for us to imagine the aroma of goats. When the congregation moved to its new building on Congress Street in 1949, one of the neighbors already had goats in a small barn behind his house. The barn and its goats were immediately behind the church, just beyond the wall behind the pulpit. If the church building had been designed like the temple in Jerusalem, the goats would have been just outside the Holy of Holies where the sacred scrolls were kept and only special priests could enter.

The man who owned the home and barn had only a few goats, but it didn't take many goats to make their presence known on a hot, humid summer night when all of the windows of the church were open. Their smell gave specific, added meaning to the biblical passage about separating the sheep from the goats. One could separate sheep and goats by smell alone, it seemed to me, though I'm not saying sheep smell like roses either.

The man with the goats was the father of several children and the husband of a faithful member of the church congregation, but he didn't come to church. He was thought to be a serious drinker. There was wildness about him that even a child could perceive in his ruddy cheeks, bulging eyes, and protruding stomach. As such, he was the subject of many prayers. Most of the prayers for him were for his salvation, and there probably were some prayers whispered in private homes for his wife and children.

My father may not have been the only member of the congregation who encouraged the man to come to church. I overheard a conversation between the two of them not long after World War II. I think my dad tried to persuade him not only to attend church but also to surrender his life to God. The owner of the goats explained that he couldn't come to church, that he wasn't good enough. He said he'd shot down a Japanese plane in the war, and men had died as a result. He remembered this incident as though it had been a personal crime, not an act of war. Since he'd killed them, he said, he wasn't fit to come to church. I'm sure my father tried to explain that God would forgive him, relieve him of his guilt, and free him of his painful war memories. Like the rest of us, he could never make himself good enough to come to church. Forgiveness was God's business. No effort, including my father's, persuaded the neighbor as far as I know.

I never heard it said that he kept his smelly goats as a protest against the church even though he must have known how they smelled. Perhaps he simply liked goats' milk or made a profit selling it. But keeping the goats didn't seem to me to express any love for the Lord and the church, and it happened to coincide with his stony refusal to come to church with the rest of his family.

The man with the goats was not alone in his struggles to overcome memories from World Wars I and II. The church included many who had come through those wars with emotional scars and much on their minds. As a kid, the little I knew about the veterans and their experiences was drama on a biblical scale. The details of the goat man's wartime were reserved for grownups, but all of us in the church shared the odor of the man's goats. I thought of it as the church's small way of being persecuted for our faith like the earliest Christians.

GRANDPA WEBERT'S PANTS

Grandpa Webert wasn't my Grandpa. He was the grandpa of my cousin Norman Webert. To me Grandpa Webert seemed ancient. He was ancient because he was very old, and he was ancient because he came from another country. Actually he came from two foreign countries, Germany and Latvia, and he spoke German.

As a boy of only ten, I thought Grandpa Webert's appearance was very foreign. He had large, rounded shoulders, and he stooped forward when he stood or walked his slow, shuffling walk. He had a big, bushy moustache and large, black eyebrows. His clothes made him look old and foreign too. He wore suspenders and dull-colored, baggy pants. He seldom spoke, partly because of his poor English, partly because he was shy, and partly because he was nearly deaf.

Grandma Webert seemed even older and more foreign than Grandpa Webert. She was probably a few years younger, but still she seemed older. She kept her gray hair tied tightly in a bun, and she wore long, drooping dresses and a shawl that covered her shoulders. She spoke even less than Grandpa Webert. In fact, I don't think I ever heard her speak at all.

Grandpa and Grandma Webert always came to church early, and they always sat in the third pew from the front on the left-hand side. To see them there every Sunday was like proof that the Scriptures were everlasting. Everyone could count on Grandpa and Grandma Webert to be there, even if most people couldn't understand them when they talked, which they seldom did.

The times when the minister asked Grandpa Webert to pray in his native German language were especially solemn and awesome.

Whenever that happened, everyone stood for prayer, and a hush came over the people. Grandpa Webert took a few moments to collect his thoughts. He may have been praying silently in those moments before he began to pray aloud in German. Then he began marching out his prayer in his old, raspy voice. His German words seemed holier than most prayers in English. God understood Grandpa Webert's prayer, and the rest of us understood we were just eavesdropping on a special conversation.

Grandpa Webert's prayer began quietly but urgently, seeming to me like a deep conversation with God in a special language that God alone understood. It was the closest thing to a Latin language service most of us in our church ever experienced—sacredness clothed in another language. The only thing we did understand of Grandpa Webert's prayer was his "amen" at the end, the same as English. And another loud "amen" always followed it from his son, my Uncle Fred Webert, as we sat down.

Another glimpse into Grandpa Webert's world came on Christmas Eve. Whenever Uncle Fred was the song leader, he would sing "Silent Night" in German as a special treat for everyone. Others in our church knew some German, not just Grandpa and Grandma Webert, so they especially enjoyed it along with the Weberts.

"Stille nacht, heilege nacht," Uncle Fred would sing. Those sitting near the front could see the tears rolling down Grandpa Webert's cheeks. He would take out his big blue handkerchief and wipe his eyes and blow his nose. I didn't know German, but I could envision an old German church, deep snow, and a mysterious European forest as Uncle Fred sang "Silent Night."

Once during Sunday night service, Grandma and Grandpa Webert were in their usual place in the front of the church, and everyone else was farther back. Many rows of empty pews separated the older Weberts from the "young people," as we kids were called, in the back two rows. The service began as usual with an opening song, an opening prayer, another song, and then another. When the singing stopped, the pastor stepped to the pulpit and talked about our blessings and about troubles and illness in the world. He then said, "Let's all stand and go to the Lord in prayer."

People shuffled to their feet. We bowed our heads, and the pastor began to pray. Up front Grandpa Webert placed his huge, calloused hands on the pew in front of him and bowed his head. He seemed to be praying in his German language. The pastor's prayer ended after a few minutes, and he concluded with a quiet "amen."

Everyone sat down except Grandpa Webert. He was too deaf to hear the pastor's amen, and he was deep in his own silent prayer. Possibly he had fallen asleep while standing. The pastor looked at Grandpa Webert, still standing there directly in front of him. He didn't know what to do except go on with the service, so he began reading a passage from the Bible.

None of us kids were paying attention to the pastor. We were only looking at Grandpa Webert, still standing and praying, stooped over the pew in front of him. We saw his huge shoulders, his suspenders, and his baggy pants. To the unruly "young people" at the back of the church, he looked odd, and his behavior was so strange that we nudged each other and began to laugh, some of us pretty loudly.

Grandma Webert had better hearing than Grandpa Webert, so the disturbance at the back of the church caught her attention. She looked back and saw us laughing, and she scowled at us. To our complete surprise, she then reached up and grabbed Grandpa Webert by the seat of his pants, attempting to make him sit down.

Grandpa Webert didn't seem to notice, or maybe he just chose to ignore her, so she pulled again, harder. Grandpa Webert's suspenders stretched, and his pants sagged dangerously. Everyone gasped! Grandma Webert had nearly pulled down Grandpa Webert's pants! When Grandma Webert tugged again, Grandpa Webert finally looked at her and sat down.

There was an uproar in the young people's pews. All of us laughed and poked each other and whispered our own accounts of what had just happened. It was one of the funniest things we had ever seen in church. It must have been one of the funniest things Grandma and Grandpa Webert ever did, even if it was unintentional.

Grandpa Webert may never have known what happened. He couldn't have heard our laughter. But Grandma Webert did hear the laughing and knew what happened. She was probably very ashamed. How could she have done such a lewd thing, pulling at Grandpa Webert's pants until they nearly came down? It even happened in church! But she hadn't meant to do such a terrible thing. God would forgive her, she probably reasoned later that week. But would God forgive those unruly young people who had laughed so hard? Maybe he would if they repented.

Grandma Webert must have wondered to herself what Grandpa Webert knew or thought about the incident. As far as I know, she never told him what had happened or asked him what he thought. The story of Grandpa Webert's pants went into a deep closet of forgetfulness at the Webert's farmhouse, and Grandma and Grandpa Webert went safely to their home in heaven in the 1950s, taking this secret story with them.

Since Grandma Webert never told Grandpa Webert about his pants, I hope I can trust you to never, ever tell Grandpa Webert if you see him in heaven someday.

HOLDING OUR BREATH IN CHURCH

W hen I was about ten years old, I came to church with a mixture of
awe and enthusiasm mixed with irreverence. Several other boys
were about the same age. I suppose we were relatively well washed—
our mothers saw to that—but grooming ourselves adequately was still
a couple of years in the future except for the required wetting our hair
down for tidy combing on that one day each week.

At that age, our awe and enthusiasm for church carried us to the
front two pews. I still can't explain that period before we moved to the
back of the church as teenagers. Why did we sit up front when we were
younger? Perhaps our fresh Christian commitments and our sense of
the "majesty of the church" made us want to be in the middle of things.
I don't think our parents required us to sit in front; we probably would
have resisted if they had.

The majesty of our church was almost entirely spiritual. It certainly
was not inspired by our small, deliberately simple church building. The
walls were concrete block, painted over for better appearance. The windows were dimpled amber glass that allowed light to come through but
kept the worldly distractions outside. No, the majesty we sensed was
the power of God to move in the hearts of the people around us, as
God's power had worked among the Israelites and the early Christians
we'd learned about from Bible stories. We saw hard-hearted people
transformed after praying at the altar in front of the whole congregation. We could feel in our own hearts the soft voice of Jesus calling us
to give our lives to him. God was truly there.

Sometimes our sense of awe was interrupted by things we did to
entertain each other during less majestic moments. We would draw

pictures, whisper, nudge each other, and play silent games, especially during the sermon. A favorite game was holding our breath. A large electric clock hung on a side wall near the front of the church, entirely unlike the clock of the covenant, which had been moved into one of the Sunday school classrooms. It was the common kind, with a round white face, bold black numbers and hands, and black plastic frame. It may have been placed there by one of the laymen so the preacher and everyone else would know how long he had preached. The clock had a sweep second hand, so we boys could tell the time down to seconds. It gave us a way to measure how long we had held our breath during the sermon. We could play this game over and over, silently, unless we held our breath too long and let it out in a loud rush or until we fainted or died, which we never did.

When we first started the game of holding our breath, we found that we could do it for 15 seconds, then 30 seconds. After a few Sundays, most of us could hold our breath for a full minute, sometimes a little longer. One Sunday my cousin Miles signaled that he was going to hold his breath for an extra-long time. I watched his chest rise as he inhaled a huge lungful just as the second hand reached the 12 on the clock. He held his breath through the easy first minute and didn't let the air out at the 12, as we had expected. The second hand made another full trip around the clock, and Miles still held his breath. Finally, at three and a half minutes, he dramatically let out his breath.

I was amazed. I didn't know how he did it. I tried to do the same thing, but I couldn't get past one minute and 15 seconds. Miles smiled proudly, and for a time he had superman status among us boys. After a couple of weeks as the breath-holding champion, Miles gave up his secret and demonstrated for us after church how he could hold his breath for so long. He just inhaled dramatically, kept his chest thrown out, and breathed silently moving only his abdomen. We were no longer in awe of his breath holding, but we were impressed by his cunning.

There is an end to all good things, including our childhood contests during church. For whatever reason, the electric clock was moved to the back of the church where only the minister and song leader could see it easily. Perhaps it was our disruptive breath holding that brought the game-ending change. Maybe a new minister didn't accept the pejorative location of the clock up near the front. For whatever reason, our gang of partly Christianized boys decided it was time to take up

Sunday residence at the back of the church. For us, the majesty of God may have moved to the back of the church along with the clock, so we did as well.

SUNDAY SCHOOL IN THE NEW CHURCH

My family's life in the 1940s and 1950s revolved around church services, family devotions, and get-togethers with our cousins and other extended family members, all of whom were regular attenders at church. Even school, home chores, and school activities had slight claim on our attention compared to church. We were there consistently for Sunday school classes, Sunday morning services, Sunday night services, and Wednesday night prayer meetings. On Friday or Saturday nights, we were often at church or in private homes for youth activities. Sunday mornings, however, were the most important times of all, when Sunday school classes on the rudiments of the Bible led into the main worship service.

Sunday school started with a brief worship service in the sanctuary for everyone. It was a short, informal time with music, prayer, and a brief devotional talk by one of the Sunday school leaders. It was also the time to celebrate birthdays. Those whose birthdays were to be recognized knew to bring a number of coins equal to their age that day. At a certain moment in the service, the birthday people would be called to the front of the church to drop their coins into a slot in the top of a pink metal can. The metal can once contained candy, but it seemed well suited for its new ecclesiastical purpose. Young kids would drop in the appropriate number of pennies one at a time. The clink of the coins announced their ages. Older youth and adults were supposed to deposit larger coins to save time, so sometimes we would hear the resounding clunk of quarters or even a half-dollar coin. The recognition ceremony would end by the congregation singing "Happy Birthday" while the honored ones blushed modestly.

This largely secular birthday celebration eventually was modified by Viola Cronin, wife of Brother Charles Cronin, our minister at the time. According to her plan, after the coins had been deposited in the pink metal box, we were to sing a new, spiritual version of the standard birthday song: "Happy birthday to you / only one will not do / take the gift of salvation / and then you'll have two!" Everyone knew this version was a more spiritual birthday song and spoke a biblical truth, but it seemed to take some of the fun out of the song.

After the Sunday school worship time, everyone scrambled to the Sunday school classrooms according to ages. All classes were in the basement, except one room upstairs was reserved for older people who would have had trouble getting down the steps.

When we moved to the new church, I was in Intermediate Class, the one for boys and girls aged eight to ten. Usually one of the serious, determined older people in the church taught the lessons, which came from the Sunday School Quarterly. The pedagogy mimicked that of the public schools of a decade or so earlier and did not always hold our attention. Nevertheless, each Sunday morning the teacher marched us through the material, and we were supposed to show that we had learned the lesson by saying we agreed with it, or at least by refraining from arguing about it. Our agreement, sometimes only by silence, presumably showed we also had adopted its principles. Not infrequently some of us tried to inject humor and action into the lessons, which to the teacher demonstrated our need for prayer and repentance. My jokes and wisecracks must have made me the object of many prayers.

My favorite part of Sunday school class time was singing. We sang in our classrooms, and we could request songs. My favorite was "Dare to Be a Daniel." I requested it every time we sang, so often that our teachers sometimes ignored me. Here are a few lines of the song:

Many giants great and tall
Stalking through the land,
Headlong to the earth would fall
If met by Daniel's band!

Dare to be a Daniel
Dare to stand alone,
Dare to have a purpose firm
Dare to make it known.

Goliath seems to be implied by the opening line, but it was David, not Daniel, who felled Goliath. I was never troubled by mingling Daniel with David and Goliath. The militancy of the song was what mattered.

Near the end of the hour-long Sunday school class time, the teacher would select one of the better behaved kids to distribute Sunday school papers. These papers were professionally produced at the Church of God publishing house in Anderson, Indiana. They had water color painting on the cover and had stories to reinforce the Sunday school lessons—Bible stories and tales of adventure and miraculous escapes from danger and evil. I often read those papers during the sermon time that followed.

The church used an especially fascinating invention to signal the end of Sunday school class time. A small, red lightbulb was mounted on the wall above the door inside each basement classroom. About five minutes before the main worship service was to start, the red light would come on. After another two minutes or so, it would flash off and on insistently a few times to remind zealous teachers that it was closing time. I loved seeing the red light. I was always eager to move on to something different, and I usually liked the services in "big church" more than Sunday school. When we were formally dismissed, we grabbed our Sunday school papers, scrambled for the door, and ascended from the cool seclusion of the basement into the full light and warmth of the sanctuary.

To be fair, even resistant scholars like me learned a lot of Bible stories and some important principles of the faith in Sunday school. The teachers were dedicated, long-suffering people whose main training for handling classes of kids came from managing their own children or corralling livestock on the farm. In modern times, children's Sunday school is far livelier and more varied than it was when I was a kid. And, truth to be told, the students have better lesson materials and better trained teachers than I did. I prefer to think that the teachers these days have more civilized kids in their classes than we kids were in those olden times.

In spite of my resistance to learning in Sunday school class, in my adult life I have found myself teaching classes of three-year-olds, fifth and sixth graders, and senior adults. Perhaps it's God's way of punishing me for my earlier misbehavior. Maybe it's God's way of allowing me to reap rewards from what I did learn in Sunday school as a boy. Or maybe it's God's way of protecting other Sunday school classes from my presence where, God knows, I would likely be as disruptive now as I was in the 1950s.

AUTHOR'S NOTE: *No part of the church was very accessible to the handicapped or the aged at that time in its history. There were steps up to the landing in front of the front door, another step into the building, and four more steps up to the sanctuary level. There may have been ten steps up to the sanctuary from outside and perhaps a dozen steps down to the basement. Hundreds of older churches had these same impediments to older and handicapped people at that time. Possibly the value of the design was to economize on the depth of the basement and possibly to keep the basement relatively dry and light.*

TRADING KIDS ON SUNDAYS

One Sunday Aunt Eula asked if two of my brothers and I would like to come to her house after church. I had a lot of cousins, and there were four young boys in that one family, including twin boys my age. Besides those four boys, Aunt Eula and Uncle Joe also had a girl about the age of my younger brother. They also had four older kids in their family, but my brothers and I usually didn't play with them. Three of them were teenage girls and liked to talk about boyfriends. "Yuck!" we boys thought.

Aunt Eula's invitation was not uncommon. My mother took turns with her in hosting these same cousins some Sundays. She and Aunt Eula probably regained a little more sanity on those days by having some of their kids out of the house, even at the cost of inviting in a rowdy tribe on some other Sunday. At the very least, when there were cousins to play with, the mothers usually had less need to direct or supervise the activities of their own children.

One of the boys in the family my brothers and I played with was Dick, born the same day as my older brother Merl. When Merl was very young and needed a name for that batch of cousins, he named them "the Dickey Boys" after Dick, the cousin he knew best. Even the girl cousins were included as "Dickey Boys." My brothers and I were always excited about going to the Dickey Boys' house for a Sunday afternoon after church, but this particular Sunday was different from all the other Sundays.

Uncle Joe and Aunt Eula lived in a big farmhouse, and their property included a huge barn, many outbuildings, and a creek. Inside the barn were cribs of soybeans, wheat, and corn. A mountain of hay bales was stacked inside the barn on one side, and a high, second story loft of loose hay towered across from it. The whole place, house included, was like an amusement park for wild kids, which we were.

After the church service, my brothers and I somehow all crowded into the Dickey Boys' car with their family. Since several of us were under ten years old and small, seven of us were able to fit two-deep into the back seat of Uncle Joe's Model A Ford. A few older kids squeezed in front with Uncle Joe and Aunt Eula. We had no idea how exciting our play day would become before we were back in that car in the evening, heading back to church for the evening service.

After a big noontime dinner, the gang went outside with Ken, the oldest boy in the family. He had attached a long rope high in one of the trees. Kenny, as he was called, gave us rides on the rope. One kid would grab the rope as high as he could reach while standing at the base of the tree. Kenny and some of the other kids would then grab the end of the rope. When they pulled the end of the rope all together, the rider would shoot up ten feet or more in the air. On the first try that day, the rope pullers just let go when the rider was up in the air, and he slammed down into the tree. After that mishap, the rope pullers let each rider down more slowly. Still there were many bumps and bruises before we'd had enough fun and Kenny was tired of pulling the rope. We learned a lot from minor injuries when we played with our cousins.

Some of us went to play in the barn while others explored the smaller outbuildings or chased the chickens. Those of us in the barn climbed the mountain of hay bales and the pile of loose hay. We made up daring stunts, jumping from as high as we could in the most dangerous ways we could. It was hot, sticky play, and we soon were covered with sweat, dust, and alfalfa leaves. It was the kind of play we boys loved.

Toward evening, Aunt Eula called us all into the house for supper. After a quick wash, we crowded our sweaty bodies around the huge dinner table for a nutritious meal of potato soup, home-baked bread, and home-churned butter. It was getting dark outside when we finished, but Aunt Eula said we had a little more time to play. She lit kerosene lamps so we could see to play indoors. Soon our play turned into a running riot. We shrieked as we ran throughout the house, making a circuit that became something like a racetrack. While the rest of us were making a racket, my brother Owen and my cousin Lois, the youngest kids, decided to play a game of catch with a basketball.

What happened next was unlike anything that ever happened before or after on one of those Sunday trade days. Owen stood on the stair landing, and he threw the ball down to Lois in the living room. Lois missed her catch, and the ball crashed into a kerosene lamp, sending it flying onto the living room floor. Kerosene began to leak from the lighted lamp, and all of us screamed as the spilled oil burst into flames around the lamp. Aunt Eula appeared instantly, as though from thin air. She did not scream. Instead, with the determination of a warrior, she rushed to the flaming lamp, picked it up in her bare hands, marched to the front door, and flung it out. It landed on the wooden steps, shattered, and burst into flames. Miraculously, Aunt Eula was not burned.

"Put out the fire!" Aunt Eula then ordered. "Get some water!"

Someone threw a rug over the fire on the floor, snuffing it out. The older girls were screaming hysterically until Aunt Eula ordered them to be quiet. The younger kids just stood staring. The big boys knew what to do next.

"Get the buckets!" Kenny yelled. "Start pumping!"

With no electricity or indoor plumbing, the only source of water was the pump at the kitchen sink. One boy pumped furiously there, and the others formed a bucket brigade with two pails and a dishpan. They flooded the front steps with water, putting out the fire. The porch, the house, and all in the house were saved.

"Praise God!" Aunt Eula yelled.

Just then Uncle Joe came in from milking the cows. He had heard the commotion, and as the kids breathlessly told him the story, he glanced at Aunt Eula.

"That's right," she affirmed. "We pert' near lost the house and mebbe some kids in the bargain."

Uncle Joe pulled back the rug where the lantern had fallen. He stared first at the scorched floor and then looked out at the steps. "We still goin' to church?" was all he could say.

Aunt Eula had seen enough wild play to know this episode wouldn't be the end of the horseplay we kids were known for, so she just gave us all a stern speech about running in the house. The steam rising in the yard from the broken lantern helped make her point. We didn't run around in the house any more that particular night. Instead, within a few minutes, we piled back into the car for the short drive to church.

Even though it was Sunday, not a testimony night, Aunt Eula told the congregation how the Lord had spared the house and all of our lives. The usual men said "amen." Many mothers wiped their eyes, and some men blew their noses. They knew what had happened at Aunt Eula and Uncle Joe's house could have happened at their homes, and it could have been much worse.

A few years later, not long after Uncle Joe and Aunt Eula were connected to electricity, Aunt Eula testified in church. She said that they were so happy with their new lights that they turned them all on every night so people could see their house "from the Pike," which was U.S. Route 20, half a mile away. She then reminded the church of the night the house nearly burned because of the accident with the kerosene lamp, and some shuddered again. She no longer had to light kerosene lamps at her house, she said, except when the electricity went out. That night at church, nearly everyone said "amen," and someone even shouted, "praise God!"

SAYING "AMEN" IN CHURCH

It used to be common for people to say "amen" in church. I don't mean just someone saying a prayer and ending it that way. I mean lots of people saying or even shouting amen. The use of that biblical word, which means "so be it," was a kind of public church cheer. In response to a special song, people would say amen. After an especially significant announcement of good news, people would say amen. Most commonly, men would say amen after the preacher made a powerful point in a sermon. As a child, the rumbling sound of men repeatedly saying amen made me think of bullfrogs around the pond at home.

Sometimes people used other responses, such as "praise the Lord" or "praise God" or just "yes" or "yes, Lord." Only once in a while would anyone say "hallelujah." In my church, people were against what they considered "Pentecostal outbursts," so the use of that word might have seemed to cross a line. And we certainly didn't clap our hands to applaud something in church. That was clearly worldly and did not respect the sanctity of church.

Although it was mainly men who said amen, some women could do it too. Those women were usually the older women, ones who were spiritual leaders and were entitled to have their say. Grandma Emma Kardatzke would say amen, and she was certainly qualified. She had raised her nine children in the church in spite of the fact that Grandpa Fred Kardatzke had resisted salvation until he was on his deathbed. All of her children were Christians, and two of her sons were ministers. She had lots of reasons to say amen, and the people of the church never knew which reason was on her mind when she said it. Her amens were soft and thoughtful, compared to the loud ones of Fred Webert. In fact, most women said their amens quietly.

Amen seemed like something for only the mature Christians to say. It was perfectly appropriate to hear it from Uncle Fred, Uncle Harris, Harry Klinger, Daddy, Grandma, Aunt Delorous, Fred Otte, Bill Webert, and other older saints in the church. Once in a while, one of the younger men would try to say it, but it usually came out as a muffled or muttered word, not as forceful praise to God like Uncle Fred would do it. Once or twice one of us kids tried saying it when we felt especially spiritual, but the sound of our own voices made us feel self-conscious, and everyone seemed to be looking at us. We sounded like little frogs chirping in the pond, not like the big bullfrogs.

One of the problems with saying amen in church was knowing how to pronounce it. Should it sound like *ay-men* or *ah-men*? My family always said it as *ay-men* at home, so that seemed to me to be the most honest and humble way to say it. *Ah-men* seemed like something you might hear in a much fancier church than ours, one with a steeple and stained glass windows. Still, some people said *ah-men* in our church. They may have been better educated or perhaps had a "high church" background.

Maybe it was uncertainty about pronunciation that caused the amens to die out in my church. Maybe it was because people became proud and cautious and didn't want to show their enthusiasm in church. Or maybe they actually became less enthusiastic. Possibly the church just ran out of mature Christians who were qualified to punctuate the services with enthusiastic amens. Maybe clapping in church displaced amens and made them either unnecessary or embarrassing.

Whatever the cause, these days I rarely hear anyone say amen in church except when the preacher or song leader says, "And all the people said . . . " and people know it's okay to say *ay-men* or *ah-men* in a medium loud voice, as long as everybody else does the same. Since almost everyone joins in, at least in my church, people don't have to be mature Christians to say amen. Some who say it might not even be Christians at all, but they would need to have been in church enough to know what to say when the leader says, "And all the people said . . ." I probably don't need to tell you, but whenever you hear that line, for heaven's sake, I hope you don't yell out "Play ball!" or "Let's eat!" That would be worldly.

SUNDAY SCHOOL PICNICS

On the day of the annual Sunday school picnic, church followed its weekly pattern until the close of the service. But then a ripple of excitement would sweep through the congregation as the last hymn was sung and the final prayer was offered. "I don't need to remind you," the pastor would say with special mock seriousness, "that our church picnic is this afternoon at Brother Arlin's place out by the pond."

"Amen!" someone would say, and a few would chuckle.

"Praise God!" another might say.

Some of the younger kids were tempted to say amen but didn't. Even they knew saying amen was serious work, and only adults were likely to get it right. We older kids in the back rows just nudged each other and swung our legs under the pews. The annual church picnic was just a notch or two below Christmas on our liturgical calendar, and we were eager to join in. I was especially excited every year because Brother Arlin was my father, and the annual church picnic was at our property in the country.

"I'm told there will be some good food there and a wonderful time of fellowship," the pastor continued.

Again some people would say "Amen!" and "Praise the Lord!" Others just smiled and nodded to each other.

Sunday school picnic day was when sensual delights were at their highest for the entire church. This was a church event that existed for no other reason than to bind our church community in a social time the adults called "fellowship." But the word *fellowship* always sounded to me like a stuffy word to describe what actually happened. Everyone would eat together and then enjoy playing games, swimming, or sitting in lawn chairs under the massive old maple trees. Kids ran wild around the yard and explored around the pond. As many as possible would ride the "trolley," an aerial ride my father had created, something people today would call a zip line. Able-bodied young people played softball and volleyball. Even the oldest members of the church welcomed this special day of eating, visiting with friends, and worshipping God in the open air. Miraculously, the weather was perfect for nearly every Sunday school picnic.

The Sunday school picnic was held on a large vacant lot that my dad called "the park." Local people called it "the old Leatherport school-yard." My parents owned the land, but the schoolhouse had been gone for nearly forty years when they began hosting the picnic. All that remained from its schoolyard years were huge old maple trees that were already mature when my grandmother started school at Leatherport in 1890. The biggest trees provided deep shade until late afternoon when the sun was low and shown under the protective branches.

For at least a week before the picnic, my family prepared our park for the picnic. We picked up fallen branches and mowed the lawn. We cleaned up around the pond, raking moss and fallen leaves from the edge. Saturday, the day before the picnic, was setup day for the big event. In the afternoon, my Uncle Joe came on his farm tractor pulling two flatbed hay wagons that would serve as buffet tables the next day.

Shortly after noon on Sunday, less than an hour after the benediction at church, those flatbed hay wagons began to groan under a load of food. It was the most beautiful collection of food anyone would see all year, and to me it looked as if it covered an entire acre. The wagons were large, about nine feet wide and fifteen feet long, so food was placed only around the edges for easy reach. And such food! Fried chicken, roast beef, ham, deviled eggs, salads, potatoes, corn, peas, green beans, baked beans with ham, baked beans with bacon, lima beans, chocolate cake, white cake, caramel cake, strawberry cake, and all kinds of pies: apple, cherry, blueberry, banana cream, coconut cream, rhubarb, and more. In my church's branch of Christianity, gluttony was not thought of as a sin—if indeed anyone ever even used that word.

Besides eating to our hearts' content, playing with dry ice was the most exciting thing we did at the picnic. Dry ice was something we had only once a year, and only at the Sunday school picnic. Each year one of the men had the task of driving ten miles to Gibsonburg to pick up ice cream for the picnic. It came solidly frozen in an oversized, insulated bucket packed with dry ice. The ice cream was good, but we could have ice cream any time. Dry ice came only once a year, so we had to make the most of it.

As soon as the ice cream was served, kids would scramble for hunks of that super cold, solid carbon dioxide. It didn't melt into liquid like regular ice; instead it was transformed directly from ice to a vapor. It didn't melt in our hands, which was why it was called dry ice, but if we held it for more than an instant, it began to freeze our skin. It felt hot, like it was burning, not freezing. When we threw it in the pond, the dry ice bubbled as the escaping vapor came to the surface, like a witch's cauldron or perhaps the breath of a dragon beneath the water.

Even more fun than holding a chunk of dry ice or throwing it into the pond was putting it in a bottle with a little water and corking the bottle. As the dry ice turned to vapor, it expanded. In a few moments, the cork would blast out of the bottle with a bang. Every year some unruly kid would point a dry ice bottle at other kids and shoot corks at them. Those kids retaliated in kind. When that un-Christian battle erupted, the grown-ups would confiscate the bottles and toss the rest of the dry ice in the pond, suspending that form of heathen fun for another year.

The church congregation did not wholly surrender itself to these pleasures of the flesh at the Sunday school picnic: the day ended with a vesper service. Lawn chairs were drawn up in a circle for adults, and kids stood in an outer circle or sat on the grass in the middle. The pastor offered a short meditation, one or two adults gave testimonies of thanksgiving, and everyone joined in singing a song or two. In the concluding prayer, the pastor said something like, "Thank you, Lord, for this day of fellowship in your presence. We thank you for your spirit among us, and we thank you that we had all these joys today without serious injuries to any of us, not even from the dry ice and the rides on the trolley." More than one mother murmured, "Amen."

OHIO YOUTH CAMPS

Summer camps were part of the lives of children and youth in my church, even as they are today. At youth camp we learned about the Bible and did crafts such as weaving colorful bracelets from plastic coated string. We played organized sports like volleyball and softball that country kids seldom did at home, and we sometimes went swimming in actual swimming pools rather than in ponds or rivers. We explored the limits of the camp and sometimes strayed to forbidden places outside. Camps were also where boys and girls met and often had their first-ever, pristine romances.

The youth camps I attended in Ohio were at three locations. The first of those camps was the best I attended in Ohio. It was in southern Ohio in a hilly, wooded area very different from the flat land where we lived. The hills were covered with old-growth timber, which one of the counselors explained was "virgin forest," a term that made the girls blush and the boys snicker.

The buildings at that first camp looked like large log cabins. The dormitories were long buildings with two rows of beds along the walls. Bedtime in the boys' bunkhouse was a long, noisy event. The loudest boys were quite sophisticated, since they had television at home and could imitate characters from programs they watched. Most of us from Elmore were pre-television country boys, so we listened in wonderment as an especially talented older boy told us of Captain Midnight and the Junior Birdmen. He said Captain Midnight fired a machine gun or maybe a death ray that looked like a can of grapefruit juice, and the boy fired an imaginary gun for us with his spit flying everywhere.

That boy even sang the "Junior Birdmen" song for his adoring listeners, complete with sound effects and more spittle:

Up in the air, Junior Birdmen,
Up in the air, upside do-o-own!
Up in the air, Junior Birdmen,
Keep your noses off the ground!
When you hear the postman ringing,
Put on your wings of ti-i-in,
Till you know the Junior Birdmen
Have sent their boxtops in!

Naïve as we were, we found these lyrics hysterically funny and somehow heroic, and many of us repeated them through the week of camp and beyond, temporarily taking on this bit of worldly drama.

My cousin Stan Kardatzke was one of the more sophisticated boys at that camp with me, and I learned a lot from him. He was a big-city kid from Wichita, a Boy Scout, and a good swimmer. But Stan learned something the hard way at camp from a particularly brash boy. At dinner one evening, Stan carefully pulled the crusts from the slices of bread we were served with the "gruel," or whatever unmemorable food we were served. It had never occurred to me to do such a thing, so I just watched in wonder as Stan neatly trimmed his bread.

But a boy across the table had something to say. "What's the matter? Aren't your teeth *strong enough* to chew the crusts?"

Stan didn't say anything, and neither did I. We were both too embarrassed, and the boy seemed too tough to attack physically. If Stan had been some years older, his manhood would have been challenged, and a fight might have ensued. Even as a boy, Stan liked to show his masculine prowess whenever possible. But this time he silently ate the bread and its severed crusts, and we never heard from the aggressive boy again.

The best thing at that camp was the swimming hole a half-mile down the hill on a dusty gravel road. The swimming hole wasn't a pond. It was just an especially deep place in a quiet, slightly green river. The water at the surface was warm, and it was so deep that it was cool near the bottom. A rope hung over the water from a high branch ten feet from the shore. A boy could grasp the rope, get a good run, and swing far out over the river. He could drop in from high above the water, and with good luck, could plunge down to the cool, deep water and touch the muddy river bottom. Girls from the camp used the same swimming hole but at a different time from the boys. Mixed swimming would have seemed unwise if not sinful, and we boys never even saw the girls traipsing off to the swimming hole in their swimsuits.

The other two camps I attended in Ohio were less dangerous and less fun. One was at the state's church convention site right in the city of Springfield. It existed mainly for the annual Ohio state camp meeting, a gathering that attracted hundreds for spiritual renewal and learning. The camp's urban setting was offset by the fact that the campus was large, and a deep ravine ran next to it. At this camp, kids played volleyball, wove plastic bracelets, and tapped out pictures of horse heads, fish, and dogs on thin sheets of copper using nails to indent the copper. Mind you, these were not the "graven images" forbidden in the Bible but just crafts for entertainment.

As usual, I "fell in love" at this camp, something that happened to me at almost every camp. I still remember the girl's name even though she didn't answer the letter I sent after camp. Her name will remain forever my secret because she would be shocked to see her name in this book. I probably didn't even talk to that cute brunette, but we may have made eye contact a couple of times. Eye contact in itself would have been enough to unbalance my world, bringing on the strange dizziness of infatuation I experienced several times in my early adolescent period. Within a few weeks after camp, other obsessions overtook me, and the girl was spared any further attention from me.

The most exciting activity by far at the Springfield camp came during afternoon nap time, when a few boys would sneak out of the dormitory, cross a major highway, and hike along a path at the rim of a ravine. This was a strictly forbidden form of fun, and I'm relieved at last to confess having done it. The year I went, no one slid down the steep bank into the creek from the crumbly path we walked. God's hand must have been on us all, steering us from danger, even in that time of trespass.

For some kids, the most memorable part of camp happened at the end of each evening. Vesper services always included an altar call, and many young sinners went forward to get saved over the course of the week. Those spiritual experiences surely meant more to those campers than all the plastic bracelets and copper plates they took home.

The last camp I attended in Ohio was by far the least attractive. I don't know where it was, whether in a city or in the country. All I remember is its unforgiving, white frame buildings utterly lacking in personality, having all the charm of a concentration camp. The sun bore down on those barracks, and they remained steamy well into the night.

One day an older man visited the camp and encouraged us to do sit-ups on an inclined board in order to reach old age in health as good as his. He also advised us to put bricks under the posts at the foot of our beds for some obscure health reason. I believe this was supposed to make blood run to our heads to give us more healthy brains. He looked so energetic that I was almost persuaded, but I never managed to follow his advice. Perhaps I would have become smarter if I had complied.

I don't remember the girl I fell in love at this camp. In fact, I don't even remember falling in love at that unromantic site. But I must have fallen in love; it was part of the camp experience. If I did fall in love there, the innocence of my youthful infatuation kept me from any contact with girls beyond furtive glances. To the parents of early teens reading this story, let it serve as a warning. Camp life awakens more than purely spiritual longings.

I did not go to the altar during vesper services at that camp even though one of my friends there suggested I should. I think he was trying to fulfill his evangelistic duty by asking me. I'm not sure why I resisted, because I'm sure I had things to repent, except that I just didn't feel that God had chosen this new friend to take me to the altar. Besides, I had already been saved at the very first youth camp I attended, a camp in Kansas far more memorable than the Ohio camps.

AUTHOR'S NOTE: *Many different versions of the song "Junior Birdmen" exist along with discussions about its origin, but the general consensus is that regardless of how it originated, it became a camp song in the 1950s. The Junior Birdmen of America website seems to me the most authoritative source of information about the true beginnings of the song. Although it's possible that the song was featured on "Captain Video" in the 1950s, it appears to have originated in the 1930s among model aviation enthusiasts as a parody of the Army Air Corps song "Into the Air, Army Air Corps." The Army Air Corps was the predecessor to the U.S. Air Force, and the song was altered accordingly, becoming "Into the Air, U.S. Air Force." The "Junior Birdmen" version, having been created by model airplane fans, was used in jest by actual aviators in World War I and later in Air Force ROTC training. Eventually it became just a campfire song popular among Boy Scouts.*

TORNADO AT CAMP FELLOWSHIP

My very first youth camp, and the most exciting, was not in Ohio, where I grew up. It was much earlier, and it was in Kansas, when I was a mere eight years old. Kids were supposed to be nine years old to attend Camp Fellowship, and my cousin Stan Kardatzke met that requirement, having been born in April that year. But my October birthday meant I was only eight years old in the summer of 1948. Stan's father, Rev. Elmer Kardatzke, was the pastor mainly responsible for the camp, so he made it possible for me to go at age eight. Going underage was a sin I carried secretly to Camp Fellowship that year, thanks to Elmer Kardatzke. Because of it, I surmised later, I experienced an event at Camp Fellowship not unlike that of Jonah when God found him out in a terrible storm. A storm found me out too.

Camp Fellowship is about twenty miles west of Wichita, in open farm country that is plagued with tornadoes from spring until fall every year. On Sunday afternoon, July 11, we campers arrived and checked into the bunkhouses on a low hill overlooking the dining hall, chapel, and playing fields. My cousin Georgene Bruner Corbett was also there, and I was glad to see her. She was a young teenager, and I felt assured every time I saw her. Dinner was served in the Quonset building on the same hill, soon followed by the vesper service in the chapel partway down the hill. The lake at the bottom of the hill was a bay on a large reservoir called Lake Afton. Camp activities were to begin in full force Monday morning. Little did we know that the week would become our most vivid memory of youth camp ever.

On Monday evening, the vesper service opened with a talent show orchestrated by my Uncle Elmer, an irrepressible extrovert. He had decided that his two sons, Jon and Stan, along with my older brother and I, would reenact the drama of "Bill Grogan's Goat," the animal that coughed up three red shirts and flagged down a speeding train that would have spelled his demise. As the youngest, I was selected for the honor of being Bill Grogan's goat. Uncle Elmer taught the song to the other campers, and they sang while the three older boys in the skit pantomimed tying me to the railroad tracks. At the last two stanzas, I became the star of the show:

The whistle blew,
The train drew nigh,
Bill Grogan's goat
Was due to die!

He gave three moans
Of mortal pain,
Coughed up the shirts
And flagged the train!

With that, I pulled a huge red handkerchief from under my t-shirt, leaped to my feet, and triumphantly waved the life-saving red flag in the air. The crowd exploded in wild applause. It would be several years before I played another role so heroic. A few days later, that night of fun seemed weirdly out of place, given what was to come.

On Wednesday afternoon, menacing clouds appeared in the west. Camp counselors and visiting adults watched the clouds while we kids yammered excitedly and went about the afternoon activities of crafts, sports, and practicing skits for the evening talent show. At dusk all two hundred campers and adult overseers gathered in the unfinished chapel for the usual evening entertainment and worship time. The chapel at that time was only a roof supported by wooden posts all around. It was open on all sides, and light bulbs dangled at the ends of their electric cords. A stage at the front was graced with a piano, a pulpit, a table, and enough folding chairs for a small choir. Beneath that stage a tornado shelter was under construction.

A stiff breeze had started even before all the kids were seated, and the electric lights were swinging wildly in the wind. Singing was soon drowned out by the wind. At first the counselors considered moving everyone into the unfinished storm shelter, but access to it was difficult, there was no lighting, and it still had an earthen floor. They chose instead to direct us hurriedly from the chapel up the slight hill to the dining hall. The steel Quonset building would shelter us better from the wind and the rain that would surely come. The Quonset building looked like a very large two-quart juice can cut in half and tipped on its side. It had a rounded roof and flat walls at both ends. The roof was corrugated steel, riveted to strong steel arches. Nothing on the campground was as safe as the dining hall at that time, since the storm shelter under the chapel was still under construction. We later thanked God we didn't go to the storm shelter that night.

Inside the dining hall, we campers took seats at the heavy wooden picnic tables, the kind typically seen at public picnic grounds. A pianist and a song leader started us singing over the rising noise of the storm. In strong wind, rain began pelting the metal building. Some of the biggest boys tried to close the windows on the upwind side. But bang! The windows shattered, exploding glass and rain in the faces of the boys. They jumped back, girls screamed, and our shelter took on water. The lights flashed off and then on again. Our singing gave way to shouts and screams. Then the lights went off and stayed off.

A few panels of corrugated steel blew off the rounded top of the building, and lightning flashed above our heads. Campers with flashlights directed their beams to the roof, and we watched in horror as whole rows of steel panels broke loose and were blown away. Rain and hail roared down on us. In the next terrifying seconds, the entire building seemed to sigh. Its great steel beams bent, and it looked as if the building was kneeling down as the top arches failed. The building then folded on its downwind side. Beams on the upwind side were ripped from their concrete foundations. The bent beams bounced once and released heavy steel roof panels that flew end-over-end down the hill toward the lake like deadly, slashing blades. Constant lightning in the now open sky above cast weird, flashing light on the campers.

As if awaking from a dream, I found myself under a picnic table not knowing how I got there. Maybe someone pushed me out of danger. Maybe I slid under the table from my seat as the roof began to fall. I remembered seeing the roof fall and seeing the steel panels bounce down the hill. The shock of those sights may have erased my memory of what happened to me next. I learned later that people sometimes faint when the high wind of a tornado reduces the oxygen supply. By this time it was raining and hailing heavily. In the blazing lightning, I looked across the concrete floor from where I lay in water under my table. All I could see under all the other tables were kids lying on the floor. None were moving. They seemed to be dead. For a few seconds, I thought I was the only one alive.

Just then a man came through an opening in the wreckage where the long side of the building had been, the side facing down the hill to the lake. He had found a tunnel-like passage through the twisted steel. He was yelling, but I could barely hear him above the wind.

"Come with me!" he yelled to me and other kids nearby. "Follow me!"

We held hands and followed our rescuer through a providential opening in the wreckage toward the old but solid lodge at the bottom of the hill on the lake's edge. It had been spared the tornado's freakish rage. Along the way, we stepped over power lines and a trench and through pieces of steel. We kids by then were talking and telling each other how we had survived the storm. We were still chattering as we entered the lodge, but our talk ended there. On a table just inside, a woman lay motionless, bleeding profusely from her head. Beside her stood three adults, silent and helpless.

"Be quiet and go on through!" our rescuer whispered hoarsely.

As we passed, an older camper said softly, "That's Sister Lighty. She may be dying!"

In the next room, many other kids were huddled together, shivering in their wet clothes. The room smelled of mildew, and it was freezing cold and dark except for lightning and a few flashlights. I dropped to the floor and pulled the edge of a carpet over me and the kid next to me for warmth. We held each other and shook, warming each other. Suddenly a man appeared over us and threw the carpet back. "Get up! Go to that other room!" he shouted angrily at me. It was only then that I realized the other kid was a girl.

I crowded my way into a tiny room with five other boys, including my cousin Jon Kardatzke. Lightning flashed through a window, and I could see that Jon was bleeding from a small cut above his eyebrow. He and the rest of us were otherwise unharmed. We all talked excitedly about what had happened and tried to seem brave. Our clothes reeked of mildew, but we were grateful to be alive. In just a short time, our world had shrunk down to just that little room and our group of six.

We'd lost track of the hundred or so other campers who were still in the larger rooms of the lodge and the other hundred still creeping out of the dining hall or huddled elsewhere around the campground.

It may have been a short time or a long time before Uncle Elmer appeared in the room. When he came in, he seemed to me like a picture of salvation. He quickly surveyed our little group, took Jon's arm to guide him out, and told the rest of us to follow. We held onto each other and made our way out of the lodge. Uncle Elmer had found Stan somewhere too, and he led the three cousins and the three other kids up the hill, through light rain. Enough lightning was still flashing that we could see our way through the rubble and downed power lines. At the top of the hill, headlights from a row of ambulances shown out like beacons and lighted our way. Uncle Elmer had rounded up all of the available ambulances in Wichita! The rear door of an ambulance opened for us, and we six kids climbed aboard.

The ambulance rocked gently as we slipped away slowly from the chaos of the camp. The dirt roads back to Wichita were as slippery as grease. The siren moaned softly all the way. We could hear the driver tell the other man up front about other events that night. He told of the tragic death of a man who had donned a steel helmet to protect himself from flying objects or the collapse of his house. He went to his front porch to see the storm, and he was killed instantly by lightning.

Sometime that night, we reached Uncle Elmer and Aunt Vera's house in Wichita. The ambulance driver and the man with him carried us kids through the flooded street and into the house. All the lights were on, and my parents were there. I hugged them silently, too thankful and too stunned to say anything.

My parents had gone to Oklahoma to visit my mother's parents. When they heard about the tornado on the radio, they rushed back to Wichita. The tornado had not struck Wichita, but the streets of the city were flooded. They had to wade through waist-deep water in the streets to get to Uncle Elmer and Aunt Vera's house. I'm sure tears were shed that night, but I was too young to think of the enormity of all that had happened. To me it was just a big adventure. We hadn't died, so that possibility evaporated from my childish mind.

The next morning was cold for summer, and it seemed unnaturally calm and bright. The cold front that had caused the tornado had given the world an especially bright, hope-filled feel. All of us were experiencing life in a new way, safe after a terrifying storm. We learned no one had died in the tornado, and no kids were seriously injured. Two camp counselors, however, were seriously injured. The injured woman I'd seen on the table in the lodge, Sister Lighty, had head injuries. Pastor John Holder from McPherson, Kansas, had been struck by the falling Quonset roof, and his back was broken. Both eventually recovered, but Pastor Holder would suffer the rest of his life from that injury.

We also learned that day that my brother Merl and a boy named Glenn Bair had gone with other boys to their cabins when the storm started instead of to the dining hall. From there they had watched in horror as the dining hall collapsed. They sobbed, thinking they were seeing the deaths of their friends and relatives inside. Amazingly, their cabin was not destroyed, and they were not injured.

My family and my uncle's family went back to Camp Fellowship to see the damage. The roof of the chapel we had abandoned early in the storm was bobbing in the lake, only its peak showing above the water. The tornado had blown the chapel completely over, and the roof had been dragged through the rows of seats before taking flight. The seats we had abandoned were flattened and smashed to pieces. When we walked down the hill below the chapel, we found the most sobering sight. The chapel's heavy stage, along with its piano and furniture, had collapsed straight down into the unfinished storm shelter. If we had gone to the storm shelter instead of to the dining hall, many of us would have died. We kids just stared at the wreckage. Our mothers cried.

My spiritual life took a new step that night in the storm. I don't remember actually praying and repenting, but afterward I was convinced I had. I told everyone, including my dying grandfather when I was back in Ohio, that I had been saved during the tornado. Years later, when I told some other survivors of the Camp Fellowship tornado that I had been saved that night, one person said, "We *all* got saved in the tornado!"

For everyone who survived, the tornado became one of the mileposts of our lives. Decades later, my brother Merl and cousins Stan and Jon shared their memories of that night with me many times. We each probably got saved again at least once after the tornado, but not so dramatically as that night. In those later religious experiences, we were moved by an inner voice rather than a storm, but we knew what it was to face death and turn to God.

My parents wisely took my brothers and me back to attend Camp Fellowship a year later, in the summer of 1949. By that time the dining hall and chapel had been rebuilt, and the tornado shelter was ready for any storm. It was a peaceful week in camp that year, and being there again without a tornado helped heal our terror of storms.

"I'LL FLY AWAY"

In our church calendar, June meant it was time for Camp Meeting. Other churches observed Lent and Epiphany as well as Christmas and Easter, as we did, but we also had Camp Meeting.

Camp Meeting got its name from large religious gatherings in the late 1800s. Christians would meet in open fields or fairgrounds, where they put up a large tent for their main meetings and smaller tents for the attendees. Camp meetings were held in most parts of the country, and most would go on for a week or two. Some of them attracted thousands of worshippers, seekers, and the curious. Camp meetings were one of the characteristics of the revivalist tradition in America, in which believers periodically sought renewed religious purity. Revival meetings in the home church were reinforced by camp meetings that might have regional, state-wide, or national audiences. For the Church of God movement, Camp Meeting was as essential as the major Christian holidays. People from the Elmore Church of God went to Camp Meeting in the then largely manufacturing town of Anderson, Indiana.

During Camp Meeting in 1948, when I was only eight years old, I decided I wanted to go to the Early Morning Prayer Meeting. I had heard of it, and it appealed to my desire for adventure and for something sensational. "Early morning" was not hyperbole: the prayer meeting started at 6 a.m. That year my family was staying at Uncle Carl's house several blocks from the campground. He was a professor at Anderson College, and he would be going to work in his office early to prepare for his summer school classes. Everyone else was still sleeping when Uncle Carl quietly asked if I still wanted to go. The prayer meeting still sounded exciting to me, so I quickly dressed and went along.

The Early Morning Prayer Meeting was held in what was then the Anderson College gym, an oval relic of the early twentieth century that resembled a miniature version of the Mormon Tabernacle in Salt Lake City. The gym had been built in about 1905 of large concrete blocks that the founders of the Church of God movement had made on that site. It was originally a tabernacle, but when the college was formed in 1917, it was converted to a combined gym and auditorium, what some would call a "gymnatorium" or an "auduasium." Several rows of bleachers rose on the far wall opposite the stage, and a low wall separated the bleachers from the gym floor. During the school year, the Anderson College basketball team competed on that same undersize floor.

The prayer meeting was in full swing when we arrived at about 6:30 a.m. Although the event was called a prayer meeting, and people did pray there, it was better known for the singing. As we walked to the gym, Uncle Carl and I could hear singing across the campground, and many people were standing outside the crowded gym. Inside, the gym floor was packed with people in folding chairs, and the bleachers were filled. When we came near one of the entrances, Uncle Carl stopped and asked, "Do you want to go in?"

I looked at the crowd inside and heard the singing. "Yes," I murmured.

Just then an old woman walked up and stared silently at us. She had no nose. All of the flesh where her nose should have been seemed to have dissolved, and we could see the air passages in the middle of her face. She was probably hoping to find divine healing at Camp Meeting, one of the reasons people came. Uncle Carl didn't speak to her. Instead, he took me by the arm and guided me inside. When we were away from the woman, he said in a low voice, "Probably has cancer."

We listened as the singing ended and someone up front praised the good singing and asked everyone to sit down for prayer. The prayer was dramatic, as if soaring to heaven itself. Many across the crowd joined in with amens as the leader prayed, and some prayed out loud, filling the gym with a worshipful hum. After prayer, someone started an announcement that took on a momentous and dramatic tone. A feeling of excitement went through the crowd. I couldn't hear all that was said, but I heard "Sister Cotton" and "I'll Fly Away." Everyone stood, and people talked and laughed as the music began. Then everyone began to sing.

Some glad morning,
When this life is o'er,
I'll fly away!
To a home on God's celestial shore,
I'll fly away!

Far away, in the middle of the gym, people cleared an aisle. Uncle Carl lifted me up to see, and when the song reached the line, "I'll fly away," I could see a small, African American woman running and leaping in the aisle. When she leaped, the crowd roared and clapped and sang louder. Her pure white clothing gave her an almost angelic look. Again and again, she ran up and down the aisle, leaping as the song went on.

When the shadows of this life have grown,
I'll fly away,
Like a bird from prison bars has flown,
I'll fly away!

I'll fly away, oh glory,
I'll fly away in the morning,
When I die, hallelujah by and by,
I'll fly away!

At the last verse and chorus, there was so much shouting and singing that it was hard to hear the words:

Just a few more weary days and then,
I'll fly away!
To a land where joys will never end,
I'll fly away!

I'll fly away, oh glory,
I'll fly away in the morning,
When I die, hallelujah by and by,
I'll fly away!

That final chorus was like a song of triumph, and the woman dancing in the aisle, Sister Cotton, seemed to take off flying, not just running and jumping. The gym was still echoing the closing lines as the leader said, "Thank you, Sister Cotton, for leading us again in that wonderful song! We all look forward to the day when we will fly away to meet our Lord in the sky!"

Just then, across the gym, a young African American man in a suit and tie stood up on top of the six-foot high wall that divided the bleachers from the gym floor. The top of the wall was a plank only six inches wide. The man began shouting and doing jumping jacks right on top of the wall, swinging his arms overhead as he leaped and spread his legs. A hush came over the crowd and all eyes were on him. He kept doing jumping jacks as he shouted, "You have to be a real man to do this for Jesus!"

Everyone clapped and some people shouted. Some prayed for his safety. He finally stopped and sat down, and the service resumed. It was the most dramatic testimony I had yet seen in my short life, and I wondered if I would ever do anything that dangerous, even for Jesus.

That morning was the first time I heard "I'll Fly Away." I didn't hear it again for many years, but it later became a popular church song and is now sometimes sung at especially joyful Christian funerals. Every time I hear it, I remember that glowing, sultry morning and the woman with cancer and the man risking injury doing jumping jacks for Jesus. And I remember Sister Cotton running and jumping.

I saw Sister Cotton a few more times at Camp Meeting in other years, and she always wore a white cotton dress. Several years later African-American ladies were overheard talking about her. "Is Sister Cotton here this year?" one of them asked.

"No, she won't be here. She's with the Lord," another explained. "Last year, she just *flew away!* All she left behind was a little pile of white clothes!"

AUTHOR'S NOTE: *Anderson, Indiana, is headquarters of the Church of God, Anderson, Indiana movement. Since other denominations and movements call themselves simply Church of God, it became important to distinguish our movement from other groups with this name. The name also distinguishes our movement from the universal Church of God, a term that encompasses all forms of the Christian faith.*

In the 1940s, twenty thousand people attended the Anderson Camp Meeting in some years. In 1955, a headline in the Anderson newspaper estimated that 25,000 people were there. If that number were an exaggeration, it would have been thought to be for the good of the community as well as for Camp Meeting itself. By that year, the name "Anderson Camp Meeting" had been changed to the "National Convention of the Church of God," to the chagrin of many older folks. Some continued to use the traditional name, and a few relatively young people today continue to call it "Camp Meeting," perhaps because of its colorful past.

For forty-three years, the main worship services during Camp Meeting were held in a huge wooden tabernacle in the center of the campground on the campus of Anderson College, now Anderson University, established by the movement in 1917. Other meetings were held in smaller buildings and tents nearby. When the wooden tabernacle collapsed under heavy snow in 1961, it was replaced by a concrete dome that also served for forty-three years.

The song "I'll Fly Away" was written in 1929 by Albert Brumley. It first appeared in print in 1932 by the Hartford Music Company.

THE LUCKIEST MAN WHO EVER LIVED

Desire for heaven and fear of hell drove much of my religious thinking and emotions as a young boy. I knew the way to heaven was through repentance and belief in Jesus, but I also thought my salvation depended on my behavior and on sinless living. In my morally wavering childhood, I repented several times and felt I was saved each time. But I was a frequent backslider, and I feared that I might sometime lose my salvation again and not have another chance to repent before I died.

Every time I heard the story of the dying thief on the cross next to Jesus who spoke kindly about him (Luke 23:39-43 NIV), I thought he was the luckiest man who ever lived. That thief rebuked the thief hanging on a cross on the other side of Jesus. Then Jesus told him, "Today you will be with me in paradise." Never mind that he was being tortured to death along with Jesus and the other, mocking thief. That thief was lucky, I thought, because he had the chance to turn to Jesus just before he died and didn't have time to sin again. Jesus promised him that he would be with him in paradise that very day. He was assured of going to heaven by none other than Jesus! If only I could have that assurance when I was about to die, I used to think! But I knew even then it was extremely unlikely that I could go through my entire life, wavering in my faith and sliding into sin, and yet somehow be assured by Jesus of my salvation right before my death like the lucky thief.

This realization led me to become more serious about faith, belief, and theology. How would I need to live if I couldn't count on being like the lucky thief? This question was the beginning of my private theological journey. That journey was interrupted many times by sin, errors, wandering, and inattention. But along the way, my faith was renewed again and again as I thought about the lucky thief and the fact that I was not him. I had chosen to find another way.

After I was saved, sanctified, and baptized in the traditions of my church for the last time while I was in college, my understanding of faith began to mature. My college philosophy professor, Dr. Louis Hennigar, suggested that God must be at least as good as a good person. That statement turned my mind to good people I had known, especially my own father. I thought of my father's love, kindness, and forgiving nature. Although my father had potential for vast power over me if he were to withhold his love, I felt secure that he never would. My new understanding of faith was based heavily on God's forgiveness and on my dependence on him, not dependence on my good behavior that was so often lacking. This insight was not consistent with my thoughts as a young boy, but I discovered it is not far from the views of many Christians whose lives and views I admired. I still treasure the story of the lucky thief, but I'm thankful I no longer have to hope to die immediately after my last act of repentance.

THE UNDERTAKER COMES TO CHURCH

C hurch on Sunday evening was even more evangelistic than Sunday morning. Sunday nights were about God's offer of salvation and about the need to accept it. During Sunday night services, God seemed very near, and death and tragedy and judgment also seemed to lurk in the darkness outside. On some Sunday nights, falling rain or the sound of a strong wind reminded us of how frail we were and how uncertain our lives were. Many older people attended the night time services, and they knew how near death might be for them. Most of them had lived in Elmore all their lives, and they knew nearly everyone in town. They knew each person who died, and each death was a loss to them.

One Sunday night during the service, a semi-truck overturned on the highway through Elmore only three blocks from the church. The driver was trapped inside, and he burned to death while horrified townspeople looked on. Church people learned about the accident when our service was over. Everyone was shocked and saddened; some felt ashamed that this terrible thing had happened and they hadn't even known about it and couldn't prevent it. A sudden death always raised questions about the spiritual condition of the person who died. In the days following, we prayed that the man who burned to death was already saved or got saved before he died.

One rainy, windy Sunday evening in March, the church was an especially welcome sanctuary from the storm outside. We sang, heard prayer requests, and prayed. The pastor started his evening sermon, something about Paul and being shipwrecked. Suddenly a woman near the back gasped, and others turned to look at the entrance door. Women clasped their hands over their open mouths. Sister Lizzie Sabroske was already getting up and pulling her shawl over her head. As she slipped out of her pew, we saw him.

The door at the back of the church was open only a crack, but people could see the eyes of a very tall man, the town undertaker, watching Lizzie come out of the church. Fred Sabroske, her husband, had removed his black hat, but his long black coat told us his errand was serious: someone had died. A shudder went through the whole congregation. Women looked at each other, wondering who it could be. Men looked briefly and then turned back to the pastor and his sermon. Children watched Lizzie and the undertaker to see what would happen next. He had come for her help, and everyone knew it. She slipped into the night with him to help prepare a body for burial.

When the service ended, adults talked about who the dead person might be. In such a small town, it was likely that someone in the church knew or was even related to the person who had died that night. They told each other about sick people in town, and they doubted it had been an accident, since no siren had sounded.

Fred and Lizzie Sabroske must have prepared several hundred bodies for viewing, funerals, and burials over the years. It was their business, and they did it right in their own house. A body would be embalmed in a back room and displayed in a bay window alcove that protruded on one side of their house. Guests could sign the register on the sunporch as they entered, and they could greet each other in Fred and Lizzie's front parlor before seeing the body. The room was just large enough to allow people to file past the casket. Viewings there seemed comforting and natural, and they gave real meaning to the term *funeral home.*

Funerals were not scary to me or other kids at church. We were mostly just curious about them. The processes of death and burial seemed far away for us kids, but they seemed very near and real to us on that stormy Sunday night when Fred Sabroske, Elmore's undertaker, came to church.

AUTHOR'S NOTE: *Fred Sabroske harbored no ill will against the church, as far as I know, but he was seldom there except on business when I was young. In later years he came often, and it may have been his life in the funeral business that endowed him with great dignity, even in the most informal moments.*

THE FIRST WEDDING

had never seen a wedding until the first one at the new church. I had gone with my parents to the wedding reception for Luther Miller and his bride at a big home in Toledo, but I had not yet attended a marriage ceremony in a church. Luther Miller was a war veteran and a friend of my parents. He was very old when he got married: he was thirty. As a young boy I thought it was sad for a man to be that old when he got married. What was the point of getting married, at that very old age? I myself expected to be married by the time I was twenty. Thirty was half a lifetime older.

When it was time for my cousin Kathleen to be married, I thought that I would at last see a real wedding. The marriage ceremony of my cousin Kathleen Kardatzke to Jerry Rhoda on June 9, 1949, was the first wedding I ever saw and the first held in the new church. Both Kathleen and Jerry were twenty years old, just the age I thought God intended people to marry.

Kathleen, known by everyone as Nonny, was the second oldest in a family of nine children. She was slim, attractive, had dark hair, and was fairly tall for a girl. Jerry was a skinny, nervous boy who was later drafted and sent to Korea to push back the Communists. Nonny and Jerry had met through high school friends, and he soon came to church with Nonny regularly. He was a jovial kidder, and that appealed to Nonny's family.

At age nine, I didn't know much about matrimony except that it should occur at age twenty. A marriage, I thought, began with a mystical, fairy-tale wedding in which a perfect and saintly and beautiful girl in a gleaming white gown and a radiant young man in his best suit

150

would come together to announce their undying love and commitment to each other. All of the birds of spring and angels of heaven would rejoice over the bride and her happy husband, I thought, and after that everything would be perfect.

Nonny was more romantically inclined than her brothers and sisters, and her wedding showed it. The church was decorated with white ribbons all around, like nothing I had ever seen, even at Christmas. It would be many years before we again saw the church so richly adorned. My family arrived early, and soon the pews were packed with eager onlookers. The pianist played romantic music and an excited buzzing of adult conversation nearly drowned out the piano. All the while, we kids talked and giggled and nudged each other in complete ignorance of what was to come.

When the music changed to something louder and more purposeful, everyone looked toward the back of the church. I saw what I thought was a bride come in with a groom, but it wasn't Nonny and Jerry. Soon another bride and groom came in, still not Nonny and Jerry. The brides and grooms kept coming in until the whole front of the church was full of them. For the first time I noticed that Jerry was standing up in the front of the church too. All at once, those brides and grooms that had come down the aisle turned and looked at the back of the church, and we did too, just in time to see two little girls come in, flinging flowers on the floor as they made their way slowly to the front. It seemed dumb to me, but I could tell that the grownups thought it was very cute. A little boy came in after them, dressed like a preacher and carrying a small white pillow. I couldn't see clearly, but I was told that he was carrying the wedding rings.

The music stopped, and a hush fell over the congregation. Suddenly the piano began playing a tune that I recognized: "Here Comes the Bride." Everyone jumped up, and I could hardly see between the grownups for a glimpse of Nonny going up the aisle. She was holding onto the arm of her dad, my Uncle Joe. It was wonderful! This was marriage as I had imagined it: a beautiful girl in a long white dress walking gracefully toward a happy husband-to-be. Everything was perfect and would always be perfect! This was the beginning of total happiness for Nonny and Jerry!

To be honest, I don't really remember the rest of the wedding. The real bride and real groom stood up front with the other brides and grooms on each side. Things were said. The only thing that mattered to me was near the end when Jerry lifted Nonny's veil and kissed her *right on the mouth*! It was stunning, mesmerizing, and almost shocking. It went far beyond my earlier understanding of marriage. This was obviously the real thing, and I felt as though I had become more of an adult right then, better prepared for marriage myself than I had ever been before. When my time came, I would know just what to do.

THE CHRISTMAS TREAT

C hristmas was the most wonderful time of year to me, maybe even better than the first days of summer vacation. Our preparations for Christmas seemed like something Christians had been doing just like this for hundreds of years. Kitchens were filled with wonderful aromas of cookies for weeks. Closer to Christmas Day, the scent of pine boughs invaded most homes. And on the actual day, our heads spun with delight as a roasted turkey or a large chicken was brought to the table to be served with dressing, cranberries, potatoes, gravy, fresh bread, and enough desserts to clog our arteries well past Easter.

I loved to sing Christmas carols in church and at home, and the congregation was especially good at harmonizing those familiar songs. The fact that we sang carols and heard the Christmas story every year actually heightened the spirit of the season. We knew that all of our church activities and feasting were really to celebrate Jesus being born in a stable and laid in a manger, and repetition did not wear out that story. In fact, the repeated traditions even added to our excitement about the story.

In those days, Elmore seemed a lot like the biblical Bethlehem in my imaginings. It was a quiet town with about the same number of souls as had lived there soon after the Civil War. People had died, and new ones had appeared, but the population was still about twelve hundred. Seven active churches gave the town a holy feel in spite of the obvious worldly temptations. One year a very bright star appeared over Elmore, and people said it might be the same star that had guided the wise men to the Christ child. It seemed to hover over Northern Ohio the whole Christmas season. It even seemed to me to be right above the Church of God on Congress Street in Elmore. Whatever that bright star might have been that year, it made Christmas more personal, more directly from God, than ever before.

The front of the church was decorated each year with a huge hanging mural that appeared about two weeks before Christmas and disappeared shortly after New Year's Day. The mural was a view of Bethlehem from the crest of a hill, with the town sleeping silently across a small valley. In the mural, the three wise men were on the hill, and the Christmas star was shining brilliantly above the holy stable below. The wise men were seated on their camels in their fine robes, no doubt thinking of the baby they were seeking and also of the evil King Herod whom they had met on their journey. I loved to gaze at this mural and imagine myself running down the path ahead of the wise men. I would go ahead of them to the stable to see Jesus in the manger. I could help the wise men find the right stable, since there would have been many like it. Each year, that mural was my trip to the Holy Land, and I could imagine it just as I wanted it to be.

In most years, the Christmas Eve program consisted of carols interspersed with simple poems or lines of Scripture that all of the children, except for the very youngest, recited from memory. The children helped bring people in, producing a record crowd each year, and so did the Christmas treat. The treat was one of the most blessed events of my early religious life. It combined the coming of the Christ child with manna from heaven, or possibly something even better than manna: candy.

When all of the children's memorized pieces had been said and nearly all of the carols sung, the Sunday school superintendent would make a short speech, thanking everyone for the help in the year's program. She (the superintendent was nearly always a woman) thanked the Sunday school teachers and those who had helped prepare crafts and costumes. She also thanked the parents who had faithfully brought their children. Then the chairman of the Board of Trustees would present a gift to the pastor. It was sometimes a memorable object, but more often it was an undisclosed amount of cash.

During those speeches, six or eight men slipped out into the overflow room at the side of the sanctuary near the front. These men were usually farmers or factory workers who seldom took on ceremonial functions. One was Warren Draper, a sunburned farmer who had served in World War II. Another was Don Otte, a merry farmer who was active in church and always chewed gum. Junior Miller, a painfully shy younger man, performed his only public role in church by helping distribute the Christmas treat.

When all of the speeches were finished, a hush fell over the church. Suddenly the Christmas treat posse marched into the church carrying the large boxes of oranges. The sanctuary was flooded with the exotic, nearly intoxicating aroma of fresh oranges as the men came down the aisles, handing oranges across the rows until everyone was served. Right behind the oranges came those mouthwatering bags of candy and nuts that kids considered the *real* Christmas treat. The women of the church had worked together for days to pack the sacred little bags of treats. It seemed they used the very same recipe every year, and we all loved it that way. Here's what I remember being in each bag:

2 English walnuts
2 Brazil nuts
4 filberts
3 almonds in their papery shells
3 pieces of colorful ribbon candy
6 pieces of jelly-filled candy
6 pieces of hard peppermint or spearmint
1 chocolate-covered marshmallow with peanuts
1 cream-filled chocolate
1 candy cane

I may have forgotten an item or two, but this list seems to me to be at least 80 percent correct. Year after year, I knew what delight awaited me, and that knowledge added to my enjoyment of the treat. I loved the fact that the Christmas treat was completely predictable and trustworthy. To me it was a kind of liturgy. A variation in the Christmas treat would have seemed like a form of heresy or sacrilege.

At the close of service, everyone bundled up to head for home. At our house, we would have a bedtime snack and go to bed promptly so we could get up very early and open presents on Christmas morning, just as baby Jesus surely must have opened his presents on the first Christmas morning. Down the road, my cousins would open their presents on Christmas Eve, right after the Christmas program. I thought it would have been fun to get my toys that night, but I also thought that it was vaguely sacrilegious to open presents on Christmas Eve. I didn't worry about it though, because I loved my cousins and knew that God would forgive them. After all, they were Christians too and had been to church like me, and they, too, had received the blessing of the Christmas treat.

AUTHOR'S NOTE: *Adults in my present church have affirmed that they remember receiving the same or a very similar Christmas treat when they were kids. Few of those churches still have the Christmas treat, and the Christmas treat at the church in Elmore has changed. It is sometimes even given out more than a week before Christmas. Pieces of candy now are usually individually wrapped for sanitary reasons, and there are no Brazil nuts in their flinty shells. The modern treat is surely cleaner than the mix of unwrapped candy and nuts that kids received in the 1940s and 1950s, and it's probably a good treat still. But I, rooted in the past, cherish the memory of the ancient, annual Christmas treat, exactly as it used to be back then.*

NEW YEAR'S EVE

The sacred hush of Christmas Eve 1949 gave way the next morning to the excitement of Christmas Day. My brothers and I got up early, opened presents, and played with our new toys. If we were lucky, snow would be falling sometime soon, and the pond would have enough ice for skating. The week after Christmas was a dizzying sequence of playing with toys and seeing the neighbor kids and our cousins. We were allowed to stay up every night past our usual bedtimes to play caroms and table games and put together jigsaw puzzles. After all, it was Christmas break with no school. Even as we enjoyed these days of playing and holiday eating, our minds turned to the next great event: New Year's Eve.

I knew about New Year's Day, the first day of the next year, and I understood that years changed numbers on New Year's Eve, just like my age changed on my birthday. But I'd only heard about New Year's Eve, the actual time when one year passed away and a new one was born. I had never taken part in celebrating it, at least not at midnight, the actual turning of the year. We kids had always gone to bed too early. At age ten, the day took on a new importance. For the first time, I would be allowed to participate in a New Year's Eve celebration.

I was thrilled when my parents announced that we would go to church at about ten o'clock at night and stay there until midnight. I began to wonder what it would look like when the New Year came. Would there be a line across the sky just as the New Year arrived so I could see the difference between the New Year and the old one? Would the new sky have a brighter color? Would the stars be bigger and brighter? Would there be a new star like the Christmas star? One thing I did know: I wanted to be outside, looking up at the sky, at the actual moment of midnight.

My parents explained that the church would have a "Watch Night Service." Everyone would "watch and pray" as the New Year approached and then sing, stand, and kneel before God as it arrived. We often knelt to pray in church, and I felt certain we would kneel at least once during this special service. The Watch Night Service seemed awesome and holy to me, just the kind of thing that the people in Bible stories might have done. I still thought the people in our church were pretty much the same as the biblical children of Israel, especially since I thought they had brought the clock of the covenant all the way to Elmore, Ohio. But I was worried about all the singing, standing, praying, and preaching we had to get through before the New Year arrived. I wanted to be outside at the moment the New Year began. What if we were late?

The Watch Night Service began with solemn singing and Scripture reading in the sanctuary followed by a short sermon about commitment and devotion to God and the passage of time. Then the men and boys and the women and girls went to separate rooms in the basement to wash each other's feet like Jesus had washed the disciples' feet before he was crucified. In the two rooms, people paired up to wash each other's feet in metal basins of water, mercifully warmed for this purpose. I was paired with an older man. While washing my feet, he talked quietly about God's love and the humility of Jesus. The same thing was going on all around the room, and presumably in the room for women and girls. The end of the old year was like the end of a time in our lives, and we were finishing it just as Jesus had ended the time of his earthly ministry.

After footwashing, we returned to the sanctuary and sat quietly. Aunt Lucille played a slow, thoughtful hymn on the church's new organ, and we were instructed to think about the passing of the year, the passing of our lives, and the holy importance of the year ahead. When everyone was back in the sanctuary, it was time for communion, which we called "The Lord's Supper." Brother Lee, our pastor, reminded everyone of the seriousness of taking communion and of the danger of taking communion unworthily. Then he began to recite the sacred lines about Jesus breaking bread and telling the disciples it represented his body.

Following the instructions about how to receive the bread and the grape juice, symbolic of Jesus' body and blood, we went row by row to kneel at the altar for communion. As we each ate a piece of bread and drank a tiny cup of juice, we were enacting something Jesus had done near the end of his life on earth. The organ was played softly again, and again we were instructed to think, this time about the shortness of life and our purpose for being here on earth.

Anxious for what was ahead, I peeked at the sacred clock on the wall. It was 11:50 p.m., only ten minutes before midnight. Now the swift passing of our lives became more urgent and more important to me. We needed to finish the service before midnight so we could actually see the New Year arrive. I watched and waited for something to happen, but people just sat there, praying silently, while the time on the clock kept moving forward. Finally, at about 11:55 p.m., Brother Lee stood and said it would be fitting for us to begin the New Year in prayer. He asked everyone to kneel in the pews so we could "pray in the New Year."

We all knelt to pray, and my heart sank when I thought that I might not be outside when the New Year swept across the sky. We prayed and prayed, and finally Brother Lee said that the New Year had arrived. We stood, and he gave a closing prayer. Just after he said "Amen," there was a loud boom outside. Unable to wait another second, I ran to the back of the church and out the door to see the sky. Another boom sounded, and I looked to see the line in the sky I had imagined.

The night was clear, and the stars were bright, but I couldn't tell by looking at the sky where the New Year began and the old one left off. I had missed the actual midnight moment. I had missed seeing the line across the sky. The New Year had come when we were praying. The booms we had heard were large fireworks shot off a couple of blocks away, not the sound of the New Year crossing the sky. Other kids came out, and we listened to the noises in the night. Firecrackers were set off a few blocks away, people banged on pan lids, and a bell rang at a church on the other side of town.

Suddenly we heard *blam blam!* Both barrels of a double-barreled shotgun were fired one after the other only a couple of houses away. "Somebody is shooting a shotgun!" one of the kids yelled. We waited for the gun to be fired again, and for a moment the night was quiet. Then we heard something we hadn't heard before: *ping ping ping* followed by a more rapid *ping ping ping ping*. All along the row of parked cars in front of the church the pinging sounded like a rain shower beginning, only sharper.

"It's the bullets landing!" yelled one of the kids. "The shotgun bullets are landing!"

Just then there were more shotgun blasts. *Blam! Blam!* They were coming from the same yard they'd come from before. We waited, and the *ping ping ping* and then the more rapid *ping ping ping ping ping* came again.

"Yea! Yea!" we cheered and ran back into the church to tell the others. By the time everyone else was outside, the night was quiet again. There were no more shotgun blasts, so we kids could tell everyone about the shotgun bullets landing on the cars. Some of the women thought this was terrible, but some of the men said it probably wouldn't hurt anything.

While the grown-ups finished talking, we kids listened for more sounds of the New Year, but all was quiet and still. Soon we were snuggling down in the back seats of our parents' cars, heading home for our first sleep of the New Year.

It had been a good way to end the old year: a church service that included washing feet, having the Lord's Supper, singing, and praying in the New Year. I didn't see the line across the sky when the New Year came, but I heard something even better: powerful blasts from a shotgun and the clatter of pellets landing on cars. Surely it was a good start to the New Year, and 1950 would be a wonderful year of peace and happiness.

EASTER MORNING

W ithout thinking much about it, I learned a lot of church traditions, hymns, and Bible stories due to our family's relentless church-going. I had at least a superficial knowledge of Christmas, Easter, and Thanksgiving—the only religious holidays we celebrated. Truth to be told, I was most interested in the most sensational aspects of those holidays, and I was especially grateful for the school vacations they provided. The rhythms of church life provided more Christian education for me and other young "heathens" than we realized. We were gradually, inexorably absorbing our parents' beliefs and traditions.

Christmas was so exciting and so appealing to my sensual nature when I was young that I mostly missed the point of Easter. I didn't realize the magnitude of Easter until I was older. I did perceive the drama of the empty tomb, and I could feel the thrill of being there and seeing the angel inside. I could sense, at least superficially, the newness of that morning in Jerusalem; and I could feel some of its reality in Elmore, Ohio, especially if Easter was a clear, sunny day in a year when it came late enough for warm weather. I thought it would be exciting to attend an Easter Sunrise service. I thought of sunrise literally, not figuratively, and I wanted to be in a service that began in darkness and ended in the full light of day. Never mind the misery of rising that early and being in the dark on a cold spring morning: I wanted the full treatment.

One year when I was in high school, a brave Sunday school teacher gave in to my urging and agreed to have a sunrise service with the youth very early on Easter morning. We planned to meet at the church and go to a place where we could see the sunrise. I don't remember if we had in mind anything more spiritual than seeing the sun coming up over the horizon; our spirituality might not have exceeded that of ancient pagans, who worshipped the sun, moon, and stars.

We didn't make it to a scenic or holy place to see the sun rise that day. Only a handful of kids showed up at church, and our teacher's courage faded in the chill of the dark morning. Our little group disbanded, and most returned to their homes for naps. The tomb was not yet open and empty, and we had left without the garden tomb experience I had hoped we would re-create.

Determined as I was, I drove alone to the nearest shore of Lake Erie to seek the inspiration I thought would come with an Easter sunrise. But Lake Erie was a disappointment too. By the time I arrived, the sky was as dark and gray as the lake's water. Clouds obscured the sun, and the shrill cry of a few gulls seemed to stab my expectant heart rather than stirring it. I shivered, got back in my car, and went home for breakfast before the Easter morning service.

I'm sure the service that Easter Sunday was holy and good. Men, women, and children were all dressed up, many in bright new clothes, to praise God and greet each other saying, "Christ is risen indeed!" Lilies lined the front of the church, and even I could tell the music was unusually powerful. We undoubtedly sang "Up from the Grave He Arose," a song that was nearly mandatory on Easter Sunday. Possibly our little choir attempted the "Hallelujah Chorus," as it did some years. After church, most families gathered at home for a dinner of ham, sweet potatoes, and other holiday foods. For me, Easter had come and was celebrated, but it didn't bring the great, beautiful sunrise experience I had wanted.

I was much older, twenty-four to be exact, when I learned how Eritrean Orthodox Christians celebrate Easter. I had entered the Peace Corps immediately after graduating from Anderson College in June 1962. At age twenty-two, I was sent to Ethiopia to teach in a public school in the province of Eritrea, which was already engaged in a war of independence that would last thirty years. I was in the lovely little city of Adi Ugri in the Eritrean highlands at an altitude of about 6,500 feet, where the weather was nearly always pleasant. Christianity and Islam were practiced peacefully side by side there; animosity was directed outward, against the Ethiopian empire of which the Eritreans were unwilling members.

In Eritrea, Easter was the most important Christian holiday. Christmas season, in comparison, passed as barely a blip on the Christian radar. Christmas was mainly a time when Europeans and Americans decorated their homes, sang special songs, and exchanged gifts while the Eritrean Orthodox believers stood by tolerantly. Eritreans reserved their spiritual adoration for Easter.

Easter in Eritrea did not come upon the people suddenly one fine Sunday morning. It was preceded by a rigorous, forty-day time of fasting. Most people were very poor, yet for forty days before Easter, they ate no meat, eggs, milk, butter, cheese, nor any other product extracted from an animal, bird, fish, or reptile. The observant Christians ate a variety of vegetable and bean dishes throughout their Lenten season. No one perished from this fasting, and this in itself may be miraculous, given the near-starvation diets of so many.

The Eritrean Orthodox fast was broken at midnight on Easter morning. Streams of worshipers arrived carrying candles, a reminder of the Light that shone in the darkness, the Light the darkness could not comprehend and could not put out. Churches were packed, and many congregants stood outside in the chilly night. Inside, ancient chants proclaimed the resurrection of Jesus the Christ, and soon the feasting began.

At midnight on the eve of Easter 1964, I climbed to the roof of my house in Adi Ugri to see the procession of candle-bearing worshippers arriving at the Orthodox church half a mile away. The time exposure picture I took that night gave me a new mental image of Easter. Lights glowed through the church's windows, and candlelight illuminated people's pure white Eritrean/Ethiopian robes as they approached the church. The new day they celebrated divided the Christian future from the ancient past. That night I truly saw the Easter sunrise.

Having seen the drama of the Orthodox Easter, I appreciated Easter in America more profoundly than ever before. The experience helped me begin to understand that Easter, not Christmas, is the central Christian celebration, though both are crucial. Easter became so much more than my childhood perception, limited as it was to the lilies, the new clothing, Easter eggs, and special Easter music. At last I understood the significance of the first pilgrimage to see the empty tomb, newly illuminated amid the darkness outside. I had heard of it many times, but I hadn't really seen it before. Now I could see Easter as the end of a long period of fasting and the beginning of a joyful feast.

IV. SAINTS

EMMA'S WICKED WEDDING RING

At age twenty-nine, Emma Kardatzke was a respected farm wife and already the mother of six of the nine children she would raise when the Elmore Church of God was formed in 1913. A tragic train-car accident that year had claimed the lives of her sister-in-law Kate Gleckler and nephew Clarence. In the aftermath of that tragedy, Emma and many of her relatives got saved. Along with George Gleckler, they became the nucleus of the Elmore Church of God.

Emma's conversion was complete and dramatic. A natural leader, she was energized and newly purposeful. She told everyone readily about her spiritual experience. She invited new believers to her home for worship services, supported by Fred, her willing but less enthusiastic husband. For several years, the young church met in private homes, the one-room Leatherport School, and the Elmore town hall. Most of those in the earliest Elmore church were blood relatives; others were neighbors and friends.

Emma's leadership in the church grew not only from her intelligence and deep commitment but also her talents. Like many farm girls, she learned to play the piano and the family's treadle pump organ as a young girl. She often played in the home church meetings and later in the first church building. With another woman and two men, she sang in a mixed quartet. Emma always kept evangelistic tracts at home to give to visitors, including those two car thieves who spent a snowy night in Emma's home and were present during the family's morning worship time.

The Church of God movement had always seen itself as a "holiness" movement. This perspective was especially true in the early days of the

Elmore congregation. Emma was one who took holiness seriously. For the Elmore Church of God, holiness was defined by a more strenuous spirituality than what was practiced in many other churches. Holiness in the Elmore church did not include speaking in tongues and other Pentecostal practices, but it did call for outward evidence of a changed life. It called for active participation in church, good behavior, and modest physical appearance. For a time, our ministers spoke strongly against vain adornments. Men didn't wear neckties, and women didn't use makeup in those early days. Women were advised to avoid gold jewelry, fine clothing, and fancy hairdos, based on passages in New Testament letters from Peter and Paul to the early churches on Christian conduct. These words from 1 Peter 3:3-4 were especially convicting for the women of the church:

> *Your beauty should not come from outward adornment, such as braided hair and the wearing of gold jewelry and fine clothes. Instead, it should be that of your inner self, the unfading beauty of a gentle and quiet spirit, which is of great worth in God's sight.*

This message evidently struck Emma's conscience. Ever since her marriage to Fred in 1903, she had worn the wedding ring Fred gave her. She prized the ring and was proud of the way it told the world she was a married woman. She rarely took it off, even while doing rough farm work or washing dishes or clothing. After she was saved and heard the message about adornment, the ring took on a different appearance to her. It seemed worldly, almost pagan. It violated Scripture. And it associated her with immoral women of the world. The more she thought about it, the more improper the ring became. She didn't need it to proclaim her loyalty to her husband and her family. She didn't need it to claim she was a virtuous wife, fending off possible male advances with that mere circle of gold.

Emma's feelings rose to shame, then guilt, and then anger at herself for keeping this worldly decoration on her hand. Finally, while alone in the kitchen one afternoon, she decided she had to rid herself of this shining testimony against her. Twisting the ring from her finger, she threw it across the room. But there it was for the children to find, or perhaps to raise a damning question in Fred's mind: was she rejecting *him*? Was the rejected ring a confession of some secret infidelity? No! She had to banish the ring utterly, and she had to tell Fred the reason. Picking up the ring, she marched from the house, looking for a place to rid herself of it and her pride in it. She thought of throwing it down the privy, but that seemed unnecessarily defiling, and it might have been found when the privy was cleaned. No place on the property seemed appropriate, and yet she felt she had to act quickly. She had little time alone, and she wanted her act to be only between her and God.

Across the road, away from their property, the drainage ditch beckoned her. It was lined with noxious weeds, and its bottom was covered with slimy muck. Perfect! Emma walked quickly across the white limestone road and tossed the ring in the ditch. She waited long enough to see it sink beneath the water and muck, and she suddenly felt the peace and joy she expected. She had taken a decisive step of faith and was done with that worldly symbol.

Only years later did Emma testify in church about this act. She said she never regretted it, but her action astonished her children and the whole church. If any irreverent children or neighbors went searching for the ring, they kept their search secret. If anyone recovered that small treasure, it was never reported.

AUTHOR'S NOTE: *I learned of this story about my grandmother only in 2013. I have wondered since then if even now the ring could be found with a metal detector. If it is ever found, I hope it will be given to the Elmore Church of God and placed securely inside the clock of the covenant along with the promises and laws of God.*

GRANDMA WALKS WITH GOD

"Your baby sister is really sick," the babysitter said one night. "She keeps crying and crying and I don't know what to do! There's nobody to help!"

Mama and Daddy were both at work that night, and the babysitter wasn't used to being out in the country like this, a few miles out of town. My two brothers and I looked at each other and at the frightened babysitter. We had to help.

My older brother was the first to speak. "Grandma lives just up the road. She always knows what to do."

"That's right!" I chimed in. "We can go get Grandma! She knows all about babies, especially baby girls!"

The babysitter looked at her three young assistants. The oldest was eight. I was five. The youngest was four. "How can we get your grandma here? You kids don't even have a phone. We're lucky you have lights!"

"We can go get her!" one of us yelled. We were caught up in the emergency, and we wanted to be the heroic rescuers. "We'll go get Grandma right now!"

"But it's dark out. It's night," she said. "You can't go down the road at night, and I can't go and leave you here with this crying baby. Listen to her cry!" The babysitter was near tears herself.

We had forgotten it was dark outside. We thought a minute, and then I said bravely, "There's enough light from the moon for us to go to Grandma's house. We can do it. Can we go? Grandma will help us, I know!"

The babysitter was holding Sharon, trying her best to soothe her crying. She stepped close to the oldest of us, my brother Merl. "Can you go get your grandma by yourself?" she asked.

Merl nodded.

"I want to go too!" I yelled. My younger brother Owen wasn't so sure. He was only four years old, not a five-year-old like me. I could see he wanted to stay at home and help the babysitter.

"Okay," the babysitter relented, "You big boys can go get your grandma. Owen can stay here with me and the baby."

Merl and I headed out bravely on the gravel road, pacing off the quarter mile to Grandma's house. We had no flashlight, and the night was dark, lit only by stars and a half moon. The white gravel was edged on both sides by grass, so we walked in the middle of the road to make sure we didn't walk off into one of the ditches. There weren't many lights on at Grandma and Grandpa's house when we arrived, but when we knocked, Grandma came right to the door.

"Say! What are you boys doing here after dark?" She knew we weren't there just for fun. "What's wrong?"

"Sharon is real sick!" Merl announced. "She's crying and crying, and we don't know what to do!"

"Is your mama there?" Grandma asked.

"No! Mama and Daddy are both at work. We just have a babysitter, and she doesn't know what to do," I said, adding, "but Owen is there helping her."

Grandma stifled a laugh. At four years old, Owen was more likely to be a problem than a helper. "Well, we better hurry and help Owen and the babysitter," she said. "Let me get my sweater." As she pulled it on, she said, "We hafta walk back. Grampa has the car, and I don't know when he will come home. Are you ready to walk back, right quick now?"

Soon we were out in the dark on the road again, heading for home, but this time we were with Grandma. Merl and I were still worried about Sharon, even though the babysitter and Owen were with her.

"What do you think the trouble is, Grandma?" Merl asked. "Why do you think she won't stop crying? Do you think she is really, really sick like the babysitter said?"

Grandma quickened her pace a little. "We just don't know. We'll see what we can do when we get there, but we can do something right now."

Do something, out here in the dark with only the black sky and stars and a little moon overhead? And we can barely see the road? I thought. "What can we do, Grandma?" I said out loud.

"We can pray!" she said, still walking briskly. And suddenly she began to pray. "Oh, Lord Jesus! Take care of baby Sharon until we get there! Hold her in your hands of love and touch her with your healing power!"

Grandma said more, and the longer she prayed the more worried I was. Since I wasn't the one praying, I kept my eyes open to make sure I wouldn't walk in the ditch and watched to make sure Grandma didn't fall in either. When she finally stopped praying, I blurted out, "Grandma! Weren't you afraid you would walk in the ditch while you were praying? You are right next to the big ditch!"

Her answer was a surprise. "Oh! I wasn't going to walk into the ditch! I had my eyes open the whole time I was aprayin'."

We had been taught to close our eyes when we prayed, and here was Grandma, telling us she had kept her eyes open. But if Grandma did it, it must be okay.

"You can pray with your eyes open, 'specially if you are walking down the road on a 'specially dark night," she explained. "I sometime even pray with my eyes open when I'm washing dishes or peeling apples."

I was still absorbing this startling new truth when we reached our house. Lights were on everywhere, and Owen was so tired he was just sitting there, half asleep on a chair in the living room. The house was quiet. No baby was crying. What had happened?

Grandma went to the baby's room and peeked in. The babysitter came out silently and closed the door. "She's okay!" she whispered. "She stopped crying a few minutes ago, probably while you were walking here."

Grandma went in and checked on Sharon and came back out. "Yep. She's down for the night, I think. Babies can be like that." Grandma had raised nine children of her own, and she had cared for many of her two dozen grandchildren. She knew babies. "Guess the Lord musta heard me prayin' down the road and came to help."

Merl and I looked at each other, both of us remembering Grandma praying with her eyes open. God had kept her out of the ditch and had taken care of Sharon and Owen and the babysitter all at the same time. We looked at Grandma. She knew a lot about babies, and she knew a lot about God. That night we learned we could pray with our eyes open, and I'm pretty sure we still pray that way sometimes, even when we don't need to avoid going into a ditch on a dark night.

HARRY KLINGER AND THE TRAIN

Harry Klinger and his wife, Alice, led quiet, simple lives. They were known for being frugal, and they didn't rush into new things like electricity. Years after most people had electricity, the two of them still spent their evenings in the warm orange glow and the comforting smell of kerosene lamps. Their son was also frugal. When he did begin using electricity, it was produced by a propeller-driven generator at the top of an old farm windmill tower in his yard. The generator could power just a couple of small bulbs that created about as much light as a kerosene lamp, but without the smoke and fumes.

Harry Klinger was a cheerful man and was deeply devoted to the church. Each month his devotion led him to visit old people in the County Home with my father. By the time of these visits in the mid-1950s, Harry was about seventy-eight years old, but he was healthy, young in heart, and felt called to visit these "old" people, many of whom probably were in their fifties and sixties, much younger than Harry.

When Harry came to our house to go visiting with my father, he would drive up in his shiny, black, late-1930s car and park it on the lawn in the shade of the tall maple trees in front of the house. My father would take Harry in our family car the rest of the way. He referred to his car as his "machine," and he was the only person I knew who called a car a "machine." Every time he came, he said to my father, "Arlin, is it all right if I park my machine on your grass, under the trees? It's cooler there."

Harry was always formally dressed for those Sunday afternoon visits. If the weather was too hot for a suit coat, he would still wear his dress shirt and tie. On those days I could see his big, wide suspenders.

He was balding, with a little crown of hair around his ears and a little wisp of hair combed over his square-shaped head. My mother would invite him in, and if he and my father weren't late for their visiting time with the old folks in the County Home, he sometimes had a cookie and lemonade with my parents while my brothers and I went out to see his machine.

This kind, old saint was one of the reasons we never had playing cards in our house. Harry didn't believe in card playing, and he probably didn't believe in most of the other marginal entertainments that crept into people's lives in the 1950s. If ever a deck of cards somehow got into our house, it was kept concealed lest it offend Harry when he came. He wouldn't have been crabby about it; in fact, because of his sweet, gentle nature, we just wanted to avoid anything that might be lower than his standards.

It was a passing train that brought the gospel to Harry Klinger one summer day when he was in his fifties. His house was next to the main rail line between New York and Chicago, and several passenger trains came by every day. Since the part of northern Ohio where he lived was flat, former swampland, the trains passed at the best speeds possible in those days, often more than seventy miles per hour. One summer afternoon in the 1930s, Harry was working in his garden beside the railroad tracks when a thundering steam locomotive came through with its train of cars. Harry probably kept hoeing weeds, since a train was a common sight to him. Suddenly something caught his attention from the corner of his eye. He stood up to see a small magazine fluttering to the ground from the passing train. Someone had thrown it from an open window.

To keep his property tidy, Harry went to pick up the discarded paper. Its cover said the *Gospel Trumpet*, and he discovered that it was a Christian magazine from a group called the Church of God, Anderson, Indiana. He read the magazine carefully and found that its fresh, simple message met a need he had sensed already. He wrote a letter to the address he found in the magazine, and he learned that there was a tiny congregation of the Church of God in Elmore, only a few miles from his home.

It was not long until Harry visited the little church. He found the people there to be as sincere and unpretentious as the *Gospel Trumpet* magazine. They greeted him warmly, and he found real meaning for his life in the singing and the preaching. He began to understand what was missing in his good life. He and Alice both got saved, promising God they would live the rest of their lives for him.

Harry Klinger was at church every time the doors were open for many years. He was generally reserved yet kindly and cheerful. His presence suggested the very gospel itself. He must have been a constant encouragement to the preachers and song leaders, beaming his approval from his regular seat next to the center aisle on the right-hand side of the church. During Wednesday night prayer meetings, he usually had a testimony or a word of encouragement for the others. Though his Christian life had its beginning in an unusual way, with a *Gospel Trumpet* magazine thrown from the window of a train as an act of high speed evangelism, Harry Klinger became one of the most devout and memorable of the saints of the Church of God in Elmore.

AUTHOR'S NOTE: *Harry Klinger's introduction to the Church of God may have been different from and more complex than my account here. In May 2015 I met his granddaughter, Doloris Dellinger, at a funeral in Toledo, Ohio. In a note she wrote to me later, she said one of Harry and Alice Klinger's sons found some copies of the* Gospel Trumpet *beside the tracks and gave them to her. Alice made her way to the Anderson Camp Meeting one year and was baptized on the campgrounds. After that time, both Alice and Harry learned of the Elmore Church of God and began to attend. Doloris added, "Years later Ma and I found out that a man who attended the church (Church of God in Toledo) was an engineer for a railroad that passed the Klinger homestead. We always wondered if he was the one who tossed the* Gospel Trumpet *out of the train as a witness. If so, his crown will have many stars."*

When Harry and Alice Klinger first came to the Elmore Church of God, one of the people who showed a special interest in them was my mother, Ruth Kardatzke. Perhaps the Klingers reminded Ruth of her parents in faraway Oklahoma. The Klingers were about the age of Ruth's parents, and their way of life was similar. Harry Klinger always appreciated my mother's kindness to him and his wife. As a show of friendship, Harry turned a piece of oak on a lathe, creating a rolling pin for my mother, one as solid as any rolling pin ever could be.

WILL HARRY KLINGER DIE IN CHURCH?

Harry Klinger was one of the most steadfast and holy saints in the church. His kind manner and spiritual testimonies made it clear that he belonged to God and would go to heaven when he died. Since he was an older man by the time he became a Christian, everyone at church thought he was likely to die soon and go to his heavenly reward.

In the winter of 1950, when I was ten years old, the church was planning to hold a revival. The adults began praying several weeks in advance for people to be saved. Preparation for the revival was especially intense during the Wednesday night prayer meetings, and the faithful made it a special point to be there. They prayed for the revival, talked about the preaching power of the visiting evangelist, prayed some more, and heard testimonies from people in the church whose lives had been changed in earlier revivals. Parts of these prayer meetings were exciting, even for young kids.

During one Wednesday prayer meeting, Harry Klinger rose to testify. He told of the wonderful works of God in his life and how he knew that his life was near its end. He praised God for saving his soul, and he talked of his wife and her faith, living at home as a shut-in due to chronic bronchial infections and related weakness. Then he began to talk of the coming revival.

"I want to live to see this next revival," Harry said. "If just one soul is saved at this revival, I will be ready to leave this earth to meet the Lord!"

I heard what he said, and I was electrified by what might happen. In Sunday school I had just heard of Elijah being taken up to heaven in a chariot. Maybe that would happen to Brother Klinger right in our revival service! Maybe the roof of the church would open just long enough for a beautiful chariot from heaven to swoop down and carry him away. Even if he just died there in church and had to be carried out by the undertaker, it would be a great thing to see. I resolved to get my schoolwork done so I could be at the revival, at least for the first night and for as many nights as it took for someone to go to the altar to be saved.

On the weekend when the revival started, I didn't have much home-work, so it was easy for me to be prepared. My whole family got dressed in our church clothes, and we were at church before the Sunday eve-ning service started at 7:30. Harry Klinger sat at his regular place on the middle aisle on the right-hand side of the church. That night I sat on the aisle on the left-hand side, farther back than him, so I could see clearly when Harry either died or was carried bodily to heaven.

The service started with inspired singing, followed by prayers, an offering, and finally the sermon by the visiting evangelist. I focused as much as I could on each part, but I was waiting for the big event at the end, the altar call. Finally it came, and several verses of a song of invitation were sung so people could think about their souls and make decisions. Several unrepentant sinners must have been there that eve-ning, but no one went to the altar. I kept watching Harry Klinger, but nothing happened to him, probably because no one got saved. I would have to come back the next night to watch and see if Harry would be swept up into heaven.

On Monday, I did my homework as soon as I was home from school. I was unsure whether I could keep doing my homework, going to church, and staying up late every night of the week in case it took that long for someone to be saved. I went with my family to church as before, early enough for my parents to talk with people before the service started. The service followed the same pattern as the night before, except there was a quartet and a solo in addition to the congregational singing. The evangelist began his sermon, and he made it easy to understand the struggle between good and evil in the world and in our lives. He held out the promise of eternal salvation as he built up to his conclusion. Then came the altar call.

We sang two verses of "Just as I Am," but no one went to the altar, so we sang all the verses and then two more invitation hymns. I thought I would have to come back the next night or maybe every night that week. Suddenly two people went and knelt at the left end of the altar.

The pastor went to pray with them, and I wondered if one of them was being saved or if they were there only for a recommitment to Jesus or sanctification. I still thought that only a person being saved would send Harry Klinger to heaven that night. I looked over at him, but he was just sitting there, probably praying as he watched. I watched the group at the altar too, but I mainly watched Harry Klinger. The group at the altar stood, and it seemed to me that at least one of the people had been saved. The evangelist stood beside those who had been and the altar. He raised his hand for attention. Everyone was already watching him, especially me.

"Praise God!" the evangelist proclaimed. "Praise God for his saving power and grace! These blessed people have laid down their burdens of sin at the foot of the cross and are saved! I'm sure in the coming days they will testify to you and to their friends out in the world about what God has done for them." With that, he allowed the saved people to return to their places.

I was right about them getting saved, so I kept my eyes fixed on Harry Klinger. But nothing happened. Instead, everyone stood and sang a closing hymn. The pastor prayed the benediction and walked down the center aisle with the evangelist so they could shake hands with everyone as they left. Then everyone, including Harry Klinger, came out into the aisle and followed them. I watched Harry as he went past me to see if there might be at least a heavenly glow around him, but all I could see was his regular blue suit, white shirt, and tie. He was smiling with contentment, but he sure wasn't dead or caught up in a fiery chariot.

Maybe he would die that night, I thought, or in a few days. After all, more than one person was saved, and he had said that he would be ready to die if just one was saved. If it happened tonight in his home, I would be sorry that I wouldn't get to see him caught up in a chariot, but it still was good to know the path had been cleared for him to go to heaven.

AUTHOR'S NOTE: *What I didn't know, and Harry didn't know, was that he still had twenty-six years to live on this earth. He lived the entire second century of the United States, from 1876 to 1976. He died in 1977, less than a month before his 101st birthday. Harry didn't go to heaven on the night I expected, and I learned that the date of his passing, like the end of the world itself, was not something for anyone to know, only something to be awaited.*

THE HUNDRED-YEAR-OLD MAN

In 1976, Harry Klinger and the people of the United States celebrated the nation's 200th anniversary, called the Bicentennial. Celebrations took place all over the country. Tall sailing ships glided into New York Harbor, and jet fighter planes roared over crowds in small Midwestern towns, including Elmore. There were great picnics in public parks and schoolyards, bands played, and the night skies were lit up with fireworks on the historic evening of July 4, 1976, that marked the anniversary of the signing of the Declaration of Independence. It was party time.

Born in Ohio in 1876, only eleven years after the end of the Civil War, Harry Klinger was raised in a state that had been pivotal in national politics during that war and its aftermath. But politics did not interest Harry. He wanted a quiet life of hard work, family responsibility, and righteousness. He was the kind of person that America needed in that second century, and there were millions of people like him. They were the kind of people for whom the United States had been created, though the nation needed others who lived more publicly and who found ways to change the nation as it grew.

Harry and others like him learned about events in the world through newspapers, public speeches, and the sermons they heard on Sundays. On the Fourth of July each year, speeches and newspapers told glorified versions of the nation's history and of its condition in 1776. In 1976, people of the Church of God in Elmore saw America as a great place of refuge from the sin and violence of Europe, which their ancestors had left behind. They saw the United States of America as a virtuous nation, in spite of vices and violence that sometimes arose. The country was, above all, a land of freedom and responsibility. It was not their parent or caretaker; it was their place to live good, full lives.

When he was young, Harry Klinger was like other kids born in 1876, a hundred years before the Bicentennial. He started school in a white frame schoolhouse when he was five years old. Children of all ages shared the same large classroom and were led by one teacher. First graders sat at small desks at the front of the room, and bigger kids had larger desks farther back. The oldest students were the eighth graders, who might be as old as sixteen. They sat at the back of the school at tables that could be rearranged for school picnics or local meetings in evenings or on weekends. The older students sometimes caused trouble in school, but they also helped the teacher with the wood-burning stove or even teaching the younger kids. For most kids, it was exciting to be in school learning to read and do numbers. It was a lot like going to church, since everyone was together and learned truths about the world and about people. They even prayed in school every morning.

What Harry learned in that one-room school helped him grow up to be a responsible, thinking, reading, working man. He didn't finish school. He had to leave after sixth grade to help his father and brothers on the farm. Like nearly all families at that time, Harry's family had very little money, but they lived well by raising much of their own food in addition to crops to sell that allowed them to buy tools and clothing and things they couldn't raise such as sugar, coffee, candy, and toys.

Much of the work was hard. Sometimes logs and bundles of hay made for heavy lifting. Sometimes Harry had to shovel whole wagon loads of wheat or oats into the granary. There were long, boring days of plowing, cultivating, and weeding fields by hand. Still, Harry knew it was good to be growing up with important things to do that helped the family and that made their farm better each year. The food was good, with plenty of meat, eggs, milk, butter, potatoes, vegetables, and home-baked bread, pie, and cake. And there was fun in the evenings before bedtime when his mother read stories or his father played checkers with the kids. Sometimes they shot wooden rings into the corner pockets of the carom board in a homespun game that resembled pool.

Many happy Americans like Harry thought, "What could be better?" Others asked themselves what *could* be better, and many of them discovered how to make life better. Often the improvements were little things, like better knives in the kitchen, a cream separator, or a better kind of fencing for the barnyard. Some were more complicated and took years to create. While Harry was still a boy, Thomas Edison found a way to provide light in homes without candles or oil-burning lamps. In 1905 an interurban train line began operating through nearby Elmore to provide high-speed passenger service between Toledo and smaller towns all the way along Lake Erie to Port Clinton and Lakeside, and later to Marblehead. Harry was a young man when the first automobile, called a "horseless carriage," clattered along a country road in Ohio. He was twenty-seven when he heard people talking about some Ohio men who had flown through the air on a large kite with a gasoline engine, which is how the first airplane was described. The world was changing in thousands of ways, and the changes were slowly affecting Harry and his way of life.

By 1977, men had walked on the moon. Cars were everywhere. Most homes had electricity, telephones, electric or gas appliances, and television. Near the end of his days, Harry must have wondered what would become of his beloved country. More than that, he probably wondered about the future of the church around the world, and especially the one in Elmore. He may have even wondered when Jesus would return and end the whirling advance of time. His death not long after the Bicentennial would be "little noted nor long remembered," as President Lincoln once said about his own famous speech at Gettysburg. But to those of us in the Elmore Church of God, Harry Klinger had lived for half of the entire life of our nation, and he was famous to us.

One day in the summer of 1976, Arlin and Ruth Kardatzke took two of their grandchildren, Clint and Stacy Benefield, to see "the one-hundred-year-old man." Clint and Stacy Benefield were Arlin and Ruth's only grandchildren living nearby and the only ones who had grown up in church with Harry Klinger. Clint was nine years old, and Stacy was six. Harry Klinger had declined, and Arlin and Ruth wanted their grandchildren to be able to say they had met a man who was a hundred years old. By this time, Harry was receiving professional care in a nursing home and had few visitors other than close family members. Arlin and Ruth felt they were practically part of Harry's family. Harry's daughter, Dorothy Miller, had said they were welcome to visit him. She added that Harry was feeling good that day and very alert.

The kids stayed close to their grandparents as they edged past carts of sheets and medicines in the halls of the nursing home. Smells of medicine and urine made them grimace, but they tried not to make faces. Moans from one of the rooms they passed sounded like someone dying. Finally they entered a dimly lit room and saw a very old man propped up on pillows. He looked weak and pale, but he smiled warmly at the sight of the children. His daughter stood at his side, beaming.

"Look how happy he is to see you!" his daughter Dorothy said. Clint and Stacy just stared, so she invited them to come over and say hello to him.

Ruth nudged the children toward Harry Klinger's bed. His smile became even broader. He seemed too weak to talk, but he said, "Ever see a man a hundred years old?"

The kids continued to stare. Dorothy prompted them. "What do you say?"

"No," was all they could manage.

"Harry, you are the only hundred-year-old man I have ever seen too!" Ruth said.

Harry smiled. He had accomplished many things in his long life, but living beyond the century mark was about the only success he could think of right then. "I hope you kids live to be a hundred," he said. His voice was stronger than Arlin and Ruth expected. "Be sure you get saved and live for Jesus as long as you live," he advised.

Those words were the wish and the blessing Harry Klinger gave to young Clint and Stacy Benefield. In about a month, a phone call came to Arlin and Ruth that Harry had died and entered heaven. No one saw him go in a fiery chariot, as the prophet Elijah in the Bible had gone, but none who knew him would have been surprised to learn that a chariot was waiting for him.

UNRELATED BROTHERS

In the Church of God in Elmore were two brothers who were different in important ways. One brother, Fred Webert, was a devout, serious Christian. He was a devoted stay-at-home man, rarely traveling beyond the stores in Woodville or the church in Elmore. A Prussian in spirit and heritage, he was legendary for the war he waged by hand against weeds in his bean fields and for the impeccable, almost military tidiness of his farm buildings. Fred loved God and children, and in his sixties he amused his nieces and nephews by hopping on a pogo stick longer than they could. In contrast, Fred's brother Emil Webert was angry and worldly. Emil rarely came to church. When he came, he remained aloof, wore a scowl on his face, and left promptly after the service. He had a reputation for rough talk, fast driving, and pursuit of many women.

Everyone thought Fred and Emil were brothers because they were both raised by the same German-speaking couple we knew as Grandpa and Grandma Webert. The parents' names were Carl and Matilda, but they seemed so distant and were held in such awe that no one outside the Webert family ever used their first names. The truth was, Fred and Emil were brothers only because they shared a household in their young adult years. They had no parent in common, thanks to the confusion and madness of the First World War.

Fred Webert was born in Newport News, Virginia, in 1901 to Carl and Paulina Webert, who had immigrated to the United States only a few years earlier. When Fred was ten years old, his father learned that he could have a farm in Latvia, a country on the Baltic Sea then governed by Russia. The call of free land was too strong for Carl, so he returned to Europe with his wife and young son in the spring of 1912. As it turned out, a worse time could scarcely have been chosen.

The family had barely settled on their farm in Latvia when Carl's wife, Fred's mother, Paulina, died. Then came the fateful year 1914, when the First World War began. By then Carl Webert had met and married his second wife, Matilda, and was farming his own land. But his new life was soon shattered when Germany attacked Russian-controlled Latvia. Carl, along with 40,000 other patriots, joined the Latvian Riflemen to fight the Germans. Carl went off for training in Russia, leaving his new wife at home with his son, Fred, now a young teenager.

The First World War raged for a few months before settling into a long, slow killing time along a line across Western Europe that came to be called the Western Front. Back home in Latvia, young Fred Webert did what he could to support his stepmother through farming and local manual labor. But the battle lines soon pressed near their farm again when the German army advanced against Russia and occupied Latvia on what became the Eastern Front of the war. A German army unit came one day and announced in the town square that all men over the age of fifteen must report for duty by the end of that day. Those who failed to report would be considered deserters and would be shot.

Fred Webert reported for duty, and his new German masters took him to a camp in Latvia for training. He then faced the prospect of meeting his father in battle, since his father's Latvian unit was part of the White Russian Army. Fred and Carl were now on opposite sides of the war. It was possible that one might shoot the other in the heat of battle. At the time, Russia was descending into civil war as the Russian Revolution consumed the country. Fred's German Army unit was on the Eastern Front on the border of Russia, waging war against both the royal White Russian Army and the Communist Red Army.

Fred's stepmother, still on the farm in Latvia, worried she might never see her husband or stepson again. Her husband had been gone three years, and word came every day of massive casualties on the battle front, but no word came from him. She struggled to maintain the farm without Carl and Fred, but it was a losing battle. One day when she was nearly exhausted, a German man wandered in and offered to help. Too tired to decline, she accepted his help. He helped again the next day and again the next until he had become a permanent resident with her. Before long, she was pregnant and gave birth to a son. That son was Emil Webert.

When World War I ended, Carl Webert was released from a prison camp somewhere beyond the Eastern Front where he had been held by the Communist Red Army during most of his absence after being captured. When he returned to Latvia, he was shocked to learn his wife had a new son that was not his. Before he could take action, the German who'd been living in his home with his wife vanished into the postwar chaos, leaving his illegitimate son Emil behind. As his shock and dismay dissipated, Carl's anger gave way to sympathy for his wife and the boy she had borne. Their shared sense of duty rejected any thought of abandoning little Emil. He became their son.

Fred Webert eventually was released by the defeated German army and returned home to find that he had a baby stepbrother, the son of his stepmother by a man other than his father. Even though Fred was not related by blood to either of Emil's parents, Emil was being raised as if he were a blood brother. In time, Carl Webert was able to sell his Latvian farm for just enough money to move the family back to the United States. After landing in New York, they made their way to Ohio, where other Germans were living.

The two brothers, Fred and Emil, grew to become very different men. They looked different: Fred had thick black hair and heavy black eyebrows; Emil had blond, wavy hair, pale eyebrows, and fair complexion. Their actions were different too: Fred devoted himself to God. He bought a farm outside Elmore, traveled as little as possible, and was at the church for every service. During the war, he had promised to serve God the rest of his life, and he was true to his promise. Besides the annual cycle of his crops, Fred's life revolved around the church. He was there every Sunday morning and Sunday evening and for Wednesday night prayer meetings. He often led the singing and sang solos and in duets with his wife, Lucille. When the church building needed repairs or expansion, Fred was there to help. Carl Webert never said it, but he must have been proud of his thrifty, serious, hard-working, religious son.

Emil Webert was another story, and people marveled that the two men could actually be brothers. Few, if any, knew the truth of their relationship. Emil lived near Elmore but was wild and restless. A farm accident took his lower left arm when he was twenty-five. He became bitter about life and remained so for many years. Even so, he farmed Carl Webert's land successfully alone, using a prosthetic clamp on his left arm for detailed tasks. He supplemented his farm income as a truck driver, always seeming lonely. Emil didn't travel widely, but he traveled fast. For many years he was better known around town than in the church. He bragged about driving ninety miles an hour in one of his fancy cars to Cleveland for the night life in one of its dance halls. He bragged about his wild times at amusement parks and other worldly places. Emil had many women, but he never married. In his final years, he was reconciled to the church and apparently to God. He settled down and began attending church. Only then did he find the peace that had so long eluded him.

AUTHOR'S NOTE: *Emil's relationship with his assumed father, Carl, was chilly at best. Only late in his life did Emil learn of his actual parentage. It explained at last his father's distant, formal relationship with him. Perhaps this revelation led Emil to the church. Perhaps there he found the familial love his life had lacked.*

FRED WEBERT'S SALVATION

Horrific war memories dominated Fred Webert's testimonies on Wednesday nights. He lived in the security of his Ohio farm home, yet he still shuddered at the cosmic horrors that had led him to God. Memories of those events were perhaps the most dramatic stories I heard on prayer meeting nights, and I heard them often. By the time I heard of Fred Webert's salvation, there had been a second world war, and Fred's conversion during the first war was more than twenty-five years in the past.

Fred Webert's testimony usually included his memory of being left alone with his step-mother in Latvia when he was a teenager. His father had left to fight for Latvia on the Russian side, he recounted, but not long after his father left, the German army gained control of the Webert area. Troops surrounded the village, and ordered all men between the ages of fifteen and fifty to appear in the town square within an hour. At first he hid, Fred said, but then he decided that his chances among the Russians would be better than his chances in front of their firing squads, so he came out of hiding and was enlisted to fight against his father's army. This was the first wartime horror that Fred related in his testimonies: he might have met his father in battle. Either one of them might have killed the other. He was forever thankful this hadn't happened. His dramatic retelling of the story made a deep impression on everyone in the church, perhaps especially young boys.

Fred's second conscience-searing experience happened while he was a conscript in the German army. He was herded from place to place and ordered to shoot, even to kill, sometimes outside combat. One memory was so shocking he didn't tell it in his regular Wednesday testimonies. One day when I was an adult he told me privately about a time when he and other German soldiers were forced to shoot Communist prisoners.

"We had a bunch of Bolshevik prisoners, and we couldn't keep them," he said. "We were out in farm fields, and we had to travel. We couldn't take prisoners. So our officers told the Bolsheviks, 'Go! Run!' and the Bolsheviks ran out into a field. Our men shot them down like rabbits! 'Oh!' I said to myself, 'Those men are dying and being sent out into eternity! They will face God with sin and blood on their hands!'"

He shook his head, looked at the floor, and repeated parts of the awful memory. "Just like that, those men went out into eternity. Those atheistic Bolsheviks didn't know God, and our men just shot them like rabbits and sent them into eternity." He didn't say whether he joined in the shooting. I suspect he did not, yet the horror of the shootings remained with him the rest of his life. The incident was not lost on me either. It was a story of spiritual horror as well as physical death.

In a third crisis later on, his unit came under heavy artillery bombardment when they were in an exposed area without walls or trenches for protection. Fred dived under a farm wagon as shells exploded overhead and on the ground nearby. His only protection was his helmet and his own arms over his head. It was in this sea of evil that Fred Webert gave his life to the Lord. "Oh, Lord," he prayed, "Please spare my life! If you let me live, I'll live for you the rest of my days!" When Fred told about this bombardment at church, we could practically hear the scream of descending shells and the thump of explosions on the ground. We could feel his desperation as he prayed.

Fred Webert's conversion and his Prussian nature made him sternly against any form of sin and most forms of fun. He had huge, bushy eyebrows, and his little toothbrush mustache was like Hitler's. But he was no fan of Hitler. He considered Hitler an utterly evil man, perhaps an antichrist, the very kind of man he had watched shooting Bolshevik prisoners during World War I. He was shaken by the horrors of World War II, since he knew from his own experiences about the violence, destruction, and evil of war. He seldom strayed from his farm on the Portage River and the road from there to the church. His immaculate farm was an expression of gratitude to the God who had saved him from the Communist bombardment and from what might have become a life of sin and murder.

Fred Webert's salvation experience became something of a model for young people in our church. From him we learned that we should give our hearts to God before we got into trouble or danger. We also learned that we should turn to God when in danger, even if we hadn't been praying, going to church, or leading a holy life already. We didn't envy Fred his serious, intensely spiritual adult life, but his harrowing experiences helped us understand the value he placed on church and his salvation, and they taught us something about the battles and bombardments we might face in the years ahead.

For many years, Fred had the job of winding the clock of the covenant at church. No one would have placed greater value on order and punctual attention to duty than this man who had been saved for God while hiding under a hay wagon during a wartime bombardment.

AUTHOR'S NOTE: *Fred Webert died alone in his farmhouse in 1984. His wife, Lucille, had died in 1977 of a heart attack in their stranded car during a blizzard while he walked to seek help. Their son, Norman, a championship body builder, died of a massive heart attack in 1988 at the age of forty-four.*

ART GLECKLER'S MISSING EAR

"Hah!" Fred Kardatzke yelled to his horses, and they resumed pulling the hay rake through the newly cut field. This team was the most peaceful and reliable he owned. He felt powerful when he worked with these huge animals. The field he was working in was utterly flat, having been once the floor of a vast swamp. Fred's father and men like him had cleared and drained the swamp, and it now produced endless crops, rooted in fourteen inches of black topsoil. The year was 1915, and crops were selling well, even as the nation wavered on the brink of war. Fred was thirty-two, physically strong, and successful in his farming.

As Fred rounded a turn, he saw his twenty-two year old nephew Art Gleckler, who was cultivating beans in the next field. The men waved to each other but didn't pause in their work. German farmers didn't waste time on pleasantries when the weather was good. Art was working for his father, George, who also owned the brick and tile factory in front of the field. Fred continued to the far west end of the field and turned his team just in time to see something horrible. Art's team of horses was running away, and Art was no longer sitting on the cultivator, holding the reins. He had fallen under the blades of the cultivator and was being dragged by the horses.

Fred stopped his team, tied off the reins, and ran to Art and his team. Art's horses bolted when Fred came near, but he ran to their blind side and grabbed the harness violently. "Stop! Whoa! Whoa! Stop, horses! Whoa!" he yelled as he wrestled them under control. He unhitched the horses and let them run free. He then turned his attention to Art, who was covered with blood and wedged under the cultivator.

"Art! Art! Let me help you!" he yelled. Art didn't move. "Oh, God, help him!" Fred cried.

The terrible sight gave Fred more than his usual great strength. He was angry at the horses and angry at the cultivator. In his fury he lifted the heavy cultivator up and off of Art's body. He leaned his back against its steel frame and pushed Art out from under it with one foot. He then let it crash to the ground.

Art began to stir. "That you, Fred? That you?" He saw the blood on his shirt and on Fred's hands. "You okay, Fred?"

"I'm okay! *You're* the one that's hurt! Look at you!"

Art tried to sit up but couldn't.

"Stay there, Art. Let me get help."

Fred ran to the road just as George Gleckler, Art's father, came by with an empty truck. "Art's hurt bad! He might die!" Fred yelled as he jumped in the truck.

George drove to the first farm lane and out into the field where his son lay bleeding. The two men lifted Art as carefully as they could onto the truck bed. Fred picked up Art's severed ear and wrapped it in his handkerchief. George turned the truck toward the road and slowed as he passed by the front of Fred's house. Fred yelled to Emma, and she ran to the road. She shrieked when she saw Art.

"Oh, Lord God, care for him!" she prayed. "Don't let him die! Let him live!"

In town they found Doctor Louis Gahn in his basement office. The men carried Art in to him and told him what had happened. It was only then they could see clearly the extent of Art's mangled head and shoulders. Three large gashes ran over the top of his head, and his right ear had been sheared off. Nothing of his outer ear remained attached.

"Here, take this," Fred said, handing the ear to the doctor.

The doctor looked at the mangled ear. "Don't worry about the ear," he said. "I'll sew it back on, but it may not take. Art has bigger problems." He thought a moment and then asked, "What made the horses bolt like that? Do you think Art had one of his seizures?"

The doctor had seen Art more than once and knew about his seizures, but he had no treatment for them. A sudden seizure may have prompted the accident; the team of horses was not known to be skittish, but any horse could panic at a sudden disturbance. Dr. Gahn went to work, cleaning, stitching, and bandaging as best he could. He then carefully sewed on the injured ear and bandaged gashes in an ankle. When he was finished, he sent Art home to recuperate. As he had warned, the ear did not reattach. When Art returned for a checkup, Dr. Gahn removed the blackened ear and gave it to him. Not knowing what else to do, Art buried the ear in his garden, or at least that's what people said he did with it.

Since Art made his living as a house painter, helping his father on the farm when he could, he had no money for an artificial ear. He had no choice but to live with an exposed ear canal. He didn't like to talk about the accident, but new people sometimes asked about it, and he sometimes told about it during testimony time at church.

Many years after the accident, when Art was about fifty-five, he rose during Wednesday night prayer meeting to testify about the cultivator accident. He was shy, and he spoke softly and rapidly. People had to listen carefully, and he didn't tell the whole, long story. He only told what it had meant to his life and to his soul.

"I was out cultivating one day, and I fell down under the cultivator. My horses started to run away. I yelled to them horses, but they didn't mind. They just drug me till I was hurt bad." In a rare moment of openness, he confided, "They even cut off my ear," and he pointed to where the ear had been.

Everyone who was there that night waited expectantly for Art's next words.

"Well, I coulda died, but I didn't. I knowd then God saved my life," he said. "First chanst I got, I went to church and got saved. I been saved ever since. Sanctified and baptized too. Like the preacher tells us, God loves us. I thank God for saving my life and saving my soul."

A chorus of amen and praise God circled the church when Art sat down.

We kids were excited to hear Art tell his story and think about the way he might have died, but what we liked best was seeing the hole in Art's head where his right ear used to be. Even though he testified about the accident, he was still shy about his missing ear and didn't want us looking at his ear hole. He always sat on the right hand side of the church, where only people coming down the outside aisle might get a glimpse of it.

A Sunday school teacher once told us the story of how the apostle Peter had cut off the right ear of Malchus, the high priest's servant, during Jesus' arrest in the Garden of Gethsemane. Jesus put the ear back on and told Peter to put his sword away. When we heard that story, we thought of Art Gleckler and wished Jesus had been there the day of the accident to put Art's right ear back on. At least Jesus had let Art live, even though he had to go through the rest of his life with a hole where his ear used to be.

AUTHOR'S NOTE: *On March 17, 2016, Jennifer Fording, the local history librarian in Elmore, found a newspaper clipping about this 1922 accident. The paper reported that Art was subject to "epileptic fits," and an auto accident a few years later was blamed on one of his "fits."*

EMIL WEBERT'S MISSING ARM

Unusual features of people's bodies are interesting to kids. In my church, we kids wanted to see the place where Aunt Eula's finger had been cut off when it became infected by a needle she used to remove a splinter for Uncle Joe. Even the moles and warts on the faces of some of the older women were fascinating to us. Sometimes a woman with a goiter visited our church, and we secretly stared at her bulging neck. We tried to see the hole where Art Gleckler's ear had been after it was cut off in a farming accident. In another farming accident, Emil Webert had lost part of his left arm. He seldom came to church, perhaps partly because we kids stared at that empty, folded sleeve where his arm should have been.

As a younger man, Emil was strong and healthy and good looking. Even though he didn't play sports at school, he was proud of his work with his father and his stepbrother Fred on their farms. The farm accident that cost Emil his arm was a common one. He had been driving a tractor, pulling a corn picking machine in the fall of the year. Some corn stalks got jammed in the narrow slot where they were pulled into the machine between two large moving chains. Emil stopped the tractor, but he didn't turn off the engine, and he didn't disengage the power-takeoff. The corn picker kept running, roaring and chewing and pulling at the corn stalks.

Emil climbed down to examine the problem. Reaching in with his left arm, he pulled the corn stalks out of the machine. Suddenly the machine started churning again. His sleeve was caught by the moving chains, and his arm was pulled in almost up to his elbow. He screamed for help, but no one was near enough to hear. The machine kept pulling and chewing on his arm until he could pull free. He was bleeding heavily. Finally another farmer who had seen the accident from several fields away got to him and pulled him away from the machine.

Emil was taken to the hospital in Fremont. Doctors stopped his bleeding and sewed up the end of his wounded stump of an arm. They gave him medicine to control his pain and help him sleep. When he woke up, he at first didn't know his arm was missing. He couldn't remember the accident, and he thought he could feel the injured arm lying beside him in the bed. When he realized that part of his body was gone, he was at first only shocked and surprised. Then he felt sad, missing the arm that he had used all his life. He tried not to cry because he wanted to be tough and serious. Then he felt angry. How could this have happened to him? How had the corn picker grabbed his arm? Why had he even tried to pull the corn out with the machine running? What would happen to him with only one arm? Could he still be a farmer? What would girls think of him, a one-armed man? Thoughts like these boiled in his mind as he lay in the hospital bed.

When Emil was sent home to recover, he felt like only half a man. Whenever people said they were praying for him, he became angry and blamed God for his accident. He sometimes felt that he had died because he had changed so much. At other times, he wished he *had* died. But there he was, alive, looking out on the farm fields where he had expected to work all of his life.

Emil didn't die then, and he didn't stop working. His body was strong, and God caused his arm stump to heal. He found that he could work around the farm with his right hand, though some things were slower than before. As his strength returned, he found that he could even do some heavy work like baling hay, using his right hand and the baling hook to pull bales of hay against his body and toss them onto stacks on the wagon. He learned to drive a tractor, a farm truck, and a car using only his right hand, and some years later he had a job driving a large semi-truck. He even received an artificial hand in the form of two prongs that could squeeze small objects. Whenever people tried to help him or give him easy jobs, he would get angry. He wanted them to know that he was still tough and strong even though he had only one arm. People who knew him stopped trying to help him, and most people stopped trying to be nice to him because that made him angry too. He thought they were just feeling sorry for him.

Emil fought back against his handicap and was a successful farmer. He supported himself well, drove late-model cars, and in his later years drove a luxurious motor home to Florida each year. But unlike Art Gleckler, who was happy even though he was missing an ear, Emil always seemed lonely, living alone with memories of his missing arm and thoughts about how that loss had changed his life. His family and others from the church tried to befriend him, but he kept himself away from family and church for most of his life. Only late in his life did he begin to attend church again, and it was like the story of the return of the prodigal son in the Bible. Those who knew him were happy to see him there again, and he felt better then about the church and about his life.

Emil Webert must have gotten saved in those later years, because he changed so much. He even specified that when he died, memorial gifts were to be directed to the church. Maybe when he was older he could see that he had lived a strong life and one that was successful in spite of losing his arm. Maybe he gave up his anger and sadness when he could look back at last and see that God had given him a good life even without his missing arm.

ELEPHANTIASIS AND THE MISSION FIELD

Missionaries visited our church from time to time, perhaps as often as once a year. Most of them had served in Kenya, which was at that time Kenya Colony, British East Africa. The Church of God established an active mission presence in western Kenya in the early 1900s, and a steady stream of missionaries went there to continue the work with local pastors. The missionaries I remember were mostly middle-aged women, and they seemed very old to me as a boy under ten.

Missionary visits were among the most interesting events at our church, especially since they usually came with colorful 35-mm slide or filmstrip presentations. The slides showed African people dressed in European clothing or in colorful local dress, brick churches with tin roofs, grass-roof native houses, open market places, smiling school children, red dirt roads, and people with a disease called elephantiasis.

Of all the pictures the missionaries showed, those of people with horribly swollen legs and feet were the most fascinating to me. The swollen limbs were so large and gnarled that they resembled elephants' legs. A picture of a woman seated on a chair under a spreading shade tree is still fixed in my mind. Her legs looked like large tree trunks. To me this woman represented Africa. She was poor like nearly all villagers, she was handicapped by this awful disease, and she probably was shunned by the people in her village because of her ugliness and her need for help. No other missionary picture filled my imagination like the lady with elephantiasis.

The people in our church knew that Christians were called to carry the gospel to the whole world, but how could we in Elmore do it? Some of our congregation had never even left Ohio. Some seldom even left

Ottawa County. Most of those who had been overseas had been in one of the world wars or had immigrated from another country. Few of us were equipped to carry the gospel beyond the walls of our church, let alone to the whole wide world. We needed missionaries, and missionary visits to our church made us feel as though we were a part of their work.

Since we couldn't send our own missionaries, we sent money and goods. The Women's Missionary Society involved nearly all the women in the church, and they made quilts and conducted projects to raise money for missionaries. Kids' birthday pennies, nickels, and dimes went for missions, and the church often prayed for missionaries. Some people sent them cards and letters. We kids usually just thought of the African kids we'd seen in slides that were our ages or the woman with elephantiasis.

The world of missions and missionaries began to change significantly in the 1950s. People other than preachers and evangelists began to go to the mission field. Sometime in the 1950s, our congregation sent out its first "missionaries." My uncle Carl and his wife, Eva-Clare "Tip" Kardatzke, went to Kenya for two years. Carl advised the Kenyan education authorities and the leaders of the Church of God mission schools. He was a college professor, so his reports from Kenya were analytical, thorough, and inspiring.

The fact that these relatives had spent two whole years there attracted me to Africa even while living in Ohio. Carl and Tip were exposed to African diseases, including the one I dreaded most: elephantiasis. Tip Kardatzke was bitten by a different type of mosquito and came back from her first trip to Kenya with permanent paralysis on one side of her face, the result of a mosquito bite, yet she returned with her husband for another year. Her kind, generous smile still shone through a face distorted by paralysis.

Also in the 1950s, my uncle Elmer and his wife, Vera Kardatzke, went to Kenya and came back bursting with stories about their adventures. They visited many of the same mission stations where Carl and Tip had served, and they also went on a big game safari. They even brought gifts to nearly everyone in our extended family, and those gifts became our links to a larger, more exciting world than we could have known without their travels.

The visiting missionaries and my two uncles and aunts planted a thirst for adventure in my restless little mind too. I had no idea how I would ever be able to travel outside my home country, but then the Peace Corps started in 1961. In 1962 I applied and was invited to go to Ethiopia. I was very excited, but I had to hurry to the Anderson College library to look up that ancient land in an encyclopedia. Some of the others in my Peace Corps group said they too were puzzled about where they would be going. One thought Ethiopia might be near Albania because he knew it had been invaded by Italy.

For two years I taught math and science in a beautiful little city called Adi Ugri in Eritrea, which was at that time part of Ethiopia. Those two years influenced the rest of my life. I didn't think of myself as a missionary like those who came to our church in Elmore or like my aunts and uncles, but my desire to go and serve began with them. I didn't see a case of elephantiasis while I taught in Eritrea or on any of my subsequent trips to Africa, but the lady with the swollen legs to this day still reminds me of the enormous needs in that vast, wonderful continent.

The Elmore Church of God has never had a large congregation. It now has fewer than one hundred souls, as it has had through most of its history. Like other small congregations, however, it reaches far beyond its walls. It finds some of its purpose in far-flung medical, educational, and evangelistic efforts, as well as in its vigorous presence in Elmore, a town that has itself remained a small, sending community.

AUTHOR'S NOTE: *It's easy to assume that elephantiasis disappeared from Africa long ago, but the disease is still rampant in tropical countries, not only in Africa but in most tropical parts of the world. Elephantiasis is spread by mosquitos that suck blood from people who carry a certain worm in their bloodstream. The mosquitoes go on to infect others. The worms affect the lymphatic system, and it causes swelling of the lower body parts and legs of the victims. The disease is associated with many other infections as well. More than one-hundred-twenty million people are believed to have elephantiasis right now, and forty million are currently affected in Africa. More than ten million in Africa are incapacitated and are so disfigured that they are objects of horror.*

SHUT-INS

When prayers were requested at church in the 1940s and 1950s, someone usually reminded the congregation to pray for "the shut-ins." As a young child, I had little idea of what shut-ins might be and how they lived. I sometimes thought they were lucky because they didn't have to come to church on bright, sunny days when it would be fun to play outside. But when I finally learned more about the shut-ins and why they were shut in, I knew that they weren't having fun or playing outside.

Nearly all of the shut-ins were old women. Often they became shut-ins after breaking a hip, which was usually a death sentence in those days. When they were able to come to church, I noticed they had gray hair, and even their skin sometimes looked gray. They usually walked awkwardly, and their voices were soft and quavering and crackling. In my imagination, there was even something ghoulish about them. When I thought of them sitting at home all the time, they seemed to grow even more ghoulish. I could imagine them deteriorating, becoming sick often and looking more like ghosts than like the people who came to church. I could picture them at night, sitting in the golden glow of kerosene lamps or dim electric lights surrounded by old furniture and lace curtains. They seemed to be from another century. In fact, most of them *had* been born before 1900.

As a young boy, I didn't really get to know any of the shut-ins well except my Grandpa Fred Kardatzke in his last year of life. He was shut in by "heart trouble," as people called it then. Grandpa had to stay in bed nearly all the time for many months, but he didn't look like the old ladies who were shut-ins. His cheeks were rosy, his hair was a thin wreath above his rounded head, and he always had a smile when I went to see him. I never thought of him as a shut-in because he seemed so different from the way I imagined those old women. People prayed for Grandpa at church, but I don't remember them ever calling him a shut-in. Maybe only women could be shut-ins, I thought. Maybe men who stayed at home because they were sick or old might were called something else. They were not like people who were able-bodied yet stayed at home by choice. Those who went to church faithfully didn't call those voluntary stay-at-homes "sinners," but they did pray for their salvation.

Some shut-ins, I learned when I was older, were not called shut-ins. They were the people at the Shady Rest Home west of Elmore. It was a place where old people went when they couldn't be cared for in their homes, like the senior living places we have now. Shady Rest was a large, two-story brick house on River Road just outside of town, set back from the road at the end of a long gravel driveway. It had been built in about 1890 and looked very old-fashioned, with green wooden shutters and big screened-in porches with lattice enclosing the area underneath to keep out animals and small children. Our family didn't have relatives living in the Old Folks' Home except for Aunt Laurie and Uncle Andy, who ran the place and cared for the people there. Aunt Laurie Neipp was one of my Grandpa Fred's sisters, and Uncle Andy was her third husband.

We drove past the rest home on our way to Woodville, a nearby town, but we didn't go in as a family. Our church's youth group did go there once or twice a year, mainly at Christmas time to sing Christmas carols. The old people would gather in one of the parlors to hear our little group of singers perform. We mainly sang to old women, but sometimes a disheveled old man was there with them. The people beamed with joy to see us, but we were too young to realize how much it meant to them. Even then I was struck by the contrast between the baggy, saggy, gray old folks and the cherubic, healthy, rosy children who sang to them. It was a sight of life and death together in one room. To the residents, it might have been a glimpse of their fading life in contrast to the new life that awaited them when they stepped beyond this life into the next. Maybe we were like angels to them.

Those old folks could have told us many interesting things about our town, the farms, the river that ran behind the home, and the fires and accidents and crimes in earlier years. Some could have told us what life was like during the First World War. A few of them must have heard their parents talk about the Civil War as well. But we were too young and unaware to even think of asking questions. All we wanted was to sing our songs and get back into the fresh air outside.

Today people at church don't call anyone a shut-in, maybe partly because the label *shut-in* sounds a little bit scary, like *inmate*, someone in prison. Or it may be partly because church words have changed over the years. Possibly if they were still called shut-ins, people might be more concerned and feel they had to do something for them.

People who are at home with illnesses or injuries now usually get well and come back to church, and we aren't surprised when they do return.. They aren't shut in permanently the way the shut-ins were in the 1940s. Medicine is better now too, and people are healthier than those in earlier years. We still pray often for "the sick" at church, but we don't write them off as "shut in." It's good to see how often older people return from their illnesses even if they can serve the Lord only by their presence in church.

People recovering from illnesses at home now aren't nearly as isolated as the shut-ins people prayed for in the 1940s or the people at Shady Rest. Back then their only contact with the outside world was occasional visits from family members and church people. Some might have been able to listen to a radio, and occasionally they may have read a newspaper. Today convalescing people have telephones, e-mail, and cable TV. Many of them have cars, so they aren't really shut in. If they can't drive, they have other ways to get out of their houses to medical appointments, church, the bank, and the grocery store.

Today's shut-ins have their own kind of work to do, like those in the 1940s. For many of them, their work is to pray and encourage others. They send cards to people who are sick, even if some of those sick people are not shut-ins. They pray for those who are praying for them. They pray for other shut-ins who are sicker than they are and for people who need the Lord. They pray for people who don't yet pray.

If we ourselves become shut-ins when we are older, it will be good to remember the lives of the early shut-ins and the examples of the heroic shut-ins around us now. When our only work is encourage-ment and prayer, we will have examples to follow and reasons to be thankful that we have lived long enough to be shut in now, and not in those earlier times.

AUTHOR'S NOTE: *In researching this book, I learned that my great-grandfather, Harmon Kardatzke, and his third wife, Emma Shirk Kardatzke, died at Shady Rest Home when I was too young to have known them. My parents told me that my great-grandfather was never one to express overt affection, so he always called this wife "Mrs. Shirk."*

V. HOW WE "DID" CHURCH

THE RELIGIOUS CONTEXT

I mean no disrespect in titling this section "How We Did Church." I admit it's a recent colloquialism that may have evolved from "doing lunch." The title may seem to deny the reality that we don't just "do church" like an empty ritual: we *are* the church if we are Christians. My intent here is to describe a few specific ways we practiced our faith in the Elmore Church of God from about 1945 to 1955. I can only describe some of the things we did and some of the things we believed. I can't describe the invisible internal conditions of people's minds and souls; those are seen only by God.

In telling you about some of the practices of the Elmore Church of God, I don't mean to deny the existence and value of the other churches in Elmore, Ohio, at that time. In 1951, at Elmore's Centennial, there were seven Protestant churches serving a population of about 1,200 souls, not counting worshippers living in other towns or in the country-side. There was no Catholic church in Elmore, though there had been one earlier, but there was one nearby in Genoa. The other Protestant churches undoubtedly "did church" in ways that differed in detail from what we did. I know very little of the internal workings of those other Elmore churches at that time or their histories. I can only focus on what I heard and saw in the Elmore Church of God, even if I saw some of it "through a glass darkly."

WE WERE A NEW TESTAMENT CHURCH

A driving aim of the Church of God movement (Anderson, Indiana) was to be a New Testament church. We wanted to re-create the purity, energy, and devotion of the earliest churches as described in the New Testament. Several of the following essays and stories tell the things we did differently from some other churches in order to be a "New Testament church" in as many ways as possible. We looked for clues and descriptions in the Bible, and we sometimes had to guess at the way the first churches did things.

Our urge to be a New Testament church made us a "restorationist" group, seeking to restore the church to its earliest form. We assumed that most of what had become "Christian" in the intervening centuries was unnecessary if not sinful or misleading. It didn't occur to us that the church and its teaching might have matured in some positive ways over time, in spite of episodes of corruption and false teaching in past centuries. So we looked only to Scripture and the Holy Spirit for our guidance, and those sources nurtured our fellowship and our fervor. We intended to be a broad Christian "movement" rather than a denomination circumscribed by a set of traditions and rituals. As time passed, we developed our own traditions and rituals.

Although our church eschewed formal creeds, formulas, and other identifying marks of denominations, the steps in the Christian life were clear to me as a boy, and they were a kind of formula. First, you had to get saved. Even if you were growing up in a Christian home and living an honest, well-behaved life, you needed the experience of getting saved, being born again. This belief is firmly rooted in Bible passages such as John 3:7 (KJV): "Ye must be born again." This step usually

207

required a direct encounter with God through prayer and a revolutionary change in the character of the person who was saved.

The second step in becoming a Christian in our church was to be sanctified. In this step, our church differed from many other parts of the Christian world because we believed sanctification was a "second work of grace." In our church, sanctification was expected to occur sometime after you were saved, and it would happen in a moment during a prayer, just as getting saved did. It required you to ask the Holy Spirit to enter a prepared mind and heart to equip you to live a Christian life.

Baptism was the third step, and it could be experienced only after you had been saved and sanctified. It could come soon after sanctification, or there might be a delay of months or even years before you became a candidate for baptism. There was no catechism or specific course of study for baptism; you qualified for it on the basis of your individual testimony of salvation. We believed that baptism was a public expression of the spiritual change experienced in being saved and sanctified. Baptism was chosen voluntarily by a responsible adult or even a child who understood its meaning; it was not something the church could confer on an adult, a child, or an infant without their choice.

These three steps made you a Christian and qualified you for heaven. They also made you a member of the great universal Christian church as well as a member of our local congregation, but we didn't talk of church membership—that would have sounded sectarian to us. True church membership to us was purely a matter of being saved, sanctified, and baptized. We were careful to avoid creating the impression that the church itself accomplished these acts for us, as we thought the concept of membership implied. God alone could save us and qualify us for heaven.

Living the Christian life involved much more, of course, than taking these steps that would ultimately get us past the pearly gates into paradise. We were called to lead sinless lives of service to others, to love fellow Christians and everyone else, to share our faith with others, to tithe our income, and to have faithful, nearly continuous attendance at church. We were to be like the Israelites, a people set apart—the basic meaning of sanctification and holiness—and we were to be humble and obedient to God. We tried not to be worldly, and we were often so separate from the world around us that we were in some ways like Orthodox Jews or other religious groups that lived distinctly different lives from the culture around them.

GETTING SAVED

Readers can't really understand the stories in this book if they don't know what getting saved meant to us. It was this experience, more than any other, that kept people together in our church. It was the rock that the church was built on, and yet it was sometimes a barrier. Some people avoided our church because of what we believed about getting saved. Understanding more fully what getting saved meant to us will give you greater insight into stories about the lives of Harry Klinger, Emma Gleckler, and Fred Webert, to name only a few of the saints in the Elmore Church of God.

The term *getting saved* is largely out of the Christian vocabulary in the twenty-first century, but it was crucial to the Church of God (Anderson, Indiana) in the 1940s and 1950s. These days people talk of "coming to Christ" or "accepting God" or "having a personal relationship with God" or becoming "a follower of Jesus." There is nothing wrong with these expressions, but to me the older term, *getting saved*, suggests the crisis of guilt and awareness of separation from God that led people to repentance and changed lives. It was an experience of being freed, justified before God, and instantly given the promise of eternal life simply through faith and the grace of God.

Getting saved was a conscious decision, but it was prompted by the Holy Spirit and required a radical surrender to God, most often made known to others through a public confession through prayer at the altar in front of the church. In that moment of confession, the person being saved was assured of eternal life with God and with other believers. A person could be saved while standing in the congregation or while praying in bed or at any other place, but going forward to the altar was the clearest, most transforming way to get saved.

I saw getting saved as the sudden resolution of a spiritual and emotional crisis. When a person got saved, there was an immediate and visible outward change in attitudes and behavior that reflected a powerful inward change. The inward change, in today's vernacular, was like a computer being reprogrammed; it was a person being reprogrammed by confessing sin and accepting God's leading in life, accepting the "indwelling of the Holy Spirit." For me as a young boy, getting saved was a public admission of my rebellious attitude and unkind behavior toward my brothers and sisters.

I said that getting saved involved an "emotional crisis," not because getting saved was essentially an emotional experience, but because emotion was involved. After all, the person getting saved believed that his or her eternal life was at stake. This all-important aspect of humanity was just one of the reasons why there could be emotion in getting saved. Getting saved was often emotional because it was a more profound experience than merely assenting to a set of facts or to an intellectual concept. It was a personal change. That said, I have known Christians who experienced conversion through intellectual discovery of Christian teaching, and those teachings profoundly altered their behavior and worldview. They too experienced changed lives and an exhilarating awareness of spiritual freedom.

Although we didn't talk about the concept of Original Sin or use that terminology in our church, we did believe that everyone needed to get saved. We believed that everyone is by nature a sinner and will sin actively sooner or later, even children. We also believed all children reach an "age of accountability" when they become conscious of their sinful nature. It's something like Adam and Eve in the Garden of Eden when they suddenly felt that they needed clothes after they had sinned. The "age of accountability" was the time when a child's misdeeds became a matter between the child and God, not just between the child and parents or teachers or other kids. It was the time when the child actually became responsible for wrongdoing. At the age of accountability, one's misdeeds led to guilt rather than just shame or fear of being detected. I believed that children were under God's special protection and forgiveness until they reached the age of accountability.

I believed they would go to heaven if they died in that early stage of life, even if they had not yet been saved.

In my church, before people could be saved or would even want to be saved, they had to become aware of their sinful nature. Sermons spelled out the awfulness of sin and made us aware of the sinful nature of some things we might have done. Not all sins were described in detail in sermons, but the presence and the dangers of sin were held up before us like the bronze serpent that Moses held up in the desert so those bitten by snakes could look at it and be healed.

Sometimes people's specific acts of sinning made them aware of their basic sinful nature. Some of the "sinners" I saw get saved must have been guilty of very minor offenses, at least in human terms, because they were pious young girls and boys who would have had little opportunity for large-scale lives of sin. Yet the sense of guilt and separation from God was real, even for children and young people. Getting saved, then, dealt with cosmic, supernatural separation from God, not just a particular sin or a collection of sins. Getting saved addressed the sinful nature we all were born with, which perhaps is a way to understand what is meant by Original Sin.

Guilt, in those days, was not considered to be a psychological aberration or hang-up that needed to be cured by a counselor or a psychiatrist. It was seen as an honest reflection of a person's willful, wrong-headed, rebellious nature and the wrongful acts that came from it. Guilt was something of a sixth sense, telling a person of spiritual or moral danger, similar to the way the heat of a hot stove causes a person to recoil from the danger of getting burned.

A person's first conscious response to guilt was often to deny any wrongdoing or to make excuses for it. Another response was to put the matter entirely out of mind, to forget it as though it had never happened, to "repress" it. When I sinned, I would often secretly resolve never to commit that sin again. Sometimes that tactic worked on a specific sin, like saying certain bad words or being angry with my siblings too much. In truth, however, there were too many forms of sin for me to avoid or repress them all, even as a kid. In older people, there were even more forms of sin, and some people even left the church without repenting of their rather public sins; they had, as we understood it, "hardened their hearts" against acknowledging their guilt.

Guilt and the feeling of guilt could lead a person to "get under conviction." This active stage of guilt was often what prompted a person to get saved or to repent of some wrong and make appropriate restitution, when possible. A person who was under conviction could choose to do the right thing and confess sins, both to God and to other people; or that person might suppress the feeling of guilt, deny it, and continue to carry that burden. The guilty person might try to deal with the guilt by talking to friends about it, hiding it, trying to avoid repeating the sin by sheer force of will, or by building defenses and rationalizations around it. Sometimes it was obvious, even to children, when certain adults avoided dealing with spiritual problems, including their personal guilt.

Being under conviction often led people to pray at the altar at the front of the church. In fact, the altar was used mainly for getting saved or sanctified. The altar was seldom a place just to pray about the cares of life, which was usually done during congregational prayers or at Wednesday night prayer meetings or more likely at home in personal devotions. On rare occasions, the altar was used in a prayer for divine healing, something we believed in but was not a major tenet of our church. As a child, I fully understood that the altar was the place for people to confess their sins and ask God's forgiveness for them. It was our confessional place.

The emotional experiences people had when they got saved or gave their lives to God were not the same for all individuals. Some people were not visibly emotional at all. Some cried quietly, while others did so audibly. Some even shook with sobs or raised their hands toward heaven as they prayed and asked for forgiveness. Regardless of the variety of emotional experiences, their changed lives were evidence of God's power, love, and forgiveness.

I went forward in church to repent of my sins and be saved at least two different times during my teenage years after my earliest conversion during the 1948 tornado. When I was under conviction as a child or a young person, it was because of both bad actions and bad attitudes on my part. My guilt made me unhappy, and it separated me from my family as well as from God. I knew that I needed to repent, but I didn't want to. I didn't want to admit that I was a sinner. I was in an inner battle complicated by the dread of going forward publicly to lay down my guilt at the altar. Finally the guilt accumulated until I could no longer deny that I was away from God, and I went forward to the altar to confess my sins to God.

People usually went to the altar only at the end of a church service. Sometimes the sermon lent itself to repentance, but often the sermon had little to do with a person's urge to go forward. The latter was true for me. I was aware of my sinfulness and my separation from God. I didn't have the peace and joy that others testified about in church, and I couldn't even think about heaven and hell. I knew that I wasn't really a Christian, even though I was in church. It was one of the "altar call" or "invitation" songs that finally motivated me to go forward. Those songs had great spiritual and emotional power, and we sang them often at the end of the service to invite people to surrender to God. Two of the most persuasive of those songs were "Just as I Am" and "I Surrender All." I rarely hear those songs now except during an evangelism event or in a video from one of Billy Graham's crusades. Here are a few of the words from those songs.

Just as I Am

Just as I am, without one plea,
But that thy blood was shed for me.
And that thou bidd'st me come to thee,
Oh Lamb of God, I come, I come!

Just as I am, Thou wilt receive,
Wilt welcome, pardon, cleanse, relieve;
Because thy promise I believe,
O Lamb of God, I come, I come.

I Surrender All

All to Jesus I surrender,
At his feet I humbly bow.
I will ever love and trust him,
In his presence daily live.

I surrender all,
I surrender all,
All to thee my blessed Savior,
I surrender all.

When I was under conviction, those songs were a kind of testimony to me, a reminder of how to relate to God. Each time, as the song began, my heart would throb and I breathed heavily. I knew I should go forward, but I was afraid to do it. I didn't want to do it. Then I would imagine letting the moment pass when God was clearly calling me, and my heart beat even harder. I knew I had to go forward and admit that all was not well with my soul. If I didn't go forward that day, I might not have another chance. I wouldn't go to heaven if I died on the way home from church, and God might not call me again the way he was calling me right then. It was a spiritual crisis that required action.

Finally, in an almost dream-like state, what people today call an "out-of-body experience," I would slip out from among my friends and start down the aisle to the altar. My knees shook, and I thought I might fall down before I got to the altar. Just going to the altar was admission that I needed God. As soon as I reached the altar and began to pray, I began to feel healed of my guilt. Someone would come to pray with me, usually my mother or father or the pastor. I told whoever it was that I needed to get saved; I didn't tell all the sins I had done. If I had been saved before and was returning to repent, I might just say that I had "gotten away from God." The person with me would pray, and I would pray. In only a few minutes, we got up and returned to our seats, and I felt like a new person, with my guilt taken away. I was "born again." I felt free and able to live a Christian life.

Sometimes people talked of being "washed in the blood of Jesus." To people outside the church, this must have sounded very strange, like a lurid metaphor. To those who had been saved and forgiven, being "washed in the blood of the Lamb" meant being healed of guilt and given a fresh, clean life because of Jesus' life, suffering, death, and resurrection.

There were a few problems with my understanding of getting saved in my early years. Or maybe the problems weren't mine alone; maybe they were shared widely in my church. One problem was that we really did believe in something like a formula or a ritual of getting saved, even though the experience itself was profound and authentic. We believed that getting saved should take place in the church at the altar, and it was most likely to be genuine and lasting if it happened that way. We must have thought that conversions such as Fred Webert's during

214

an artillery bombardment in World War I or my first conversion during the tornado were an exception to the rule.

Although following the formula of salvation at the altar may have been overdone at times, it gave real power to the altar call and to the lives that were changed at the altar. Without the altar experience, it was much easier to forget about a time of repentance that was done at home alone in bed after the lights were out. I'm sure people did get saved and give their lives to Christ quietly at home without much emotion, but they may have wondered sometimes if their salvation was real when its beginning differed so much from the way getting saved was explained and practiced in church. Also, most of us kids got saved before having committed any horrific sins or having spent years in a luridly sinful lifestyle. We didn't have the same dramatic testimonies that we often heard on Wednesday nights.

Another problem with my understanding of getting saved was the belief that if people were really saved, they wouldn't sin again. If people thought they were saved and then sinned, it seemed to me, they must not really have been saved in the first place or had somehow "lost" their salvation because of the sins they committed. As I understood it back then, there seemed to be no room for simple repentance within the Christian life, so I would wait until my sins and my guilt reached an unbearable level and then go to the altar to begin the process of the Christian life all over. I would get saved, sanctified, and baptized again. I was not alone in having repeated conversion experiences. A very famous Christian musician once said in my presence that he and most of the kids he knew had been saved multiple times. I believed that those conversion experiences were the way back to God if a person had become a "backslider," which meant having returned to sinful patterns after being saved.

As I went through high school and into college, I began to question my view of the Christian life and of getting saved. I began to wonder if there was anything to the Christian life beyond getting saved because that's all that I thought our ministers preached about. There didn't seem to be any room for learning and maturation after becoming a Christian. I wondered why Christians are taught in the Lord's prayer to ask for forgiveness of debts, trespasses, or sins, when I thought being a Christian meant living a perfect life.

Since those days, my life has led me to the belief that God does forgive sins, even in Christians, though our sins are supernaturally serious because they separate us from God. We are to work with God to separate ourselves from sin. Now I simply trust God's grace and forgiveness and his resurrection of Jesus as the basis for my Christian life when I still sometimes "wander from the fold of God."

AUTHOR'S NOTE: *"Just as I Am" may be the quintessential invitation hymn. It was written by Charlotte Elliot in 1835, and it became the most frequently sung invitation at Billy Graham crusades. Judson W. Van DeVenter (1855–1939) wrote the words for "I Surrender All." The poem was put to music by Winfield S. Weeden (1847–1908) and published in 1896.*

SANCTIFICATION

The second step in becoming a Christian in my church was to be sanctified. In this, my church differed from many other parts of the Christian world because we believed sanctification was a "second work of grace." Salvation, or getting saved, was possible only because of God's grace; it couldn't be earned by good behavior. People could not be good enough to *make* God forgive them. Sanctification was a similar step, and it too was a gift from God.

In my church, sanctification was expected to occur sometime after a person was saved, and it could take place in a moment at an altar of prayer. There wasn't a definite time period prescribed, but a period of maturation and growth in the faith was expected before a person sought sanctification. A person would likely be sanctified by going to the altar in front of the congregation and praying for this gift, which would deepen the person's spiritual life and make the person more secure in being able to maintain a sinless life. Although many churches believe that sanctification is an ongoing process that begins with acceptance of Christian faith and continues throughout this life and perhaps into the next life as well, that view was not how I saw it when I was a boy.

There's little for me to tell about my childhood experience of being sanctified. To me being sanctified was mainly a rational decision. It was like completing a catechism or being confirmed, though we didn't have a formal catechism and didn't practice confirmation like many other churches. Still, this was the way I experienced our form of sanctification: it was a conscious act on my part, declaring by another trip to the altar, that I had become a Christian and intended to lead a holy, sinless life. One Sunday a few weeks after I had been saved, I decided

I needed to take that next step of faith. I needed to affirm the meaning of my earlier prayer at the altar and my conviction that I had been saved from the debt of sin. So when the service ended and the altar call was given, I calmly walked to the front of the church and knelt at the altar. When the pastor came to pray with me, he asked, "What are you seeking from the Lord today, Nyle?"

"I want to be sanctified," I whispered.

"Well, praise God!" he replied. "Have you been saved?"

"Yes," I whispered, and at this moment I felt secure in my salvation. No overhanging guilt from some recent sin cast doubt on this little, private testimony.

"When were you saved?" the pastor asked. I related the details as clearly as I could remember, and this information authenticated my salvation for the pastor.

"Good!" he said. "Then let's pray." And the pastor began quietly praying something like this: "O God, our heavenly Father, our young Brother Nyle has come here seeking the infilling of the Holy Spirit. He has committed his life to you, and he now seeks the power to live all his days in holy service to you. He has asked to be sanctified, and we know that you will not turn away one whose sins have been forgiven and who seeks you it spirit and in truth. Enter Brother Nyle now, and assure him of his presence in your kingdom today and forevermore. Keep him from sin and the snares of the world, and bring him into your eternal presence at the end of his life."

The pastor then said, "How about you pray too?"

My boyish mind was hazy about this request, so all I could pray was, "Lord, I want to be sanctified."

That was enough. The pastor reached across the altar and shook me by the shoulders. I looked up, and there were tears in his eyes. He and I stood, and he turned me to face the congregation.

"Brother Nyle came forward today to be sanctified, isn't that right, Nyle?" he said. I nodded and he continued. "He testified that he has been saved, and he has prayed for sanctification. God has richly added that gift to his salvation. Isn't this a wonderful day?"

"Amen!" said Fred Webert and "Praise God!" said Grandma Kardatzke.

I looked around, and all the adults were smiling. The young people just stared seriously and silently with unknowable thoughts. At that moment, I felt mature and "confirmed"—in the way my church confirmed young believers. The pastor had called me "Brother Nyle," and that was enough confirmation for me. It was a new mantle of belonging. I was happy after that day to just be "Nyle" most of the time and "Brother Nyle" mainly in church.

BAPTISM IN THE PORTAGE RIVER

"Shall we gather at the river,
Where bright angel feet have trod?"

Baptism was the third step in becoming a Christian in our church. It completed the trilogy of "saved, sanctified, and baptized." While we didn't believe that baptism saved a person, it was a third, vital step in starting the Christian life. It wasn't magical or even spiritual in its own right, but it was an "outward sign of an inward change." It was one of the first testimonies by a new Christian, a way of announcing to the world the person was following Jesus and that the Holy Spirit had come his or her life. Compared to getting saved, baptism was a small but essential thing, but it was *visible*. You could *see* a person actually go under water and come back up, a baptized Christian.

We believed that the person being baptized had to have experienced salvation and had to know what baptism meant. We didn't believe the church had the power to *give* salvation or membership in the great holy Christian Church through baptism, so we didn't believe babies should be baptized. Baptism was something only for Christians who were old enough to know what they were doing. In our church, baptism followed sanctification after an unspecified interval, but there were stories of people insisting on being baptized immediately after being saved and sanctified. One man was reported to have marched his congregation off to an ice-covered river to be baptized in a hole chopped in the ice. No one in our church thought baptism was *that* urgent.

Young children could be baptized if they believed they had consciously accepted Jesus as their savior. Young, new Christians in our

church were often eager to complete the three steps of "saved, sanctified, and baptized" to be sure they really were Christians and would
qualify for heaven if death should overtake them at a young age. I was
probably eight or nine years old when I was first baptized.

Yes, I said "when I was *first* baptized." It was not uncommon for
people in our church to be baptized more than once, especially if they
were first baptized when very young. Re-baptism usually came after
a lapse of faith, probably with some visible rebelliousness or bad
behavior, followed by repentance and getting saved again. As a serial
sinner myself, I was baptized twice before my final baptism when I
was a college student. Perhaps I should have been baptized additional
times later in life, but I accepted my college age baptism as final, even
though my faith and behavior were not always exemplary.

We didn't seem to know it, but our church was part of a very old
tradition in Protestant Christianity called the "Anabaptist" tradition.
The Anabaptists rejected the legitimacy of infant baptism, including
their own baptisms. They then were baptized again as adults when they
had embraced a new, more personal view of salvation and the church's
role in it. For this, Anabaptists were persecuted and many were exe-
cuted as heretics. We, of course, considered those who had persecuted
our historic predecessors to be sinners opposing the true way of faith.

We were clear in our church about how baptism should be done. We
always tried to imitate the Bible way of doing things, and we knew that
Jesus had been baptized in the Jordan River. The Bible doesn't actually
say that John the Baptist lowered Jesus under the surface of the water,
but we felt it was likely. Similarly, Act 8 reports that both Philip and the
Ethiopian eunuch "went down into the water" so the Ethiopian could
be baptized immediately after his conversion. Since they walked into
the water, we decided there must have been enough water for baptism
by immersion. To follow Christ's example, we believed, we needed to
be fully immersed under water when we were baptized. Going under
the water was seen as representing a kind of spiritual death to our sins
and our sinful natures. Coming up from the water was a kind of resurrection. Having died to the world in baptism, we were raised to a new
life to be lived with Jesus in our very souls.

Our church didn't have a baptismal tank, so we had to go somewhere else when people needed to be baptized. The Church of Christ
nearby had a baptistery, and the pastor charitably allowed us to use it

for our baptismal services. The baptistery was a long, narrow tank that was deep enough and wide enough that two adults could stand waist-deep in it. The tank was set in a window-like opening above the speaker's platform so the congregation could see the baptism.

My first baptism was at the long-since demolished Church of Christ, only a block away from our church in Elmore, halfway between the old Church of God and the new one. I and other boys went to classrooms behind the baptistery with our parents. The girls had their own dressing room. We boys took off our shoes and deposited spare sets of clothes and towels on chairs. I must have followed some other boys to the edge of the tank, and one-by-one we went down the steps into the water when our names were called. The pastor announced each kid's name and asked if we had repented of our sins and had turned our lives over to Jesus and wanted to follow him. We each affirmed this when our turn came.

"Upon your profession of faith in our Lord Jesus Christ, I now baptize you in the name of the Father, the Son, and the Holy Spirit," he would say with one hand raised. He would then use both hands to lower the person backwards into the water, submerging the person's head just briefly before lifting the person back up to a stand. When it was my turn, I held my nose as I went under, though I was not sure if holding my nose might invalidate my baptism. When I came back up and wiped my face, the pastor was smiling and I could hear a few people out in the congregation saying, "Amen! Praise God!"

I had a second baptism much like the first, and that one too was in a borrowed baptistery. The details are so hazy that I won't try to reconstruct the experience here. I note it only for the sake of thoroughness.

My last baptism was by far the most meaningful. By then I was twenty years old. I went to the altar in Elmore in the fall of my sophomore year in college, and I affirmed that action at the altar of the old Park Place Church in Anderson, Indiana, during Religious Emphasis Week the following year. At these times, I repented mainly of my rebellious attitude and the way I had rejected the church during my first year of college. My repentance this time was more about my sinful *nature* than about specific sins. When I was younger, I hadn't thought about my sinful nature at all, only about some specific sins that had gotten me in trouble at home, at school, and in my feeling of God's approval. In college, I began to see that I was basically a rebellious person who needed God's help to live right. On the basis of these more mature spiritual experiences, I wanted to be baptized again.

Our church still didn't have a baptistery at that time, and I'm glad we didn't. This time my baptism took place at a sandy beach at a fishing resort on the south side of the Portage River, somewhere downstream from the town of Oak Harbor in northern Ohio. The service was held in August on a Sunday afternoon. Four young people from the Elmore youth group were to be baptized before my turn would come. We stood on the riverbank while the pastor, up to his knees in the greenish gray water, gave a short sermon for the benefit of everyone, including fishermen and other vacationers who probably had never seen such a spectacle. The pastor talked about John the Baptist, who had baptized Jesus in a river like this one, and how the Holy Spirit had descended on Jesus like a dove. At that moment, the pastor seemed to *become* John the Baptist, and the Portage River seemed to *become* the River Jordan. It was like a scene in a painting with a blue sky overhead, a line of trees on the opposite bank dividing sky from water, and the pastor in his white shirt, seeming like a prophet.

The pastor waded into deeper water—up to his waist—and called us, one at a time, to step in and be baptized. Soon it was my turn to go in, a young adult much older than the others. My knees felt weak as my feet searched out smooth places in the uneven bottom of the murky water. The river was too shallow near the shore, so I met the pastor at a distance farther out from my watching family members. As before, the pastor asked for my pledge of faith in Jesus and announced he would baptize me in the name of the Father, the Son, and the Holy Spirit. Suddenly I was under the greenish brown water and came up dripping, surrounded by its mossy smell. I had done it! I had been baptized as an adult, and I felt more like an adult Christian than ever before.

I slogged my way to shore, my clothes dripping and water running into my eyes. Someone handed me a towel and I dried my face just in time to see a rosy-cheeked man, a vacationer, coming toward me. As he walked past me, he said, "Good luck to you!" and I said, "Thank you!"

It seemed like a strangely secular greeting right after baptism. The man clearly wasn't "one of us." I couldn't smell beer or liquor on the man's breath, but I was pretty sure beer or something like it must have been part of his Sunday afternoon. I felt I had just met "the world" as I came out of the river, a freshly baptized Christian. That man's friendly congratulation has always seemed important to me. His four words, "Good luck to you!" seemed to say something about the world and the Christian life that I was embracing as my own. He probably meant it as a blessing of sorts, or it may have been a skeptical wish for me; I'll never know.

The world and I have met many times in many places since I met that man on my baptismal day. If there is such a thing as being a life-long learner, part of it must involve learning the difference between the world and the Christian way.

AUTHOR'S NOTE: *The hymn "Shall We Gather at the River" was published by Robert Lowery in 1864 and is closely associated with baptism by immersion. If you haven't seen baptism by immersion in person, you could see it in the excellent movie,* Tender Mercies. *Robert Duvall is a fallen country and western singer who comes to faith after marrying a young Christian widow. The baptism takes place in a small Baptist church in rural Texas. You may also see an especially moving version of a river baptism in* O Brother, Where Art Thou? *The background song for the scene is "The Good Old Way," derived from an American slave song published in 1867, and possibly written much earlier. Alison Krauss sang off camera for the movie.*

AVOIDING WORLDLINESS

I've turned from the world and its follies,
Forever forsaken all sin,
I've given myself unto Jesus
To ever and always serve him.

In our church we had a strong sense of the difference between our-selves and "the world." We didn't invent this difference: the nature of the world is mentioned in many places in Scripture. The apostle Paul warned people of "the basic principles of this world" (Colossians 2:8). Even Jesus spoke often about the world in a spiritual sense.

When we talked in our church about the world, we of course didn't mean the planet Earth. We meant humanity outside the walls of our church, outside the walls of our homes, and outside the way of living we believed was right in God's eyes. We also meant the world where people worked, competed, formed friendships and alliances, spent money, voted, and did a million other things. The world could be a place of pleasant effort and sometimes success. It also could be a place of striving and self-determination and distractions and sometimes angry willfulness. It was a place of war and crime as well.

To me as a young kid, certain things clearly were "of the world" or "worldly." Not going to church was an obvious worldly thing. I assumed that people who didn't go to church didn't care enough about God to thank him, sing songs to him, or ask for help with their prob-lems. When they could have been in church, worldly people were "out in the world," even if they weren't doing anything especially bad. Those people sometimes seemed a little angry to me, even when they weren't angry. On the other hand, some worldly people seemed happy and seemed to be doing just fine. I learned that the Bible admits this seeming contradiction.

Worldly people sometimes showed it in very obvious ways. For example, one of my neighbors used to swear a lot, and he swore so loudly I could hear him clear across the empty lots between his house and mine. Now *that* was worldly. Other people drank beer until they got drunk. I don't remember actually seeing anyone who was drunk, but I heard about them and could guess who some of them might be. To people in our church, having even a little beer was considered a sin. Having a little beer would surely lead to drunkenness someday, we thought. I thought of beer as the main source of drunkenness because I hadn't heard of other alcoholic drinks. None of us knew anything then about more harmful drugs.

Smoking, too, was a clear sign of worldliness, but I admit it was one that fascinated me from the time I was a small boy. In the 1940s, just after World War II, many soldiers smoked cigarettes. The heroic, dramatic feeling I had about the lives of these soldiers may have contributed to my interest in smoking, but it wasn't only soldiers who smoked. It seemed to me that most men and women smoked except those living in my house and the people in my church. I think people knew that smoking was unhealthy and could be a fire hazard, but they went ahead and did it. It seemed to make them feel they were part of the "big world."

Movies and dancing were considered worldly in our church until after I went away to college in 1957. Movies started to become acceptable when television invaded most people's homes; it was difficult for church people to see the difference between television programs they viewed at home and movies viewed in theaters. Movies were gradually, if only partially, exonerated.

Dancing was considered worldly and a step toward other sins, probably because of the nature of dance moves and the touching between dance partners. The fact that we didn't go to dances set us apart from other kids. We were left out of a lot of social life, I'm sure, but we believed we were also left out of a lot of sinful activity that might have led us astray. Even if we doubted that dancing was sinful, we young people avoided it because it would have offended our parents. Also, our lack of experience made us want to avoid a potentially humiliating performance at a dance. I suspect that most kids in churches like mine didn't dance, even later as adults. As a result of not dancing as kids, we were so awkward on the dance floor in adult life that most of us were pleased to avoid that worldly activity, even if we came to doubt its sinfulness.

In addition to avoiding smoking, drinking, dancing, going to the movies, and other worldly things not mentioned here, our constant church going set us apart from other people in our community. We didn't just go to church once in a while; we were serious about it, and we went often. We went to church all morning on Sunday, a couple of hours on Sunday evening, and an hour and a half on Wednesday evening. We also went to youth group on Thursday or Friday and sometimes a youth party on Saturday. We didn't have much time to be worldly.

Before my time, some people in the Church of God were even more conscientious about worldliness. Some men wouldn't wear ties, and some women didn't wear jewelry and makeup. Even wedding rings were considered worldly adornments. But in my youth and early adulthood, there was no noticeable difference between the clothing, jewelry, and accessories of the people in the Church of God and that of the people who were Methodists, Lutherans, or Catholics, or even those who didn't go to church at all.

Although we avoided some visible marks of worldliness, I think even we kids knew those things were not the essence of worldliness. The essence of worldliness was following the crowd and its ways rather than any clear principles, especially those in the Bible. It meant being caught up mindlessly in passing fads and passions, using foul language, and taking God's name in vain. At its core, worldliness was pursuing our own interests, money, and power over others with no regard for God. It was being no different at all from those outside any church. It was making "the world" one's God and worshiping its false gods.

We seldom use the terms *worldly* or *worldliness* now, and most Christians probably see worldliness differently than we did in Elmore in the 1940s and 1950s. Most might be thankful that the church's outlook on worldliness has changed. But it may still be worthwhile to try to understand the meaning of that English word now that it seems so foreign.

AUTHOR'S NOTE: *The hymn quoted at the opening of this chapter is titled "Wholehearted Service." The words are by Charles W. Naylor (1874–1950). The music is by Andrew L. Byers (1869–1952). It is taken from the 1971 edition of* The Hymnal of the Church of God *(Warner Press, Anderson, Indiana).*

STAINED GLASS WINDOWS

The Church of God in Elmore didn't have stained glass windows when I was growing up, and it still doesn't. In the new building on Congress Street, the windows were simple, dimpled, translucent, yellow glass that let in light on Sunday mornings but filtered out the distractions of the world. In the old church building, once a one-room schoolhouse, the windows were plain glass that let in the beauty of the earth as well as light.

The people of our church wouldn't have wanted stained glass windows, even if we could have afforded them. Such windows would have smacked of the denominational churches our people had separated ourselves from. Also, such windows would have been reminiscent of the ancient Catholic heritage of some of us, where stained glass windows depicting Bible scenes and saints were part of the worship experience. To us, stained glass windows would have seemed like idolatry, just one step away from statues of saints.

In medieval times, stained glass windows in towering sanctuaries communicated Scripture and the majesty of God to the uneducated masses of Europe. The soaring, vertical lines of the churches directed people's minds and emotions toward God. In a similar spirit, church hymns communicated the Bible to us. The Church of God (Anderson) and our local church were especially adept at communicating the gospel through hymns that were lively, majestic, happy, or somber, depending on the subject. Those hymns were the "stained glass windows" for believers and sinners alike, some of whom might not have been so moved or edified by fine sermons.

Sunday morning services often opened with an anthem-like hymn that purely glorified God. It might be followed by a hymn expressing devotion to Christ and some aspect of personal experience. Sunday evening hymns tended to be more personal and evangelistic. Those hymns were rich in human experience: love, joy, assurance, fear, temptation, sin, guilt, forgiveness, illness, death, hope, heaven, and the need for God's guidance. A hymn's soaring exaltation of God, a memory of one's salvation, the thought of a danger overcome, or hope for heaven would stir our emotions as we sang. The hymn book we held in our hands was as close as our congregation came to a liturgy. We could turn to the hymnal for words we needed in many life experiences. Indeed, the theology embedded in the Church of God (Anderson) hymns was for decades the clearest statement of our otherwise unwritten beliefs.

Even as an indifferent or rebellious boy, I eagerly joined in singing the hymns. I learned to approximate the tenor or bass harmony lines by following the little black dots up and down on the hymnal page. In my teens I wanted to sing bass, and I was thrilled to hear the bass line sung forcefully by more mature men. If ever a soprano voice sang the descant line, I had chills. I was greatly moved when all the voices joined in harmony, and I felt it reflected the harmony among us. Fortunately the hymns usually had several verses and a repeated chorus that helped us learn the melody and harmony.

Two of my favorite hymns were "Heavenly Sunshine" and "His Yoke Is Easy, His Burden Is Light," but I often thought of fried eggs when we sang that second hymn. "Heavenly Sunshine" was an early version of the "happy news" choruses that later dominated church singing. I also liked the martial sound of "Onward Christian Soldiers" and "A Mighty Fortress Is Our God." My boyhood list of favorite hymns was fairly long, perhaps partly because our song leaders avoided some of the more formal, stilted hymns in the book.

Besides hymns, we also sang "youth choruses." They were often sung just for fun on Sunday evenings and in Wednesday night prayer meetings, but they were never sung on Sunday mornings. I liked the youth choruses, and I even liked the fact that they were distinctly lightweight and less mature than the hymns. The youth choruses often had only one verse and sometimes invited hand motions from the singers. We clapped to keep time with the music only when we sang some of the youth choruses.

I still know many hymns by heart, at least through the first verse. I often wake up in the morning with one of those old hymns going through my mind. Though I was not a model child or teenager nor a trained singer, I was one of the many "heathens" to whom the hymns spoke more clearly than Scripture itself. Even now, as I remember our church services and the beautiful, harmonious singing, I nearly forget myself and go backward in time to the simple, unadorned windows that separated us so simply from the world outside while our hearts and minds soared in songs, just as stained glass windows once spoke so eloquently to our ancient forebearers.

WEDNESDAY NIGHT PRAYER MEETINGS

W ednesday nights were reserved for the weekly prayer meetings. Those evenings were nearly as sacred as Sundays in our church's ecclesiastical calendar. No other church events were scheduled for those nights, and indeed the entire town respected the churches' claims on Wednesday evenings. Much of what I learned about the lives of adults in the church came from those prayer meetings.

Prayer meeting nights involved more than prayer, though actual prayer was the central focus, and pray we did. We prayed seated, we prayed standing, and we knelt for prayer in the pews. There might be three for four "seasons of prayer" on a single Wednesday evening. Each prayer time was preceded by a brief meditation or Scripture reading by the pastor. A season of prayer might follow a particularly powerful testimony. The number of those seasons of prayer depended on what else happened during the evening. When we prayed, anyone could chime in and lead the prayer. While one spoke out in prayer, others continued praying softly. A holy drone filled the church, sometimes punctuated with a moan or a tearful sob. When we had prayed long enough, the pastor would pray loudly enough to be heard, and the congregation would again be seated.

Prayer meeting nights always included a few songs. They were lighter and less majestic than the ones we sang on Sunday mornings, and they were less evangelistic than those on Sunday nights; only the most faithful showed up on Wednesday nights, so they needed a change of pace. Since children of the very faithful also came to church on Wednesdays, the song time included a few youth choruses. Those short, lively, devotional songs could have been sung around the campfire at youth camp or during the devotional part of a youth fellowship party. They were not to be mistaken for adult church music; they were a concession to the young.

Wednesday night also differed from Sundays in that there would be no altar call at the end of the service. Those who came on Wednesday had already given their lives to God and needed only to rejoice, pray for others, and testify about the marvelous works of God they had experienced. Beside prayer and singing, Wednesday was a time to give testimonies and listen to the testimonies of others, and that was the most memorable feature of prayer meeting nights for me.

Testimonies were personal stories of faith, primarily from adults. Testimonies could be about a flash of insight into Scripture or an experience in Christian living. They could be about a danger narrowly escaped or about a recent recovery from an illness or injury. The best testimonies were historical, almost biblical stories about how a person had come to faith. Of those, the most thrilling involved escapes from death or recovery from a near-fatal illness or accident. The stories "Fred Webert's Salvation" and "Art Gleckler's Missing Ear" in this book came straight from my memories of those men's Wednesday night testimonies.

Giving a testimony was expected at some time or another of nearly everyone who came on Wednesdays; only young children were excused from this sacred duty. Just a few testimonies were voiced on a single evening, but we all knew our turns would come. Whenever believers had an especially meaningful experience, they were expected to share it, first with those gathered on prayer meeting night and then with others out in the world. Although it was assumed that these would be spiritual or morally significant experiences, one lady testified at great length about cockroaches when she returned from her first trip to Florida.

"Coming of age" was informal in our church, but it did mean a young person was old enough to give a testimony at Wednesday night prayer meeting. This transition into spiritual adulthood usually happened at age twelve or thirteen and corresponded to other coming-of-age events in other churches and other faiths.

The adults must have yearned to hear some sign of God's goodness in the lives of the unruly young people sitting near the back of the church. The older saints surely longed for assurance that the church's mission was being fulfilled in its precious offspring. Young people, however, usually avoided giving their testimonies due to fear or embarrassment, but eventually they would be called out by the person leading the service. A youth testimony might be requested after a pause in testimony time, after the adults had shared their adventures with God or had perhaps repeated their life stories sufficiently for that night. In that pause, the silence would become heavy. A great searchlight from God would sweep over the congregation and settle on the young people huddled far from the front of the church and perhaps far from the throne of God. The voice of God might then speak through the leader to an unsuspecting youth: "Bob, how about letting us hear your testimony?"

Fear and trembling, both of which are biblical emotions, would shoot through the young man. God's searchlight had settled on him. What could he possibly say? He had been in church all his life, and he had been saved at youth camp last summer, but those facts could hardly be stacked up against adult testimonies of being saved in battle or on a death bed. Bob would then stand as if in a dream, feeling the eyes of all the adults on him. The knowing eyes of his youthful friends were on him too. He had to say something, but what? In panic, he would turn to the most familiar escape route for young testifiers, blurting out, "I'm saved and sanctified, and I'm glad to be here tonight. I want to learn more about Jesus!" He would then sit down with a thud.

Even that shriveled little testimony was enough to elicit some murmurs of "amen" and "praise God." The testimony had been approved! The searchlight of God might then move onto another of the youth, and she would rise and give a similarly worded testimony and receive the same praise from the adults of the church. When enough testimonies had been heard, the service would end with another meditation thought, a very short Scripture reading, and a closing prayer. The church was reminded to return in a week and bring more prayer requests and testimonies to share.

As a young boy, I lacked the powers of concentration needed for full spiritual participation on prayer meeting nights. It was easy to listen to the dramatic stories of the adults and amusing to see the discomfort of other young people when they had to testify, but it was difficult to stay focused during the long prayer times, so I came to church with my pockets stuffed full of little gadgets and memorabilia to play with during those times. While kneeling for prayer in the pews one

Wednesday night, I noticed a tiny worm hole in the back of the lovely wooden pew I was facing there on my knees. A worm had burrowed into the wood, probably while the wood was still part of a tree in its forest home. The worm hole needed to be explored, that was plain, and I was just the one to do it. I remembered the very thin copper wire my father had brought home from the Sun Oil refinery in Toledo where he worked. It was just the thing I needed.

The very next week, I came to prayer meeting night armed with a short length of that wire in my pocket. When everyone knelt for prayer, I was prepared. I pulled out the copper wire and slid it into the worm hole. Just as I had hoped, the hole went deep into the back of the pew. I slid the wire in as far as possible and found the tiny tunnel was at least a couple of inches long. The worm, of course, was long gone, but I was grateful for the diversion it provided during an especially long season of prayer that night. I knew the great searchlight of God might soon fall on me and I would have to stand and testify, feeling like a man facing a firing squad. But for the moment, I was safe to explore the rare little wonder of nature some thoughtful worm had been kind enough to provide just for me.

AUTHOR'S NOTE: *When I told my young nieces and nephews about the worm hole some years ago, they laughed and doubted my veracity. After a brief search, I found the worm hole again, but the pew had been moved to the right-hand side of the church, near the front, probably after new flooring was installed. If the pew had been in that spot in the 1950s, I never would have found the worm hole because I wouldn't have sat so near the front. That section of the church near the front was occupied by the older, more sincere saints. If I see you at the Elmore Church of God in this earthly life, I'll be glad to show you the worm hole, and I hope that will somehow make you think of ancient days when people went to church three times a week, including Wednesday prayer meeting nights.*

FOOTWASHING

"**E**verybody wash your feet before we go to church tonight," my mother announced. The older children knew what she meant, but the younger children were puzzled.

"We're going to have footwashing tonight," Mama explained. "We will wash each other's feet, so we have to be prepared," she said to the youngest children, who had never gone to this service before. I was a grown-up twelve-year old, and I had been to one or two footwashing services. I knew what to expect, and I knew it might feel strange again. But it was one of the most sacred moments of the year. This time I was nearly a man, so I would be included as an adult.

"Can't we just put on clean socks?" one of the boys asked.

"Not on feet like yours!" Mama laughed. "I've seen how dirty the bottoms of your feet are. You can't expect someone to wash your feet when they're that dirty. We can't have stinky feet for foot washing!"

"But if they're going to wash our feet, won't that clean them up? Why do we have to wash them just to be washed again?"

"We're not going in order to get our feet *cleaned*," Mama replied. "In fact, we're not going mainly to have *our* feet washed. We're going to wash *other* people's feet. That's the point. But when they wash our feet, we want to have clean feet for them. Okay?"

We nodded. What Mama said made sense. She fixed a big pan of water, and we all washed our feet, even my littlest brother who was only five years old and would probably just watch the service that night. Soon we were all bundled in the car for the three-mile trip to town for Maundy Thursday service, though I don't think any of us had heard the term *Maundy* back then.

At the church, we all gathered in the sanctuary upstairs. We sang "When I Survey the Wondrous Cross" and "In the Cross of Christ I Glory." The pastor spoke about the night when Jesus and the disciples gathered in "the upper room" for the "Last Supper." He read the passage in the gospel of John that says

> It was just before the Passover Feast. Jesus knew that the time had come for him to leave this world and go to the Father. Having loved his own who were in the world, he now showed them the full extent of his love. The evening meal was being served, and the devil had already prompted Judas Iscariot, son of Simon, to betray Jesus. Jesus knew that the Father had put all things under his power, and that he had come from God and was returning to God; so he got up from the meal, took off his outer clothing, and wrapped a towel around his waist. After that, he poured water into a basin and began to wash his disciples' feet, drying them with the towel that was wrapped around him. (John 13:1-5)

As the pastor read those lines, nearly everyone thought of the drama we were about to re-enact. We would perform the washing of feet just as it was described in that passage from the Bible. The pastor reminded us that Jesus had told his followers to wash each other's feet. He quoted this passage:

> Now that I, your Lord and Teacher, have washed your feet, you also should wash one another's feet. I have set you an example that you should do as I have done for you. I tell you the truth, no servant is greater than his master, nor is a messenger greater than the one who sent him. Now that you know these things, you will be blessed if you do them. (John 13:14-17)

From young to old, we knew that we would be following Jesus in the act of washing feet, just as he had done. Most children and young teens probably assumed that all Christians would be doing what we were about to do that night. The older people knew that most other churches would not have footwashing that night or at any other time. At our church, we believed the Bible made it clear that we should do it. We believed that this ceremony was one of the things we needed to do in obedience to Scripture.

Carlton Yeagle, a painter by profession, led us in his clear tenor voice in one more song and reminded us that the men and boys would go to one classroom in the basement, and the women and girls would go to another for the footwashing part of the service. Pastor Witt prayed, and everyone went to the basement.

The church didn't have a "Holy of Holies" like the Old Testament tabernacle and temple. It didn't even have a baptistery at this time, or that might have seemed like a Holy of Holies. But when we went into the basement room for footwashing, we were entering a kind of Holy of Holies. We would be performing a solemn ordinance of the church, and we would be doing it just as Jesus had done it for his disciples. Washing feet was a way of saying we intended to be humble, helpful to others, and faithful in imitating Jesus in every way possible. Washing each other's feet not only reminded us to be humble; it also underscored our caring for each other and our desire to be clean spiritually. No other event in the church seemed as holy as this one to me except the experience of getting saved.

The older men knew just what to do, and the young men and boys followed their lead. We sat in a circle around the walls facing the center of the room where towels, basins, and a large container of warm water were ready. The older men bowed their heads in a mood of deep reverence while the boys and younger men nervously awaited their cues. Sometimes we sang part of a hymn as we started, but this night Pastor Witt was in my group. He opened the ceremony in his own words: "Just as Jesus washed his disciples' feet, we will wash each other's feet in obedience to him. He showed his love for his followers through this humble act. We show our love for Christ and for each other by following his example."

With only that simple statement, the foot washing service began. Fred Webert, who had been saved during a bombardment in World War I, immediately stood and picked up a basin of water and one of the extra-long towels that were used for this ceremony. Unfolding the towel, he wrapped it around his waist and secured it, keeping one long end free. In his rough farmer's voice, he repeated in his own words some of the words in John 13:5 and 13:14: "After supper with his disciples, Jesus got up, girded himself with a cloth, and washed the disciples' feet. He said, 'Now that I have washed your feet, you should wash one another's feet. You should do as I have done.'"

With that, Fred knelt in front of Harry Klinger and gently lifted one of the old man's feet into the basin of warm water. He splashed water over that foot and washed it with both hands, all the time softly telling Harry again that this was just what Jesus had done. He washed the other foot in the same way, and then he dried both feet with the free end of the towel. The men stood and embraced. Fred said, "God bless you, Brother Harry!" And Harry replied, "The Lord be with you, Brother Fred!"

Harry Klinger then shuffled to the middle of the room for a basin of water and a towel. He was already an old man, twenty-five years older than Fred Webert. Repeating what Fred had just done, he splashed water over Fred's feet and dried them. Again the men stood, embraced, and blessed each other with those same words. In those moments of embrace, it was as though the two men's testimonies were transferred between them, shared with a supernatural intimacy. Other men watched these two devout older men, and most of them said "amen."

Although I was only a boy of twelve, one of the men came to me with his basin of water. It was Warren Draper, a shy farmer. "Can I wash your feet?" he asked. I nodded, and he nervously got on his knees and began to wash my feet. It was as strange to me as it probably was to him when it was my turn to wash his feet. The only contact between us had been brief greetings before and after church. Now we were in direct contact, washing each other's feet, and in that small way sharing something so important that we couldn't have expressed it in words.

Many years later, long after Harry Klinger died at the age of one hundred, I was again at the Elmore Church of God on a Maundy Thursday. By then I was in my thirties and had children of my own. I hadn't been in a footwashing service for more than ten years, and it again seemed as other-worldly as it had when I was twelve years old. The older men, with their life experiences and spiritual maturity, seemed to tower over me spiritually, even though I was physically taller than any of them. The room suddenly seemed as new as it was on New Year's Eve in 1949, when the church was new and the basement still smelled of fresh concrete. It also seemed like what I remembered from that previous footwashing in 1952, back when I was twelve. Nothing had changed: the same towels, pans, and tub of warm water where there. It was as though I had rediscovered an ancient sanctuary. Just as we had many years before, we washed each other's feet. And all around the room, some of the same testimonies I had heard in Wednesday night prayer meetings years ago were shared quietly again as the men washed each other's feet.

This time my father knelt in front of me and washed my feet. We were both men, and this kind of closeness seemed unfamiliar, even with my own father. When he finished washing my feet, we stood and hugged. "God bless you," he said a little nervously. "God bless you, Daddy," I replied. As it had seemed years earlier when Uncle Fred washed Harry Klinger's feet, it now seemed that something special had passed from my father to me in those moments. My father had given me a blessing for my adult years, sharing with me the faith that would continue to sustain both of us all our days.

After that footwashing night in the 1980s, we had communion in the sanctuary as we had done in 1949 and 1952 and on every other Maundy Thursday. Communion symbolized our spiritual tie to Christ. Footwashing reminded us that in the coming days, there would be times to "wash feet" in other ways. We might "wash feet" by taking food to shut-ins or picking up sticks in their yards. We might help clean the church or paint a room for a widow or give someone a ride to church. Those other forms of service to the church or to other people might sometimes be as inconvenient or distasteful as footwashing might seem, but our experience in that basement room would remind us of our promise to be humble and helpful even when we didn't want to be.

AUTHOR'S NOTE: *"Footwashing," when expressed as a single word, usually refers to the Christian practice I have described here rather than the sanitary practice of merely washing one's feet. The term is sometimes hyphenated and is sometimes expressed in two words. The term* maundy *is derived from a Latin word,* mandatum, *meaning "command." In this case, it refers to the command of Jesus to his followers that "you also should wash one another's feet" (John 13:4-17 contains the full account).*

FAMILY WORSHIP

B efore bedtime nearly every evening, my family would gather in the living room for family worship. Mama or Daddy would read a Bible story from Elsie Egermeier's *Bible Story Book* or sometimes from the Bible itself. Sometimes we sang a song or heard some reminders from Mama or Daddy, and we always finished by kneeling at the sofa and chairs to pray. The youngest child would pray first, followed by the older children and then by our parents. No one prayed very long, but everyone prayed.

Family worship included prayer requests, usually for someone in the church or someone in our large extended family who was sick or for the salvation of souls or peace in the world. When I was very young and World War II was raging, we kids would always include in our prayers, "Help the boys in the war." When that war ended, we dropped that line from our prayers, but after 1950 we began to pray, "Help the boys in Korea." In both wars we knew some of the "boys" who were there, but to me they were big men, mostly over twenty and some nearly thirty or even older. I knew that they must be boys to our parents, so we prayed for them as "boys." We kept up family worship on a regular basis until I was in high school. After I graduated and left home in 1957, the family still had family worship, but it was harder to do as the kids got older. Still, our family worship had shown us how to have church at home, even if we didn't always do it.

Grandma Bruner in Dacoma, Oklahoma, had a much more demanding family worship time. When we went to visit, we were all included in her morning worship. Grandma would fix us a sumptuous farm breakfast every morning: hot and cold cereal, toast, biscuits, eggs, bacon, sausage, fried potatoes, fruit, jam, honey, and milk. We kids couldn't eat all of the breakfast, and we could hardly wait to put on our shorts and run outside. But Grandma had her daily worship right after breakfast, and we had to join her. She would put her Bible at the head of the dining room table along with one of her devotional booklets. She would read to us from the Bible and from the devotional. She might recite one of the many poems she knew by heart or a memorized passage of Scripture. Then we all prayed, starting with us kids. Grandma finished with a prayer that seemed to have come straight from the Bible, usually a long prayer about people we didn't know and troubles we could barely imagine. Grandma's worship time was something that we knew we should learn to do when we were older and more spiritual and more disciplined, even if we wouldn't do it exactly as Grandma did.

After morning worship with Grandma, we boys would run out into the exciting warmth of the Oklahoma morning to search for horned toads and red ant dens. We were usually in Oklahoma near the Fourth of July, and fireworks could be bought in stores. We saved money for weeks before our trips from Ohio, where fireworks were illegal, so we could buy firecrackers for blowing up the entrances of the red ant hills. We didn't think about family worship while we were blowing up ant hills and disturbing the peace with firecrackers. Grandma must have been praying for our safety, since no one was seriously injured by our fireworks except a few thousand stinging red ants.

The last time I had family worship at home with my family in Ohio was the day in September 1962 when I left for two years in the Peace Corps in Ethiopia. I had come home for a few days to pack two suitcases for the epic journey. The first leg of my trip would be an afternoon flight from Toledo to New York City, followed by flights the next day to Rome, Athens, and Addis Abba. The separation was going to be long, and there would be no visits or phone calls for two years. It was clearly a time for prayer, so my mother gathered everyone in the living room for family worship, just as we had for many years. We were going to pray for my safety and the safety of the family during the two years we would be apart. The prayers that morning, it seemed, would be more important than almost any other time in the life of our family. My dad was away at work that morning, and my older brother was living in Chicago, so it was up to the rest of us to pray before I left.

We knelt at the living room couch and a couple of chairs, and my little sister Annette, eight years old, started us with her usual short prayer. Then my brother Larry prayed a somewhat more complete prayer as a teenager. My sister Sharon and my brother Owen, both young adults, added their prayers. Then it was my turn, and I began to pray, not really knowing how to pray, since I had never faced such a time. I started my prayer in the usual way, but suddenly I saw the long expanse of days and the great distance stretching out ahead. My prayer fell apart. I began sobbing, and everyone else began to cry. We cried so hard we couldn't keep praying. Finally Mama controlled her tears enough to pray and finish our worship.

With the worship time over, we all stood up. Little Annette looked around at her tear-stained family and asked, "Why is everybody crying? He's not going to *die*, is he?"

Laughter exploded around the room, blowing away the fears that had brought us to tears. We knew that I or one of them could die while I was gone, and we didn't know when we would meet again, but it was better to laugh than cry.

We all grew older and more mature about the world because of my experiences overseas those next two years, which I shared. I thought about that family worship time a lot while I was overseas. I didn't die, and we all escaped "many dangers, toils, and snares."

AUTHOR'S NOTE: *Between 1962 and 1964, I exchanged many letters with my family, and we exchanged three-inch reel-to-reel tapes in those days before cassettes. This degree of isolation is difficult to imagine now that we have email, Skype, Facetime, inexpensive worldwide phone access, and relatively easy international travel. The last line of the story contains words from the hymn "Amazing Grace" by John Newton, written in 1779.*

EPILOGUE:
THE CLOCK AND THE SAVING REMNANT

T here really is an old school clock in the Elmore Church of God. It's the same one that hung in the back of the one-room church on Harris Street, and it has been in the new church on Congress Street since 1949. The pendulum still swings when the clock has been wound and properly oiled, and the pendulum's face still can seem like a fiendish Philistine god to those with vivid imaginations just as I had when I was a young boy growing up when I imagined the old clock had been carried by my forbearers from the Promised Land to Elmore, Ohio. The clock is no longer in the sanctuary, perhaps to avoid frightening children, perhaps to avoid it being stolen by antiquities dealers. After all, it is a treasure that endured a long journey not totally unlike the journey of the Ark of the Covenant from the Sinai desert to the Promised Land more than three thousand years ago.

The clock has been with the congregation through its lean and fat years, and it has been in my consciousness from my early years. Its image became the inspiration for this collection of historic stories. In truth, a telling of the full, factual history of the Elmore Church of God would not be as entertaining as the stories in this book. I have not reported the thousands of times things went well, when the crops came in beautifully and the weather was pleasant. I haven't named all the individuals who came to church in excellent health who tried every day to enhance the kingdom of God. I know that conflicts and disappointments were somehow overcome and hurt feelings were healed over the years; these are not recorded here either. The stories I have included offer dramatic glimpses of life in my home church from its founding to the present. I hope these stories ring true not only with those in my home church and my home town, but with some who have experienced church life in similar small churches elsewhere.

The Elmore Church of God reached its largest attendance in the late 1950s. Later the church experienced turbulence over issues that have arisen in most churches in the past fifty or sixty years. There were disagreements over church music and worries about budgets being met and which translation of the Bible to use. Young people sometimes drifted away from the church, and at other times there were so many young people that the church struggled to find enough adult volunteers to help guide them. In the early 1990s, the church ambitiously opened a day care center to serve young mothers and attract young families to the church, and this effort led to management challenges. For these and other reasons, the congregation has gone through some difficult and discouraging times as well as its times of peace, renewal, and stability.

The Bible mentions a "remnant" repeatedly in the Old and New Testaments when only a few survived a catastrophe and carried on God's work. A "saving remnant" refers to a small group of the faithful who are preserved like a seed that can flourish again. More than once the Elmore church survived when only a tiny remnant kept the doors open after a fractious exodus. In one instance, the church dwindled to hardly more than three or four couples and a handful of single individuals and children. The church's future seemed in doubt. But that remnant persevered, and new leadership was found. New followers came, and the church revived. As I write in mid-2016, the Elmore Church of God is thriving and is having a positive impact on its community.

Churches are made up of imperfect humans living in a fallen world, so it's not surprising that churches have flaws like other human institutions. Yet needy people continue to be drawn to church—not just this particular congregation but to the great universal Church of God in its great variety all around the world. People come like patients to a hospital or clinic, needing healing of their souls, minds, and bodies. They come in fear and in poverty, and in the middle of divorce or grief or the approach of death. Some come with burdens of shame and guilt and binding habits. People seek direction and rightness in their lives, and they often find it in a church. Like thousands of other congregations in large cities, small towns, and rural areas around the world, the

Elmore Church of God continues to be a light that shines in the darkness, unconcerned that it may never be a great city set on a hill.

Many more things have happened in the Elmore Church of God, and more lives have been changed than are recorded in this book. Only a few of the many stories about the Elmore Church of God and its people and community are recorded in this book. To paraphrase the closing lines of the gospel of John, if all the stories could be written, they would fill a much larger book than this.

CHRONOLOGY OF THE CHURCH OF GOD OF ELMORE, OHIO

1913	Passenger train hits George Gleckler's car, killing his wife and son; George Gleckler experiences salvation and helps start the Church of God; house church meetings begin.
1925	The church buys the one-room St. John's Parochial School building on Harris Street at the urging of Carl Kardatzke with financial support from Henry Otte and George Gleckler.
1944	Parsonage on Fremont Street is purchased along with a vacant lot on Congress Street where the Trinity Lutheran Church once stood.
1947	Construction begins on the new church
1948	Cornerstone is laid in March; first service is held in the unfinished building on October 31, 1948. Full occupancy is in early 1949.
1949	First funeral in March; first wedding in June in the new church.
1949	Dedication of new church in August.
1953	Mortgage burning.
1955–58	Highest Sunday morning attendance of 155, on average.
1965	Fellowship hall, baptistery, and classrooms are constructed.
2000–2001	Attendance dips to twelve for several months.
2004–Present	Attendance returns to long-term average of about 70.
2013	Centennial of the church; more than 175 visitors come from far and wide.

PASTORS OF THE ELMORE CHURCH OF GOD

Pastors are listed by the years in which they were appointed.

1913–1925	Itinerant pastors for house church meetings were John Osborne; W.J. Henry; men named Hoeflinger and Wilson; and others whose names are lost
1925	George Edes, first full-time pastor at first church building on Harris Street
1928	Lester Worden
1931	Nathan Yoder
1934	Walter Veitch
1935	John Call
1937	Clyde Steepleton
1938	John Peoples
1942	Joseph Richardson
1948	W. Curtis Lee
1951	Forrest Witt
1953	Charles Cronin
1956	Aubrey Bates
1963	John Call (Same as 1935)
1966	J. Louis Larimore
1969	Charles Miller
1972	Paul Nice
1979	Lois Salsman
1986	Richard Luckett
1989	Ken Fairbanks
2001	Tom Willhardt, pastor in 2016 at this writing

ABOUT THE AUTHOR

Nyle Kardatzke now lives and writes in Indianapolis, Indiana. He retired in 2009 after a varied career of teaching and school administration. He grew up near Elmore, Ohio, and graduated from high school there in 1957. He graduated from Anderson (College) University (Anderson, Indiana) and earned a master's degree and a PhD in economics from the University of California, Los Angeles. He has three children and nine grandchildren, and he is active in the Church at the Crossing, Indianapolis.

The author's other books are *Widow-man: A Widower's Story and Journaling Book* (2014) and *The Brown House Stories: A Child's Garden of Eden* (2015). Both are available in print and Kindle editions on Amazon.

CPSIA information can be obtained
at www.ICGtesting.com
Printed in the USA
FSOW03n1727101016
25985FS